BHUBANESWAR

FROM A TEMPLE TOWN TO A CAPITAL CITY

Ravi Kalia

SOUTHERN ILLINOIS UNIVERSITY PRESS
Carbondale and Edwardsville

Printed in India
Designed by Loretta Vincent
Production supervised by New Leaf Studio
97 96 95 94 4 3 2 1

Library of Congress Cataloging-in-Publication Data

Kalia, Ravi.
Bhubaneswar : from a temple town to a capital city/Ravi Kalia.
p. cm.
Includes bibliographical references and index.
1. City planning—India—Bhubaneswar. 2. Orissa (India)—Capital and capitol. I. Title.
HT169.I52B475 1994
307.76'0954' 13—dc20 92-46696
ISBN 0-8093-1876-8 CIP

The paper used in this publication meets the minimum requirements of American National Standard for Information Sciences—Permanence of Paper for Printed Library Materials, ANSI Z39.48-1984. ♾

For Professors Bipin Chandra, B. B. Misra,
Amba Prasad, Tapan Raychaudhuri, and Stanley Wolpert,
each of whom introduced me to
India from a personal point of view

CONTENTS

ILLUSTRATIONS

Pages 79–98

MAPS AND PLANS

PHOTOGRAPHS

PREFACE

Bhubaneswar before becoming the capital of Orissa in 1948 had been a temple town. As a temple town it prospered and thrived, becoming an important Hindu cultural and religious center. Although the early history of Bhubaneswar is mired in myth, based largely on legend and tradition, it is generally believed that the town probably developed around the Lingaraja temple, erected to commemorate Lord Shiva. Thus the name Bhubaneswar: the Lord of the Three Worlds, Tribhuvneshvara.

Bhubaneswar experienced several changes in its physical form, its ethnic composition, its religious character, and its role as a subcontinental socioreligious center from one century to another: the city's character alternating with Buddhism, Jainism, Shaivism, and Vaishnavism—religions which found a home in Bhubaneswar at one time or another with the changing dynasties of Kalinga, the ancient name for Orissa. The presence of different religions gave Bhubaneswar its pluralistic character, but not without making the Oriya people suspicious of outsiders; and it also gave Bhubaneswar its definite religious character, which has endured into the present.

The same religious character of Bhubaneswar ultimately became responsible for its selection as the new capital of Orissa, although the city had never been the political capital of the region. But the Oriyas—proud, sometimes too proud, brave, loyal and religious, often too religious—signally searched for a city that exemplified Oriya spirit. In their drive to build a city that symbolized Oriya unity, the Oriyas occasionally displayed intolerance, inherently remained suspicious of new ideas and people, lacked a capacity for analysis, showed a strong inclination to act from feeling rather than from thought, possessed a narrow concept of community, invariably were fond of fiction and folklore, above all possessed too great an attachment to the romantic past, displaying sentimentality, even a lack of realism—such was the make-up of the Oriyas; and such they remain today, despite the onslaught of modernism and secularism.

But, for all the changes that were going on and being made in independent India, and the bold commitment to secularism and scientific progress that was being made by Nehru in new India, the Oriyas displayed little enthusiasm for being weaned away from their ancient past. If Old Bhubaneswar had suffered from years of neglect and decay, its power over the Oriyas would remain tremendous, even conclusive, and would exhibit itself with great distinctness, in the building of New Bhubaneswar.

But the decision to place the capital at Bhubaneswar was not as unusual as it might appear at first glance. Soon after independence the Punjabis decided to build their capital at Chandigarh, which derives its name from a temple of the goddess Chandi (Power) located at the site. Through what process did the Oriyas arrive at the decision to place the capital at Bhubaneswar? Does the process have any other parallels in India? Can the construction of Bhubaneswar explain trends in urban planning and government in postindependence India?

The need for building a new capital was first expressed when Orissa was constituted as the eleventh province of British India in 1936. The Oriya movement for a separate province in the first half of the twentieth century had at its core the old Kalinga spirit—the desire to recapture the romantic past of Orissa—and construction of the new capital at Bhubaneswar was to be its culminating expression. Just as the people of Kalinga had built thousands of temples in praise of the gods to solicit their divine benediction for salvation and prosperity, so, too, were the people of the new province inspired to consecrate the new province by building the capital at Bhubaneswar.

There is in the Oriya struggle for a separate province—and consequently in the decision to build the capital at Bhubaneswar—the beginning of a fissure which was potentially important, since it threatened and continues to threaten the national solidity to which the Indian National Congress aspired from its inception. Henceforth the Oriyas would stand—wholly apart from the Congress body politic? Of course not. But increasing numbers of them, at any rate, would display a suspicious sullenness toward Congress leaders and contempt for their programs. The struggle for a separate province by its very nature could not be made part of the national program of Congress, and for its success depended as much on regional sentiment as on the goodwill of the British masters.

Paradoxically, it was the British who had been responsible for dismembering Orissa in the nineteenth century for the sake of administrative convenience and efficiency, scattering the Oriya-speaking territories in the neighboring administrative units of Bengal, Madras, and the Central Provinces. The Oriya movement that finally evolved in the early twentieth century fed on two seemingly conflicting sentiments: on the one hand, Oriya nationalism drew its strength from linguistic chauvinism and consequently was directed against the exploiting Bengalis, Tamils, and Hindi-speakers of the Central Provinces; on the other, cooperation with the British was considered important, even essential, for the realization of the Oriya goal of a separate province. Madhusudan Das, the chief architect of the Utkal Union Conference, which spearheaded the Oriya struggle, strongly believed that Orissa had much to lose by confronting the British. The logic of regional considerations demanded practical politics. It also meant finding regional symbols for Oriya unity—and Bhubaneswar best served this purpose, although there were a few who believed that its sacred character was at variance with independent India's commitment to secularism.

So at the core of the Oriya political consciousness was the concern for the unification of Oriya territories under a separate province, which was viewed by the Oriyas as not only essential for safeguarding their language and identity against the onslaught of Bengali, Tamil, and Hindi, but also necessary for protecting local administrative jobs from slipping to the English-educated *babus*. Having its origin in linguistic passions, Oriya nationalism came to be directed against the Bengalis, Telegus, and Hindi-speakers who displaced the Oriyas in jobs, which—in the Oriya view—rightfully belonged to the people of Orissa.

However, the Oriya question—as the demand for a separate province came to be called—remained moribund until the viceroyalty of Lord Hardinge, when the government of India announced the creation of the new province of Bihar and Orissa on December 12, 1911. The government of India had reasoned that, because the Oriyas and Biharis have little in common with the Bengalis, this arrangement would receive the enthusiastic support of both the Oriyas and the Biharis. Instead, the Oriyas overwhelmingly rejected the proposal, and the debate on the future of Orissa was kept alive by Oriya leaders in the newly constituted Bihar and Orissa Legislative Council.

Meanwhile, the government of India's failure to grant Orissa a separate status contributed to rapproachment between the Utkal Union Conference and the Indian National Congress, although Congress's adoption of the principle of linguistic nationalism as the basis for forming of Indian provinces in 1920—a move that legitimized Orissa's right for a separate province, and a move that later became the basis for the reorganization of states in postindependence India—greatly helped in bringing the two organizations together. But the struggle between the regionalists, who viewed the backwardness of Orissa and unification of the Oriya territories as the two interrelated problems of Orissa separate from national politics, and the nationalists, who viewed the Oriya question as part of the larger national struggle for independence, was to continue until 1931, when Congress officially adopted a resolution for the creation of a separate Orissa. Five years later, the government of India in the face of growing Oriya discontentment finally created the new province of Orissa on March 3, 1936.

No sooner had the new province of Orissa come into existence than the controversy on where to locate the capital city broke out. The most serious contenders for the position were Cuttack and Puri. Cuttack was eventually ruled out because of its overcrowded character and Puri was ruled out because of its religious character, which was considered incompatible with the secular character of new India. For nearly ten years the Oriyas debated where to place the capital. Some secular-minded Oriyas were opposed to converting a religious city into a capital; others viewed conversion of a small town like Cuttack into a capital incompatible with the modern urban aspirations of the new province; still others viewed the selection of a capital as an opportunity for building an administrative colony for the "brown" bureaucrats of the new province in the same manner that the British had built civil lines as residential colonies for the European civilian administrative staff and cantonments as military stations.

So when the postwar Reconstruction Department recommended Bhubaneswar as a possible choice because it contained large tracts of open space, the Oriyas saw that city becoming a symbol of past pride—and thereby preserving the hard-won Oriya unification—and also offering hope for a modern future. The modern urban mission was articulated by the Maharastrian-brahman B. K. Gokhale, special advisor to Governor Howthorne Lewis, who saw Cuttack remaining the principal commercial center, Chowdar, a Cuttack suburb on the north bank of the Mahanadi, developing into a modern industrial complex, and Bhubaneswar, about twenty miles south of Cuttack, becoming the capital city as well as the chief cultural and educational center of the new province.

To implement their urban mission the Oriyas hired the German planner Otto Koenigsberger. From the beginning, Koenigsberger and the Oriyas disagreed in their vision of the capital city. Reared in the tradition of the German Reformation, Koenigsberger viewed the development of New Bhubaneswar along secular lines, having political autonomy, organized commercial relationships, and brave new architecture that would accommodate the requirements of modern life. The Oriyas, given the tendency to idealize, had the old pattern of planning still too powerfully stamped upon their minds to break away from the past. Having experienced no Hindu Reformation, the Indian town retained its close relationship to religion and continued to grow more or less organically with people living together pretty much without a sense of community.

From the beginning the temple town and the capital city exerted influence upon each other to establish dominance the one over the other. The development of Bhubaneswar represents that struggle: on the one hand, between man and his gods, and on the other, between man and technology. The final shape and style of Bhubaneswar bears as much the imprint of religion as that of rational scientific knowledge imported from the West.

Nowhere did this struggle express itself more clearly than in the selection of the architectural style. The record of the prevailing thinking in Orissa governmental circles clearly shows that the demand for adopting temple architecture in Bhubaneswar was widespread, and Indian politicians felt duty-bound to have an Indian style city because it was seen by them to make a politically correct statement. Governor Asaf Ali clearly instructed the PWD that "the architecture of the new capital should conform to the . . . ancient art of Orissa." Koenigsberger, on the other hand, maintained that since the new India was intended to be a secular state, there was no place for temple architecture in the capital city—although he was prepared to include important religious monuments of the old town in his master plan to "form interesting view-points at the end of the main roads."

Although mixing of interests resulted in achieving mixed results in Bhubaneswar, the Indians were able to work out their ideas far more freely in Bhubaneswar than in Chandigarh, where Le Corbusier and his European team of architects retained close control of all architectural developments. Other than the master plan which was provided by Koenigsberger, the architectural developments in Bhubaneswar were carried out by British-trained Indians eager to find their own identity. The conflict thus generated naturally created confusion—but in the long run this opportunity allowed Indian planners and architects to define their own positions in regard to the modern international style and to prepare themselves for the replanning of old cities and the designing of new ones.

ACKNOWLEDGMENTS

In reconstructing the story of Bhubaneswar I incurred debts to many people, some among whom had helped earlier when I wrote *Chandigarh*. The Honorable Minister Inder Gujral and his gracious wife, Sheila, were throughout encouraging, introducing me to individuals who could be of assistance in my research, reasoning and suggesting ways out of dead ends, and always generous in their hospitality.

I am equally indebted to Mrs. Manmohini Sahgal, who not only provided important insights into the characters of Jawaharlal Nehru and Kailash Nath Katju, the late governor of Orissa, but also introduced me to Orissa Chief Minister J. B. Patnaik. My special thanks are due Chief Minister J. B. Patnaik for giving me the permission to consult the Capital City Project Papers in Bhubaneswar. Also, my gratitude to the venerated Biju Patnaik for sharing his ideas on Bhubaneswar with me in 1987; he later came out of retirement to become the chief minister in 1991. Dr. R. K. Nayak, special secretary to the Orissa government, General Administration Department (GAD), and his fine staff were extremely helpful in photocopying the material relating to the development of Bhubaneswar; and Mr. M. N. Mohanty, IAS, Chief Minister's Office, skillfully guided me through the administrative procedures.

My special thanks are also due Governor B. N. Pande, himself a distinguished scholar, for supporting my research. Mr. L. Mishra, IAS, secretary to the governor, kindly introduced me to key individuals in Bhubaneswar, and instructed various departments of the government to assist in my research. To Mr. P. K. Mohanty, Housing and Urban Development Department; Mr. S. M. Patnaik and Mr. R. N. Bohidar, Tourism Department; Mr. M. P. Modi, Mr. R. N. Mishra, and Mr. P. B. Das, General Administration Department; and Mr. P. K. Hota, Bhubaneswar Development Authority, my sincere thanks for facilitating my research.

I thank Dr. Harish Chandra Das and his fine staff at the Orissa State Museum for photocopying material on Bhubaneswar. My gratitude and appreciation is extended to Professor D. R. Kalia, director, Orissa State Library, Bhubaneswar, for his assistance and good humor, even when I appeared frustrated in my long search.

Warmest thanks are extended to Mr. Abdul Ali and his excellent staff at the Directorate of Town Planning, Bhubaneswar. The Directorate literally became my home in Bhubaneswar; D. C. Misra, B. K. Roy, and D. Padhi provided valuable information on the developments in Bhubaneswar. I incurred an additional debt to Abdul Ali and his family for their warm hospitality and for looking after my needs in Bhubaneswar.

Warmest thanks are also extended to Chief Architect A. K. Biswal and his excellent staff for providing drawings and maps of Bhubaneswar. A special word of mention must be made of R. C. Padhi and his staff, Miss Smrutirekha Mohapatra and Miss Ratnamala Swain, for quickly reproducing Otto Koenigsberger's drawings.

To D. R. K. Patnaik, who guided the early developments in Bhubaneswar, and M. P. Kini, who served under Government Architect Julius L. Vaz, sincere thanks for sharing their experiences; and I am especially grateful to the latter for providing a singularly sensitive understanding of Vaz's ideas and personality. I thank Professors M. N. Das and Karunasagar Behera, Utkal University, for their many valuable suggestions. My best efforts notwithstanding, I deeply regret for not being able to interview Mr. Bhatru Hari Mahtab, the late Harekrushna Mahtab's adopted son. However, the historically conscious Harekrushna Mahtab, certainly aware of his role in the development of modern Orissa and sensitive to the Oriya character, left behind his autobiography and deposited his personal papers not at an institution in his native Orissa but at the Nehru Memorial Museum and Library in New Delhi, where I was able to consult them.

My continuing gratitude and appreciation to the staffs of the excellent National Archieves of India and the Town and Country Planning Organization, New Delhi, with special thanks to Chief Town Planner E. F. N. Ribeiro, who was singularly helpful in steering me toward new material. A word of mention must be made of M. P. Modi, special assistant to the chief planner, for assisting me with administrative details. To S. S. Shafi, D. S. Meshram, O. P. Mathur, Dr. Dinesh Mehta, Dr. H. D. Kopardekar, Professor Asish Bose, Professor Ramashray Roy, and B. G. Fernandes I am indebted for their insights on Indian cities. I thank A. R. Nanda, registrar general and census commissioner, government of India, for providing the census data and for sharing his ideas.

My grateful appreciation is extended to Eugene W. Huguelet for letting me use the interlibrary services of Randall Library, University of North Carolina at Wilmington, to the maximum; and I thank Mary Ladner, June Suermann, and John F. Mohr for their assistance and support. I also thank the staff of Perkins Library, Duke University, for giving me extended borrowing privileges, with special thanks to Professor John Richards for recommending me to Perkins Library, and to Rebecca Gomez and Cliff Sanderson for approving my countless requests. My thanks are due the staffs of the India Office Library and Records, London; Nehru Memorial Museum and Library, New Delhi; and the University of Chicago Library for promptly furnishing material. A special word of mention must be made of my distinguished colleague and friend, Ravinder Kumar, director of the Nehru Memorial Museum and Library, for his personal interest in and support of my research.

I thank the Council for International Exchange of Scholars for the Fulbright grant, which made it possible for me to spend an extended time in Bhubaneswar in 1988. I am also grateful to the University of North Carolina at Wilmington for the faculty and research development grant in 1989.

To Professor Otto Koenigsberger and his gracious wife, Renate, I owe special gratitude. Otto spent long hours with me, recounting his days in Bhubaneswar and the details of his master plan for the city. He put at my disposal all his personal papers relating to his work in Bhubaneswar and other Indian cities; and Renate made sure that we were kept well supplied with food and drink. She also kindly assisted in procuring material from the India Office Library after I left London. Otto later read the manuscript and made valuable suggestions. My heartfelt thanks to both of them for their support.

I started my research on Bhubaneswar while I was still living in Los Angeles and completed the manuscript after moving to Wilmington, North Carolina. In between I made five trips to India, and in the process I incurred a personal debt to many friends who helped in many ways; and although there is not space to mention each by name, I wish to thank them all for their support in my long search. To Joe and Mary Robinson, Rob and Esther Huey, George and Charlene Groff, Barbara Longsdon, Carolyn Mayfield, Raul Gonzalez, William Diemer, Jeff Pupp, Anand and Patsy Daftry, Jim and Eileen Ray, Ashok and Rita Beckaya,

O. P. and Veena Bhardwaj, Sharda Nayak, Andrea Singh, M. N. Buch, Professors R. P. and Shusheela Kaushik, Professors Partha and Narayani Gupta, and Professor Tom and Martha MacLennan my heartfelt thanks. I incurred an additional debt to Tom for reading the later chapters of the manuscript, and to Martha for many a delightful meal.

Many colleagues helped me stay the course in this long search as well, and I especially thank my distinguished colleague, guru, and friend, Stanley A. Wolpert, for his continuing support, as also to my esteemed colleagues, Eric Monkkonen, Gerald Barrier, Frank Conlon, Ainslie Embree, Ved Prakash, Leo Jackobson, Wellington Chan, Bhagwan Dua, Steve Berk, Bruce Kinzer, and Melton McLaurin.

I thank Professor J. F. Watts, the members of the Executive Committee, the history faculty, and Deans Paul Sherwin and Martin Tamny for their help and encouragement, which made it much easier for me to settle quickly into the rich environment of The City College of The City University of New York (CUNY).

I also thank my editor, Richard D. DeBacher, and his successor, Curtis Clark, and my copy editor, Stephen W. Smith, for their help in bringing this book to press; I thank the production director, Natalia Nadraga, her excellent staff, plus New Leaf Studio for the design, artwork, and other work; and I thank S. K. Mookerjee and his successor, Neil O'Brien, Oxford University Press, New Delhi, for their support in bringing out the Indian edition. Also, I deeply appreciate the thoughtful critiques and valuable suggestions made by anonymous referees for the publishers, which greatly helped improve this volume. For the word-processing wizardry, my thanks to Pat Wilson and Cathy Johnson.

I can never adequately thank my family in India, especially my mother, Sheela, my nephews, Himavan and Vikas Varma, and my nieces, Shivani, Rohini, and Radha Patel—whenever they are also in India—for making my visits home so enjoyable and eventful. Without their love, support, and kindness the completion of this work would indeed have been difficult.

BHUBANESWAR

.1.

THE TEMPLE TOWN

Bhubaneswar, the heavenly city on the east coast of India in the Puri district of Orissa state, is at heart a Hindu town—with its warrens of markets, temples, and sacred water tanks. Hindu pilgrims from all corners of India come to this celestial city to seek divine bounty from the countless deities who reside in the inner sanctums of the scores of temples scattered all over Bhubaneswar. The temple town, which rose and fell in importance for centuries before finally becoming the capital of Orissa in 1948, contains a series of ancient sandstone temples that vary in size from the towering structure of the Lingaraja, 128 feet high, where Lord Shiva, the city's presiding deity, resides, to the miniatures a few feet tall scattered all over the town or along the banks of the ancient water tanks, where holy men submerge themselves several times at the crack of dawn before propitiating the gods.

In the old temple town very little has changed. Tens of thousands of Hindu pilgrims still visit the sacred city to pay homage to deities and to seek their bounty; and holy men still submerge themselves in water tanks before propitiating their gods. The streets in the sacred city are lined with sweetshops and flower vendors selling their wares to the pilgrims who take them as offerings to the Hindu deities resting in splendor in the inner sanctums of the temples. Outside the temples, youngsters under the close scrutiny of their elders press visitors to the sacred city for baksheesh; women with young children carried under their arms follow worshipers around, demanding loose change to feed the family; holy men in lotus position sit in blissful meditation wherever they can find a quiet corner; and brahmans sit cross-legged promising to read the future of the visitors. Men, women, children, stray dogs and cows, cars with blaring horns, bicycles, bullock carts, horse-drawn carriages, rickshaws, and motorscooters freely intermingle in the streets, competing for space in good humor.

In the midst of tradition and continuity, the old temple city of Bhubaneswar represents a kaleidoscope of images and sequences.

But in the neighboring planned township of Bhubaneswar, built after 1948 as the new capital city of Orissa, a new pattern of life has emerged. Populated mostly by government employees, the new town has in its chameleon way now begun to reflect another new age that began in postindependence India. Laid out in broad intersecting avenues on which rows of elegant government-approved houses are built after the British cantonment model, the new city represents a striking contrast from the old one. These houses, with fenced front yards and indoor plumbing, are assigned on the basis of rank in the civil service hierarchy rather than in the caste system. A capitol complex, large and spacious government buildings, and a modern marketplace in the heart of the new city serve as the temples of new faith; the people of Orissa come here to seek solutions to their problems and pay homage to the new political icons. The service population of the new township—made up of washermen, cowherds, small tradesmen, rickshaw-pullers, sweepers, manual labourers, and others who have failed to find housing in the capital city, the old town, or the nearby villages—live in squatter colonies and unauthorized dwellings which have cropped up on the periphery.

Old Bhubaneswar, as a Hindu cultural and religious center, included an area much wider than the one occupied by the present temple town. The orthodox Sanskrit text *Svarnnadri-Mahodaya*,[1] a topographical manual for the pilgrims, defines Bhubaneswar as lying between modern Khandagiri on the west and the temple of Vahirangesvara situated on the top of Dhauligiri (Dhauli) on the south. The entire area lying between these two prominent points, stretching approximately twelve miles, constituted the extent of old Bhubaneswar, and much of the remains of the earliest habitations and monuments have been discovered in the precincts of the present temple city.[2]

Bhubaneswar derives its name from the temple city's chief deity, the Lingaraja: the Lord of the Three Worlds, Tribhuvneshvara. Remembered in ancient Sanskrit literature as *Ekamrakshetra* (mango forest), named after the mango groves in the area, old Bhubaneswar probably developed around the Lingaraja temple, erected to commemorate the *Svayambhu lingam* (literally, phallus made out of natural stone) that stood under a mango tree.[3] Tradition has it that the Lingaraja temple, the quintessence of Kalinga architecture, was built over a period of forty-three years encompassing the reigns of three of the later Somavamsi kings[4]—Yayati Kesari, Ananta Kesari, and Lalatendu Kesari—and probably was completed toward the close of the eleventh century.[5] The majestic temple dominates the landscape surrounding the old city and is representative of the accumulated and crystallized experience in temple building of several centuries. Standing within the spacious compound of laterite measuring 520 feet in length and 465 feet in breadth and having the imposing portal on the east and two secondary gates on north and south, the temple's towering size, the magnificent proportions to which it has been built, its carefully crafted embellishments, its lavish carvings, the graceful curve of its *shikkara* (spire), and its Kalinga-inspired elegant architecture and plastic decoration render the temple "one of the greatest creations of Indian architecture."[6]

In fact so strong was the architectural influence of the Lingaraja on the Indians that Government Architect Julius Vaz later would want to duplicate the temple complex in his designs for the capitol complex in new Bhubaneswar. The Lingaraja is a combination of four chambers running west to east in the same axial alignment, i.e., *deul* (sanctum), *jagamohana* (audience hall), *natamandira* (dancing hall), and *bhogamandapa* (dining hall), the last two being later additions, which is borne out by the fact that "they are built of an altogether different type of sandstone and . . . their sculptures bear the obvious signs of the artistic development and peculiarities of a later period."[7] The *deul* is, like other temples at Bhubaneswar, a *rekha* (line) structure, the spire giving the optical impression of one continuous line, while the other three are *pidha* ("wooden seat"; the pyramidal structure) in form. Both the *natamandira* and *bhogamandapa* are open halls and the former has a flat roof.

Lying on longitude of 85 degrees and 50 minutes, east, and latitude 20 degrees and 15 minutes, north, Bhubaneswar is situated to the south-west of the three great rivers—the Baitarani, the Brahmani, and the Mahanadi—which, together with their numerous branches, intersect the coastal plain of Orissa in the Cuttack district. Rocky, with an undulating surface, Bhubaneswar and its surrounding area is mostly unfit for cultivation, providing an ideal location for the growth of habitation and religious monuments. Bhubaneswar proper and its immediate neighborhood are full of laterite formations occasionally broken up by hillocks of sandstone, the former providing excellent material for secular buildings and the latter for religious monuments. The mild climate of the coastal region and the existence of natural springs possessing curative properties must also have contributed to Bhubaneswar's uneven and protean history.

Bhubaneswar, which first witnessed the prolific activity of temple building in the seventh century A.D., experienced several changes earlier in its physical form, its ethnic composition, its religious character, and its role as a subcontinental socioreligious center from century to century or decade to decade. The celestial city's character alternated with Buddhism, Jainism, Shaivism, and Vaishnavism, religions which found a home in Bhubaneswar at one time or another with the changing dynasties of Kalinga, the ancient name for Orissa. The presence of all these religions gave Bhubaneswar its sacred character, blending sanctity with beauty and art with religion. Old Bhubaneswar promised *moksha* (salvation) to the Hindus, and the city has come to be viewed as the domain of Lord Shiva, the Destroyer, Lord of the Three Worlds. A local legend has it that as many as six thousand temples were erected in old Bhubaneswar and about ten million *lingams* existed in the city and its vicinity. Different in style and size, some more magnificent and elaborate than the others, and not all surviving into the present, most of these temples are dedicated to Lord Shiva. The use of sandstone in each of these temples tells the story of Bhubaneswar—*Ekamratirtha* (sacred place)—and attests to the craftsmanship of local artists in handling sandstone for building even in the pre-Mauryan period. Many of the temples are built near or around the Bindu Sagar, a lake which, according to a legend, was formed by collecting a drop each from all the sacred waters of India. A Hindu pilgrim to Bhubaneswar must begin, therefore, with a bath in this sacred lake and follow by worship of Lord Shiva, which will deliver him *moksha*. The ancient *Brahma Purana* declares: "He who undertakes the pilgrimage to this *tirth* [holy place] and performs due ceremonies, with his senses controlled, liberates his twenty-one generations and goes to the heaven of Shiv. One may bathe in the Bindu [Sagar] any day and if he has the *Darshan* [vision] of (1) Shiv, (2) Parvati, (3) Chanda, (4) Kartikeya, (5) Ganesh, (6) Nandi, (7) Kalpavriksha, and (8) Savitri, one goes to Shiv's heaven. The *Ekamra* is the *Shiv kshetra* as sacred as Kashi and one who takes a bath here will certainly attain liberation."[8]

The Buddhist *jatakas* (birth stories) and the Brahmanical *sutras* (traditions) reveal that art in India in the pre-Mauryan period was mostly of perishable materials such as clay, bamboo, wood, and brick. It is, therefore, not clear when and how Bhubaneswar emerged as the center of civilization, and much of its early past is mired in myth and tradition; but the city is one of the few places in India which have archeological remains from the earliest period down to the end of Hindu rule. By most accounts old Bhubaneswar was not the political capital of the region; however, it served, along with Puri, where the great temple of Jagannatha—Vishnu, Lord of the World, the Preserver—stands, as one of the twin religious centers for the Hindus. "Even then," one observer of Bhubaneswar has noted, "there must have been a dual pull because . . . the stronghold of the [Shaiva] priests was not Bhubaneswar but Jajpur—corruption of Yagyapur, City of Sacrifice, or Yayatipur, City of Yayati, [the] legendary founder of the Kesari or Somavamsi dynasty."[9] Bhubaneswar's history enters into a clearer period in the days of Mauryan emperor Ashoka (Sorrowless), who reigned from 269 to 232 B.C. and who chose a hill outside of Bhubaneswar for the promulgation of his rock edicts, including the two special Kalinga edicts, and for erecting a pillar. The excavations at Sisupalagarh, five kilometers to the southeast of Bhubaneswar, take the origin of the old city back to the fourth or third century B.C., lending credence to the belief that the city of Tosali, the regional administrative capital of Ashoka, might have been situated in the neighborhood of Dhauligiri,[10] eight kilometers south of Bhubaneswar.

Sisupalagarh was "a well-planned and well-fortified city, square in shape, each side measuring three-quarters of a mile and each having two elaborately constructed gates and some small exits."[11] The Gandhavati river (modern Gangua) served as the city's natural moat on the western and northern sides, and the excavations at the site have led to the conclusion that the city was intimately connected to a northern culture in its early period and to a southern culture in its later period. A few archaeological relics from the site have been linked to the Mauryan period, but they do not substantially add to the early history of Bhubaneswar. Ashoka's monuments near Bhubaneswar, therefore, remain the main source for the early history of the city. The idea of making rock-inscriptions may have originally come to Ashoka from the Persian king Darius, and, considering the Mauryan emperor's missions to the Greek kingdoms, it is not surprising that the capitals of Ashokan pillars bear a remarkable similarity to those at Persepolis and may have been sculpted by craftsmen from the northwest province. The two special Kalinga edicts at Dhauligiri and Jaugada in the Ganjam district were probably specifically meant for the people of Kalinga.[12] The Dhauligiri inscription omits edicts twelve and thirteen to make room for the special

Kalinga edicts. Clearly, the omission by Ashoka of edict thirteen was deliberate because that edict describes pithily the emperor's conquest of Kalinga (c. 261 B.C.), involving great carnage, many captives, and misery of the people. The scale of the casualties and the extent of the human misery indicates the might of the Kalinga kingdom to have put up such a strong resistance against the mighty Mauryan emperor. The omitted edict at Dhauligiri recorded the sentiment of Ashoka:

> When he had been consecrated eight years the Beloved of the Gods, the king Piyadassi, conquered Kalinga. A hundred and fifty thousand people were deported, a hundred thousand were killed and many times that number perished. Afterwards, now that Kalinga was annexed, the Beloved of the Gods very earnestly practiced *Dhamma*, desired *Dhamma*, and taught *Dhamma*. On conquering Kalinga the Beloved of the Gods felt remorse, for, when an independent country is conquered the slaughter, death, and deportation of the people is extremely grievous to the Beloved of the Gods, and weighs heavily on his mind. What is even more deplorable to the Beloved of the Gods, is that those who dwell there, whether brahmans, *sramanas*, or those of other sects, or householders who show obedience to their superiors, obedience to mother and father, obedience to their teachers and behave well and devotedly towards their friends, acquaintances, colleagues, relatives, slaves, and servants—all suffer violence, murder, and separation from their loved ones. Even those who are fortunate to have escaped, and whose love is undiminished (by the brutalizing effect of war), suffer from the misfortunes of their friends, acquaintances, colleagues, and relatives. This participation of all men in suffering, weighs heavily on the mind of the Beloved of the Gods. . . . Today if a hundredth or a thousandth part of those people who were killed or died or were deported when Kalinga was annexed were to suffer similarly, it would weigh heavily on the mind of the Beloved of the Gods.
>
> The Beloved of the Gods believes that one who does wrong should be forgiven as far as it is possible to forgive him. And the Beloved of the Gods conciliates the forest tribes of his empire, but he warns them that he has power even in his remorse, and he asks them to repent, lest they be killed. For the Beloved of the Gods wishes that all beings should be unharmed, self-controlled, calm in mind, and gentle.
>
> The Beloved of the Gods considers victory by *Dhamma* to be the foremost victory. And moreover the Beloved of the Gods has gained this

victory on all his frontiers to a distance of six hundred *yojanas* (i.e. about 1500 miles), where reigns the Greek king named Antiochus, and beyond the realm of that Antiochus in the lands of the four kings named Ptolemy, Antigonus, Magas, and Alexander; and in the south over the Cholas and Pandyas as far as Ceylon. Likewise here in the imperial territories among the Greeks and the Kambojas, Nabhakas and Nabhapanktis, Bhojas and Pitinikas, Andhras and Parindas, everywhere the people follow the Beloved of the Gods' instructions in *Dhamma*. Even where the envoys of the Beloved of the Gods have not gone, people hear of his conduct according to *Dhamma*, his precepts and his instruction in *Dhamma*, and they follow *Dhamma* and will continue to follow it.

What is obtained by this is victory everywhere, and everywhere victory is pleasant. This pleasure has been obtained through victory by *Dhamma*—yet it is but a slight pleasure, for the Beloved of the Gods only looks upon that as important in its results which pertains to the next world.

This inscription of *Dhamma* has been engraved so that any sons or great grandsons that I may have should not think of gaining new conquests, and in whatever victories they may gain should be satisfied with patience and light punishment. They should only consider conquest by *Dhamma* to be a true conquest, and delight in *Dhamma* should be their whole delight, for this is of value in both this world and the next.[13]

Clearly the destruction caused by the war filled Ashoka with remorse, and in an effort to seek expiation he was drawn to Buddhist thinking. The Mauryan emperor's conversion to Buddhism was gradual, however; over a period of two and a half years he became a zealous devotee of Buddhism. This led him eventually to renounce his ambition of *dig-vijaya* (military conquest) in favor of *dhamma-vijaya* (spiritual conquest). The new Mauryan policy of *dhamma*, besides introducing Buddhism to Orissa,[14] included measures which today would be considered welfare programs: building of new roads, sinking of drinking-water wells, construction of resthouses every nine miles on highways for travelers, and so on. But Ashoka was careful to make a distinction between his personal belief in and support of Buddhism and his duty as emperor to remain unattached and unbiased in favor of any religion. "The Beloved of the Gods," he declared in one of his edicts, "honours all sects and both ascetics and laymen," and considers essential "the advancement of . . . all sects."[15] The pluralism of India dictated a more tolerant socioreligious policy which could be ignored only at the risk of disturbing the concord among men of different sects.

Hinduism must have coexisted with Buddhism in Bhubaneswar under Mauryan rule. However, because of the royal patronage, the entire artistic expression of this age, whether architecture or sculpture, centered on Buddhism, and wealthy merchants and prosperous guilds (*shreni*) also came to give their support for Buddhism. Representations of religious architecture are the Buddhist *stupas* (literally "gathered"), the largest and most famous of which was built at Sanchi in central India, and Buddhist cave-temples, the most impressive of which are at Ajanta and Ellora, completed several centuries after Ashoka's death. Having links to pre-Buddhist burial mounds, the *stupa*, a hemispherical dome of solid stone, supposedly contains the ashes of the Buddha. Tradition credits Ashoka with having built no fewer than 84,000 *stupas*, which several hundred years later were embellished with elaborately designed stone railings and "gates" (*tornas*), topped with many tiers of umbrellas above the "little square house" (*harmika*), set over the egg-shaped dome, through which the Buddha's spirit was said to pass from terrestrial to celestial release and eternal repose. Symbolizing the universe, the *stupa* is believed to be a primitive ancestor of the Hindu temple; and Ashoka's monuments near Bhubaneswar clearly inspired the later Buddhist and Hindu temples of the city—just as they were to influence the architecture of new Bhubaneswar in the twentieth century.

The language used by Ashoka in the Dhauligiri inscription is extremely conciliatory, clearly meant for the pacification of the newly conquered people. Composed in the *Brahmi* script, considered to be the predecessor of the *Devanagri* ("City of The Gods") script of Sanskrit and modern Hindi, phonetically the earliest developed *script*, the two special edicts express the Mauryan emperor's intense solicitude for the welfare of the people of Kalinga, proclaiming them to be his children. At Dhauligiri, which has been identified as the Mauryan administration's regional capital, Tosali, Ashoka issued a code of conduct for his officers (*mahamatras*) by which they were to govern the people of Kalinga:

> By order of the Beloved of the Gods: the officers and city magistrates at Tosali/Samapa are to be instructed thus: . . . You are in charge of many thousands of living beings. You should gain the affection of men. All

men are my children, and just as I desire for my children that they should obtain welfare and happiness both in this world and the next, the same do I desire for all men. . . . You should strive to practice impartiality. But it cannot be practised by one possessing any of these faults—jealousy, shortness of temper, harshness, rashness, obstinacy, idleness, or slackness. You should wish to avoid such faults. The root of all this is to be even-tempered and not rash in your work. He who is slack will not act, and in your official functions you must strive, act, and work. . . . There is great advantage in conforming to this instruction and great loss in not conforming to it. For by disregarding it you will gain neither heaven nor the favor of the king.[16]

In the second special edict at Dhauligiri and Jaugada, Ashoka exhorts the hill people, apparently outside his imperial control, to have confidence in Mauryan rule and promises a relationship with them based on the new doctrine of *dhamma*:

. . . All men are my children. . . . If the unconquered peoples on my borders ask what is my will, they should be made to understand that this is my will with regard to them—"the king desires that they should have no trouble on his account, should trust in him, and should have in their dealings with him only happiness and no sorrow. They should understand that the king will forgive them as far as they can be forgiven, and that through him they should follow *Dhamma* and gain this world and the next."[17]

That the full force of Ashoka's rule and proselytization was felt in coastal Orissa, leaving out the peoples of the hilly tracts, possibly explains the Mauryan emperor's decision to place his special rock edicts near Bhubaneswar, which must have formed the center of his missionary activities. Whereas Jaugada on the northern bank of the Rishikulya River in the Ganjam district, where Ashoka placed his second set of inscriptions, was probably a large town and the presence of the fort there suggests to its having been a military center, its proximity to the sea served as an added advantage for trade and maritime activities. Bhubaneswar, according to the orthodox Sanskrit texts that provide hyperbolic legendary accounts of the city and the Jagannatha temple chronicle *Mandal Panji*, included Dhauligiri and Sisupalagarh, possibly making the city into a metropolis.

Ashoka's rock edicts at Dhauligiri provide the earliest specimen of sculptural art in Kalinga, and are incised on a rock with the sculptured forepart of an elephant at the top. The elephant sculpture, about 1.22 meters in height, represents the sacred symbol of the Buddhists. (In Buddhist tradition, the great preacher is believed to have entered his mother's body in the form of an elephant.)[18] Due apparently to the inferior quality of the rock, the sculpture lacks the typical Mauryan finish; nevertheless, the sculpture represents accomplishments of Mauryan craftsmanship in the treatment of the figure and the handling of the bulky material.

There are two other major sculptures which have been assigned to the Ashokan period in the Bhubaneswar area. First of these is the upper part of a lion, about three feet in height and eight feet, seven inches in circumference, which was discovered near the Bhaskaresvara temple. There already existed near the temple a colossal *lingam*, nine feet in height and twelve feet, five inches in circumference at its base, which was considered to be a Shaivite symbol but which is now being linked to the lion figure. Both monuments are now being assigned to the Mauryan period. Because both monuments are made from the same sandstone material, which is not similar to the stone used in the temple itself, and because a lion figure usually served as the capital of an Ashokan pillar, archaeologists have concluded that the Ashokan pillar was converted into a Shaivite *lingam* at a later date.[19] The other piece of sculpture at Bhubaneswar which can be assigned to the Mauryan period is "a portion of the capital consisting of the abacus, the torus and the so-called bell," thirty-two inches in height and nineteen feet, five inches in circumference near its upper bulge. Lying near a water tank known as Ashoka jhara just behind the Ramesvara temple, situated halfway between the railway station and the Lingaraja, the bell capital represents "certain divergence" from other Ashokan bell capitals. This has generated a controversy about its belonging to the Mauryan period; however, it is now considered to be a part of another Ashokan pillar near the Ashoka jhara.[20]

Because these remnants do not manifest the Perso-Hellenic influence generally associated with stone architecture from the Ashokan period, the authenticity of their once belonging to Ashokan monuments has been cast in doubt. The explanation may be that the original monuments were crafted by local artists, probably under the direction of imperial supervision, who left a local imprint on these monuments. The presence of other pre-Mauryan monuments in the Bhubaneswar area strongly suggests that Kalinga artists were well experienced in handling sandstone, and the Mauryan emperor must have employed local artists to build his monuments in Bhubaneswar. Although Ashoka had defeated Kalinga, he had not succeeded in extinguishing the independent spirit of the people; and this spirit must have flourished even under Mauryan rule and expressed itself in cultural and artistic accomplishments. The quickness with which Shaivism reasserted itself in Orissa after Ashoka's death, combined with the subsequent conversion, destruction, and vandalism of Buddhist monuments by Shaivites, serves as testimony to that Kalinga spirit—and Orissa was later to respond with the same fervor against attempts at domination by the Mughals, the Marathas, and the British. The same Kalinga spirit was to reappear in the first half of the twentieth century, providing the basis for the creation of a separate state of Orissa in 1936, and the construction of the new capital at Bhubaneswar was to be its culminating expression. Just as the people of Kalinga had built thousands of temples in praise of the gods to solicit their divine benediction for *moksha* (salvation), so, too, were the people of Orissa inspired to consecrate the new state by building the capital city at Bhubaneswar.

Political events in India—and Orissa—after the close of the Mauryan period (c. 180 B.C.) became diffuse, involving different dynasties and eras and peoples. Evidence is tentative and an effort is made to reconstruct history from many sources, including Chinese. The second century B.C. saw India divided into a number of political regions, each with its own ambitions. Kalinga, which remained a source of anxiety to imperial Magadha, rose to power under the Chedi kings of the Mahameghavahana family, probably in the first century B.C. King Kharavela, the most noteworthy of the Chedis, left a long inscription, which includes a biographical sketch, at Hatigumpha—the Elephant's Cave—in the Udayagiri hills; but because it is badly damaged, sections of the inscription are difficult to read, making it hard to determine either this king's dates or the chronology of the monuments he apparently left behind in the sister hills of Udayagiri (ancient Kumari Hill) and Khandagiri (ancient Kumar Hill, named for the son of Shiva). Consequently, scholars remain divided on Kharavela's dates, some placing him in the second century B.C., others placing him in the first century B.C., and still others placing him much later in the second quarter of the first century A.D.[21]

Prevailing local legends have further obscured the origin of the Chedis. Perhaps the most romantic of these legends, and certainly the one to have generated literature in Telugu, tells a story of Princess Karuvaki, a maiden from a local community of fishermen who was noted for her beauty and valor and who eventually married the prince of Kalinga. She fought alongside the prince and the king of Kalinga against Ashoka. Both men were killed in the war, and Ashoka carried her away to Magadha, where he proposed to marry her. But Karuvaki made the condition that she would marry the Mauryan emperor only if he converted to Buddhism. After Ashoka's conversion, Karuvaki married him and requested that the emperor have sculptured the events of their romance at Ranigumpha—the Queen's Cave—in the Udayagiri hills near Bhubaneswar. Although the sculptures in relief on the walls of the Ranigumpha "appear to have some congruity with the above legend," verification of the story remains elusive for historians. The same legend tells about Ashoka renaming Kalinga as "Cheti," probably after the family name of Karuvaki. "Cheti" literally means fisherman, and in the course of time the kingdom of Cheti became "Chedi."[22]

The most plausible date for the beginning of Kharavela's reign can be placed in c. 159 B.C. A devout Jain, Kharavela displayed equal passion for military conquest and conducted a number of successful campaigns in various directions. The Hatigumpha inscription describes his conquest over the king of the western Deccan, his occupation of Rajagriha to the north, his encounter with the Greeks in the northeast, his victory over the Pandyan kingdom in the south of the peninsula, and finally his two invasions of Magadha, whence he regained possession of a sacred Jain statue which had been carried away earlier by the Nandas, the predecessors of the Mauryas. Besides referring to military conquests, the inscription refers to Kharavela's spending vast sums on the welfare of his subjects. There is a special mention of irrigation canals built by the Nandas, and Kharavela takes special pride in his own efforts in this direction. The inscription is ornate and hyperbolic in style, meant for royal propaganda.

Kharavela's reign witnessed the rise of Jainism, and under his patronage the Udayagiri and Khandagiri hills, 6.5 kilometers away from the capital city of Bhubaneswar, became strong Jain centers. The Jain caves from the two sister hills represent a changing trend in cave art, displaying definite preference for ornamentation. The Ranigumpha sculptures provide information on the life-style of the Kharavela court. Sir William Wilson Hunter, the noted nineteenth century Indologist who served as the director general of statistics and who completed his famous work *Orissa*, in two volumes, in 1872, mistakenly described these caves as

Buddhist but provided a faithful description of the sculptures at the Ranigumpha:

> The upper verandah of the QUEEN'S MONASTERY is adorned with a sculptured biography of its founder. The first tableau, worn almost level with the rock, seems to represent the sending of presents which preceded the matrimonial alliances of the ancient dynasties of India. A running figure stands dimly out, apparently carrying a tray of fruit. The second appears to be the arrival of the suitor. It delineates the meeting of the elephants, and a number of confused human forms, one of whom rides on a lion. From the third tableau the biography becomes more distinct. It represents the courtship. The prince is introduced by an old lady to the princess, who sits cross-legged on a high seat, with her eyes averted, and her arms round the neck of one of her maidens below. The fourth is the fight. The prince and princess, each armed with swords and oblong shields, engage in combat. The fifth is the abduction, depicting the princess defeated and carried off in the princess [*sic*] arms, her sword lost, but her shield still grasped in her hand. The prince holds his sword drawn, and is amply clothed. The princess is scantily draped, with her hair done up in a perpendicular chignon, rising from the top of her head, and a long tress falling over her bosom to her waist. She wears heavy anklets. The sixth is the hunt. A tree forms the centre of the piece, on one side of which the prince and princess are shooting at a bounding antelope; while a led horse stands near, and attendants armed with clubs. The prince draws his bow in the perpendicular fashion. It is about two-thirds his own height. A lady looks down upon the chase from the tree. A court scene follows, in which the prince sits on a throne on the left, with attendants holding fans on either side. Dancing girls and musicians are grouped in front, and the princess appears on a throne on the extreme right. The eighth and ninth tableaux are effaced. Three scenes of dalliance between the prince and the princess follow, and the series in the upper story ends in a mysterious running figure with a snake twisted round him. The lower verandah exhibits the sequel. A convent scene discloses the princess retired from the vanities of life, sitting at her cell door in the upper storey of a sculptured monastery, with her ladies, also turned ascetics, sitting at separate doors in the lower one. The remaining tableaux, four in number, represent the prince, princess, and courtiers as hermits, with their

> hands on their breasts in an attitude of abstraction, freed from human passion, indeed even from the necessity of religious observances, and wrapt in contemplation of the Deity.
>
> Throughout, the prince is generally fully dressed, with a cotton garment falling from his girdle, but leaving the leg bare from the knee. The lady wears a feathery headdress, with her hair done up in a towering chignon. A scroll of birds and beasts and leaves runs the whole way along. The battle and hunting scenes are given with much spirit, the animals being very different from the conventional creatures of modern Hindu art.[23]

Higher up in the hill facing the south is the Ganeshgumpha—the Ganesh Cave—named after the elephant-headed Hindu god figure inside. Apparently a work of later date, the cave sculptures provide another version of the same story told in the Ranigumpha:

> In the first scene, a lady watches over her husband, who is sleeping under the sacred Buddhist tree. In the second, a suitor makes advances to the lady, who turns her head away. He has seized one hand, and she seems to be in the act of running from him, with her other arm thrown up as if crying for help. The third is the battle. The husband and the lover (or perhaps it is the lady and her suitor) fight with oblong shields and swords. In the fourth, the warrior carries off the vanquished princess in his arms. In the fifth, the successful paramour is flying on an elephant, pursued by soldiers in heavy kilts. The prince draws his bow in the perpendicular fashion, as in the previous series, and a soldier has cut off the head of one of the pursuers. The sixth is the home-coming. The elephant kneels under a tree, the riders have dismounted, and the lady hangs down her head, as if in shame or sorrow. The seventh represents their home-life. The lady stands with her hand on the prince's shoulder, while he has one arm round her waist, and in the other hand grasps his bow. The series ends in a scene of dalliance.[24]

There must have existed a number of other caves in the hills of Udayagiri and Khandagiri which had a socioreligious significance. The reference in the Hatigumpha inscription to the recovery of the Jain statue by Kharavela clearly establishes the existence of Jainism in the Bhubaneswar area before Ashoka's conquest of Kalinga, and it would appear that the rivalry between Buddhist Magadha and Jainist Kalinga was fueled as much by political ambitions as by religious fervor. Jain sacred literature also points to the existence of the faith in the Bhubaneswar area before Ashoka's conquest of the region. The loss of political independence to the Mauryans and the missionary activities of Ashoka must have created feelings of resentment among the people of Kalinga, who must have been looking for ways to maintain their own cultural and religious identity even under the Mauryans. Kharavela's deliberate omission of any reference to the Mauryans in his inscription was probably intended not to remind the people of the bitter memory of the Kalinga war, just as Ashoka himself had considered it prudent not to mention the war in his Dhauligiri inscription. By choosing to place his inscription in the Udayagiri hills, which are in the close vicinity of Dhauligiri, Kharavela was perhaps hoping to overshadow the memory of Mauryan rule of Kalinga. "The monuments of Udayagiri thus mark," one scholar has persuasively argued, "the height of the glory of Kharavela's dynasty, when freedom had been won, the defeat from Magadha avenged, the sacred seat of Jain recovered and the revival of Jainism was in full force."[25] The vast wealth accumulated by Kharavela from his conquests supposedly provided the necessary financing required for cave art and the first temples of Bhubaneswar. In the course of time Buddhism was to disappear from the region, although Jainism continued to retain a small following even in the days of Shaivite ascendancy. On Kharavela's death, however, Kalinga—and Bhubaneswar—were to fall into nearly eight hundred years of quiescence.

Although not until the seventh century A.D. did Kalinga once again enter a period of historical activity, there are evidences available to indicate that in the intervening centuries Bhubaneswar remained an important cultural and religious center for the Buddhists, Jains, and Hindus. The bulk of the population remained Hindu, even when Buddhism and Jainism received royal patronage. Recognizing the predominantly Hindu character of India, both Ashoka and Kharavela were prudent to propogate religious toleration in the inscriptions near Bhubaneswar, and not until the Kesari period did Hinduism receive royal patronage when that dynasty imported thousands of brahmans from the north and offered them land grants to settle villages known as *sasanas*.

Even before the Aryan colonization of Kalinga by the great influx of the brahmans, the collapse of the Mauryan empire in the second century B.C. had exposed India to a series of central Asian and Persian invasions, removing the northwest from indigenous control and causing political fragmentation of the subcontinent from which Kalinga did not escape. In the first century B.C. the northern Deccan played a significant role in shaping the course of the history of the subcontinent on the rise of the Andhra-Satavahanas, who established their rule in Magadha in 27 B.C. Apparently originating in the Andhra region, homeland of the Dravidian Telugu-speaking peoples in the delta between the Krishna and Godavari rivers on the east coast, the dynamic Andhra-Satavahanas ruled much of south and central India from the second century B.C. to the second century A.D. Their rule signifies Aryanization of the Dravidian Andhras, as the Sanskrit word *Satavahana* is believed to have meant "seven mounts," a legendary allusion to the seven-horse chariot of the Hindu god Vishnu, whose mounts each represented one day of the week.[26]

Satkarni was the earliest of the Andhra-Satavahana kings to have received wide recognition for his military conquests and is believed to have performed a horse sacrifice (*Ashvamedha*), a Vedic Aryan practice, to establish his claim to an empire. Establishing their capital at Paithan on the Godavari, about a hundred miles northeast of modern Pune (in the northwest Deccan), the center of subsequent Maratha power, the Andhra-Satavahanas were eventually to control the Deccan, thus providing the connecting link between the north and the south, not only in terms of politics but more importantly in trade and in the exchange of cultural ideas. Amaravati, on the banks of the Krishna, which later became the southeast capital of the Andhra-Satavahanas, "flourished on its trade with Rome, Ceylon, and Southeast Asia and may have been the most prosperous city in India during the second century of the Christian era."[27] The discovery of four *yaksa* (folk divinity) images near Bhubaneswar and their miniature prototypes in the Khandagiri-Udayagiri caves has led one scholar to conclude close cultural contacts between Bhubaneswar and Sanchi in Central India.[28] Considering that Kalinga was contiguous to Andhra and considering that the Andhra-Satavahana king Gautamputra is believed to have occupied Mount Mahendra in Kalinga, it may not be "unreasonable" to suggest "that there was a period of Andhra-Satavahana supremacy in Orissa and this supremacy began with the fall of Kharavela's dynasty and ended about the third century A.D."[29] Because the Andhra-Satavahanas supported the brahman orthodoxy, when necessary even in an armed conflict, as Gautamputra ruling in the first half of the second century A.D. did in a bloody conflict with the *Shakas* (Scythians) in the north to preserve the purity of the Vedic *varnas* (caste), Kalinga—and Bhubaneswar—must have experienced the resurgence of Hinduism during their rule. The discovery of two *Nagaraja* statues in the suburbs of Bhubaneswar indicates the existence of the popular Hindu folk cult of *Naga* worship in the region. "A careful comparison of the ornaments, garments and swords worn by these *Nagarajas* with those of the sculptures in the Udayagiri cave temples . . . shows that they belong to a conception entirely dissimilar and different";[30] and these figures belong to a period when the style and tradition and religion of the north again make themselves felt in Orissa, possibly after the decline of Buddhism and Jainism which flourished under Ashoka and Kharavela, respectively.

Buddhism reasserted itself in Kalinga under the Murunda dynasty in the third century A.D., however, when parts of Bihar and Orissa came under the rule of Murunda kings. Originating in the northwest, the non-Hindu Murundas were easily drawn to the more accepting Buddhism. Ruling from Pataliputra (modern Patna), the Murundas, like their Indo-European speaking nomad cousins, the Kushanas (Yueh-chih), had arrived in India after being driven from their homeland in central Asia by the Han dynasty of China (founded in 202 B.C.). The Murundas styled themselves after the Kushanas, striking coins similar to the Kushana coin types and taking the imperial Kushana title *Maharaja-rajadhiraja* ("king of kings"). The Kushanas, too, had been patron kings of Buddhism, and Kanishka, who ruled for more than two decades around A.D. 100, hosted the Fourth Buddhist Council in Kashmir to discuss matters pertaining to Buddhist theology and doctrine. The impetus given Buddhism under Kanishka may also have influenced the religious proclivities of the Murunda kings, who came to be named as the "Puri Kushanas" by the nineteenth-century British Indologist A. F. R. Hoernle, after the other temple city of Orissa, Puri.

The period between the fall of the imperial Kushanas and the rise of the Guptas in the fourth century A.D. is a fragmented period in Indian history, but north India took a distinct turn toward brahmanical Hinduism under Gupta rule. The temple architecture, known as *Nagara* in the *Silpa-sastras* (Hindu canonical texts on architecture), that first developed in the north during the Gupta period ultimately exerted its influence in Orissa as well, where it became assimilated with the local tradition. Hereafter, Bhubaneswar became the center of the distinctive Orissan style of Indian art and architecture, and, with a few exceptions, the new art form was completely pressed into service of Lord Shiva and his female counterpart, *Shakti* (Female Power). The two Hindu cults dominated the scene until the ingress of Vaishnavism in the thirteenth century.

A controversy remains as to whether the Guptas (c. A.D. 320–550) occupied Orissa or not. One early history of Orissa has unequivocally maintained that "there is no evidence, whatsoever, to prove that any part of Orissa or Kalinga was included in the Gupta empire."[31] A more recent study has argued that there are evidences "to show that the Guptas were in occupation of at least the coastal districts of Orissa."[32] Controversy notwithstanding, the sheer size of the Gupta empire, which extended to the Punjab on the west and Bengal on the east, and in the north included Kashmir and the Deccan in the south, must have exerted enormous influence on Orissa from its imperial power base in Magadha. The discovery of Orissa copperplates bearing the Gupta dates and the discovery of sculptures at Bhubaneswar and Dengaposi bearing Gupta characteristics point to the presence of Gupta cultural influence in Orissa—which was to shape the region's later history. Moreover, the conversion of the Buddhist pillar into a Shaivite phallic emblem in the fifth century points to a struggle between the two faiths, the latter having replaced the former by the fifth century. According to the account in the apocryphal version of the *Ekamra Purana*, a Shaiva work on palm-leaf manuscript possibly completed in the thirteenth century, there was a dreadful war between the gods and demons on the banks of the Gangua (ancient Gandhavati) near Bhubaneswar in which the gods, with the help of Shiva, defeated the demons. The story is an apocryphal reference to the Shaivite and the Buddhist struggle in the Bhubaneswar region, resulting in the triumph of Shaivism.

The Hindu cultural renaissance of the Gupta period survived into seventh-century India, which saw political rivalries between the Buddhist king Harshavardhana (reigned 606–47) of Kanauj in the north, the Hindu Chalukya king Pulakesin II (reigned 610–42) in the southwestern Deccan, and the Shaivite Gauda king Sasanka in the east for the control of Kalinga. While tradition tells about Sasanka's rule of Orissa, it provides no clear dates of his reign. But he is believed to have ruled Orissa until the end of his life in A.D. 619. A devout Shaivite, Sasanka was an implacable enemy of the Buddhists and is believed to have built several Shaivite temples on the ruins of Buddhist monuments in the Bhubaneswar region. Although Shaivite worship existed in Bhubaneswar before Sasanka, tradition credits him with making Lord Tribhuvanesvara, the Lord of the Three Worlds, the Destroyer, the chief deity of the celestial city and commemorating the occasion by erecting the famous Tribhuvanesvara temple from which the city derives its name. Supreme status notwithstanding, the shrine of Lord Tribhuvanesvara continues to honor the old tradition of paying respect to earlier shrines of the city, when it is carried to them on fourteen festive occasions celebrated annually in the Lingaraja temple. The itinerary of the traveling shrine is planned in the order of the antiquity of the fourteen shrines, the first two containing the remnants of Ashokan pillars.

None of the monuments built by Sasanka have survived, but it is possible that the eleventh century Lingaraja in Bhubaneswar was built on the ruins of the Tribhuvanesvara. The *Ekamra Purana* tells about the existence of a *Svayambhu lingam* under a mango tree which revealed itself to the people of Bhubaneswar in the *Dvapara* age, and in the subsequent *Kali* age Sasanka commemorated the sacred symbol by erecting the Tribhuvanesvara temple. (In Hinduism, the cosmic time cycle revolves in the sequence of four yugas [ages]: 1] Krita, 2] Treta, 3] Dvapara, and 4] Kali.) Eventually, the *lingam* came to be called Krittivasa, another name for Lord Shiva. Known also as Hemakuta, Hemadri, Svarnnakuta, Svarnnadri,[33] all different names for Lord Shiva, Hinduism's "Great God" (*Maheshvara*), Bhubaneswar came to be regarded as *Kailasa*, Shiva's mythic mountain home in the Himalayas.

The trend toward monotheism in brahmanical thinking, born out of the eighth century B.C. philosophy of the *Upanishads* (literally "to sit down in front of," hence the name given to esoteric Vedic texts consisting of philosophy and religion with the concept of the Absolute or the Universal Soul) and the subsequent successful attacks of the sixth century B.C. heretic sects of Buddhism and Jainism on Vedic sacrifices and gods, had resulted in the idea of the trinity of gods: Brahma, the Creator; Vishnu, the Preserver; and Shiva, the Destroyer of all evil in the universe. The idea also represented the cyclical conception of nature where creation, preservation, and destruction were seen as the natural order of things; and of the three gods, Vishnu and Shiva ultimately emerged as the popular gods, developing a large following among Hindus as the Vaishnavas and the Shaivas, respectively.

Shiva evolved from the Vedic rain god Rudra and the Tamil god Murugan, incorporating a number of fertility cults, such as those of the phallic emblem (*lingam*), the bull (*nandi*), and was also associated with a number of fertility goddesses, chief among them being *Shakti* (Power). The devotion to the *lingam* became the most important aspect of Shaivite worship from about the beginning of the Christian era, and Shaivism itself became the embodiment of Hinduism's reconciliation of extremes: erotic passion and ascetic renunciation, frenzied motion and controlled calm, violence and passivity.

A gradual shift in Hinduism from ritualism to a more personal relationship between god and the devotee further helped in making Hindu salvation (*moksha*) accessible to the peasant masses of India as well as to the brahman elite. Under the new monotheistic doctrine, both Vaishnavism and Shaivism offered a devotee the opportunity to receive God's grace (*prasada*) through devotion (*bhakti*). The idea of personal devotion served as the dynamic force of later Hinduism, resulting in the frenzied activity in temple building in India of which Bhubaneswar is the supreme example. Henceforth, Shaivism was to remain the dominant religion in Bhubaneswar and, in the absence of royal patronage, both Buddhism and Jainism receded into the background.

The form of Shaivism that established itself in Bhubaneswar represented the *Pasupata* sect (founded by the Shaiva teacher Lakulisa) which had flourishing centers in the north as well as in the south.[34] The various sects of Shaivism represented Shiva's various incarnations: He was "at once the auspicious creator of life, Lord of Beasts (*Pashupati*), and King of the Dance (*Nataraja*) and the dark destroyer, haunting burial grounds and consuming poison; fiercer than the tiger; death and time incarnate."[35] The Shiva temples of seventh-century Bhubaneswar were predominantly Indo-Aryan in inspiration, although later they came to incorporate indigenous characteristics. Both the Pasupata sect and the Indo-Aryan temple style (*nagra*) may represent the free mixing of south and north India in Orissa—and Bhubaneswar—a free mixing which one scholar has attributed to the "borderline spirit" of the region.[36] The Pasupata sect's practice of building *lingams* to memorialize its deceased masters led to the construction of innumerable Shiva *lingams* in Bhubaneswar. The later rulers of Orissa were familiar with the sect, the influence of which can be seen in many a temple they built in Bhubaneswar.

The sudden outburst of temple building in Bhubaneswar in the seventh century "can only be understood [in light of] a long period of Buddhist predominance, bridging the 'gap' between the 1st century A.D. and the 6th with nothing but Buddhist monuments—and surely, some Jain monuments too."[37] The Buddhist architects that preceded the Hindu architects provide historical continuity to Orissan temple architecture, which came to combine the best of traditions from the north and south. It is generally maintained that, being a border state, Orissa is ethnically nearer to the Dravidian south than to the Aryan north, notwithstanding the Sanskrit antecedents of the Oriya language. In any case, the resulting "free mixing" of ideas and cultures produced the miracle of Orissan temple architecture, which unhesitatingly burst "into a passionate and almost frantic activity, raising temple after temple, always [faithful] to [the Orissan] style, always ready to make minor changes, but never stopping until in 1250 A.D. . . . the ultimate and triumphal Sun Temple at Konarak is [raised]."[38]

The earliest group of temples to have survived in Bhubaneswar, of which the Parasuramesvara temple is the best preserved, was probably built by Madhavaraja Sailodbhava II of Kongoda (modern Ganjam), who was feudatory of the Gauda king Sasanka and who probably declared his independence at the end of Sasanka's rule in A.D. 619. The political fragmentation of Kalinga that followed the death of Sasanka to which the Chinese Buddhist traveler Yuan Chwang refers on his visit to the region in A.D. 639 resulted in the rise of three separate kingdoms of Odra, Kongoda, and Kalinga. Andhra and Kosala were the two neighboring kingdoms. The Sailodbhava kingdom included both Bhubaneswar and Puri, which has been determined by the discovery of the Sailodbhava copperplates from the two areas, but it remains undetermined whether the Sailodbhavas built any monuments in Bhubaneswar.

Nor do the *Ekamra Purana* and the *Mandala Panji*, the Jagannatha temple chronicle at Puri, credit the Bhauma-karas, who succeeded the Sailodbhavas, with the building of many temples in Bhubaneswar. Their origins and dates of rule remain obscure, but they are believed to have been of non-Aryan origin, which explains their omission in the two works. Another tradition traces their origin to a brahman mother and a non-brahman father.[39] One scholar has tried to link them to the Bhuyan tribe that still resides in the mountains and plains of Orissa[40] because, like the tribal Bhuyan woman who enjoys greater freedom than her Hindu counterpart, the Bhauma-kara woman also enjoyed greater freedom, and the dynasty produced no fewer than six sovereign female rulers of Orissa. With the exception of Rudramba of the Kakatiya dynasty and the Kashmiri queen Didda, the Bhauma-karas were perhaps the only Hindu dynasty to allow women to succeed their husbands and fathers until the democratic election of Indira Gandhi as prime minister of modern India.

Occupying Bhubaneswar sometime before A.D. 736, the Bhauma-karas must have been forced by their non-Aryan origins and unorthodox practices to embrace Mahayana ("Greater vehicle") Buddhism. Conversion to Hinduism was technically difficult because of the caste system's dependence on birth. Although a large non-Hindu group could be gradually assimilated by becoming a subcaste, the conversion of a single individual was virtually impossible because no caste could be assigned to him. It was therefore easier for the foreigners invading India—the Greeks, Kushanas, and Shakas—to become Buddhists. Brahman orthodoxy, however, could not treat people of non-Indo-Aryan origin who held political and economic power as outcastes; this contradiction was reconciled by the clever practice of conferring the "fallen *kshatriya*" (Hindu warrior; the second class in the Hindu caste system) status on them.

Bhauma-kara rule of Orissa must have created considerable socioreligious problems and also must have challenged the theoretical structure of caste and orthodox practices of Shaivites in Bhubaneswar. It was during this period that tantric (occult) practices entered Shaivism, and Mahayana Buddhism, which fosters tantrism, became the dominant religion in the region. The Sisiresvara and other Shaiva temples in Bhubaneswar were renovated by the Bhauma-kara artists, who introduced Buddhist images and motifs into them. The Mahayanic images of gods from this period come so close to the contemporary sculpture of Hindu gods that they help in providing continuity to Orissan architecture.[41] The period also witnessed the rise of the *Shakti* (power) cult for the first time in the region. The syncretism of *Shaktism*, Shaivism, and Mahayana Buddhism is best reflected in the sculptures of the Vaital temple. This syncretism also led to some esoteric practices—wearing of skulls, drinking, howling, human sacrifice, erotic sculpture[42]—all becoming part of the extreme Shaivite cult of *Kapalika*, which worshipped Shiva and Shakti in their tantric manifestations of Bhairava and Chamunda, respectively.

For nearly a hundred years after the end of Bhauma-kara rule, believed to be about A.D. 830, Bhubaneswar underwent yet another period of political uncertainty. Not until the rise of the Somavamsi kings, popularly known as the Kesari kings for their wide use of the dormant local regal title *Kesari* (lion), in the first half of the tenth century does stability return to Bhubaneswar. Possibly having origins in Kosala in central India, the Kesaris established their rule in western Orissa. The Kesari line was Brahmanical rather than Buddhist from the beginning, and under its patronage Shiva worship was to prosper for over two centuries. No evidence exists of the immediate disappearance of Buddhism, and Buddhist hermits continued to dwell in the sister sandstone hills of

Udayagiri and Khandagiri. But temples to the All-Destroyer Shiva formed the new focus of the public works under the Kesari kings, three of whom—Yayati, Ananta, and Lalatendu—are credited for committing royal resources to the completion of the monumental Lingaraja temple at Bhubaneswar. The Kesaris are also credited with building the famous Jagannatha temple at Puri, the city destined soon to become the center of the rival worship of Vaishnavism, but nothing of the original temple has survived, the present temple having been built in the twelfth century by Anantavarman Chodaganga.

The religion of royalty slowly became the accepted faith of the people and Shaivism's ceremonial practices eventually came to supplement the ascetic rites of Buddhism. But Shaivism did not solely depend upon its new converts; rather the Kesaris encouraged great migrations of brahmans to Orissa from north India, the most dramatic migration apparently occurring in the reign of Yayati Kesari who is credited by tradition for importing ten thousand brahmans from Oudh to perform a great Vedic sacrifice. That tradition signifies the Aryan colonization of Orissa, and later brahmans were to claim descent from these ten thousand brahmans. Whether or not the tradition exaggerates the numbers, the migration of the brahmans must have resulted in introducing an urban culture in Orissa. Aryanization thus refers not to an ethnic but to a cultural transformation of people in different parts of India, including Orissa. The majority of the people who came under the Aryan influence consider themselves Aryans, although they are not Aryan ethnically.

The Kesaris are credited with performing *Ashvamedha* (horse sacrifice) at Chaudwar near modern Cuttack, which became their capital; however, the later Kesaris are believed to have shifted the capital to Bhubaneswar, though the claim remains unsubstantiated. There is yet another suggestion that the Kesaris held their court alternately at Bhubaneswar and Jajpur.[43] Certain it is that the Kesaris established their capital at Cuttack because of its strategic location, and that city remained the capital of Orissa until it was replaced by Bhubaneswar in 1948.

Kesari rule brought Orissa under one administration, and the royal support for the arts and architecture and tolerance of different cultures culminated in what came to be known as the distinctive Orissan culture. Both Buddhism and the Kapalikas cult receded into the background without royal patronage. Buddhism in Orissa had failed to assimilate with Shiva worship, and when at length it disappeared, it melted not into Shaivism but into Vaishnavite rites of Jagannatha. Krishna, who enjoys the double distinction of being the fluting lover of India's milkmaids and one of Vishnu's most popular incarnations, came to be included for the first time in the sculptural representations in the temples of Bhubaneswar, thus heralding the arrival of the new religion. Tradition claims that Kesari rule finally passed away in the early twelfth century with the death of Ananta Kesari, although there is some historical speculation that the dynasty ended with the rule of Karna, but not before it had handed back to the people of Orissa their proud Hindu heritage.

The vacuum created by the lapse of the Kesaris was finally filled by the Gangas, who introduced into Orissa the new religious creed of Vaishnavism, the other major sect of the Hindu belief system. The origin of the Gangas remains a matter of dispute, which has led to their also being called the Eastern Gangas to distinguish them from an earlier dynasty of the same name that ruled in south India. Tradition credits the Gangas for carrying with them on their successful expedition the Vaishnavite doctrine from the south to the east. It is certain that, taking advantage of the waning rule of the Kesaris, Anantavarma Chodaganga established and extended the hold of the Gangas on Orissa, starting in the last quarter of the eleventh century from a small principality between the present Ganjam district and the Godavari River in southern Orissa that had been annexed by his father, Devendravarma Raja Raja I. The indefatigable Chodaganga, a descendent of the vigorous Cholas on his mother's side and the energetic Gangas on his father's, ruled for nearly seventy-four years, during which time he was married to at least six wives, raised a large family, extended the frontiers of his empire from the Godavari in the south to the Hooghly in the north, and built several monuments, including the famous Jagannatha temple at Puri, which he completed in the first fifty years of his reign. His salutary career, which remains unparalleled even by the mighty Kesaris, unfortunately has left no evidence that will allow his association with any of the temples in Bhubaneswar. However, an inscription in the Lingaraja and the legendary association of his name with certain monuments in the Bhubaneswar area attest to his influence on that celestial city.

The first act of the new dynasty, which was to rule Orissa for the next three centuries, was to revolutionize the religion of Orissa. Just as the Kesaris had been the patron kings of Shaivism, and the rulers before them had been the patron kings of Buddhism and Jainism, the Gangas became the new patron kings of Vaishnavism, which has remained the reigning religion of the region. It must be noted, however, that in all instances the royal patronage of religion resulted not so much in mass conversion of the people but in a royal obsession with building temples to the new gods. The Ganga kings' patronage of Vaishnavism notwithstanding, their rule ushered in a period of great syncretism during which Shaivism and Vaishnavism, the two great traditions of Hinduism, coexisted in divine harmony—to which the later-day Oriyas were to aspire.

The thirteenth century Orissa experienced the last of the best expressions of Hindu art before the force of Islam under the mighty Mughals swept the subcontinent. "From 900 to 1300 A.D.," one nineteenth-century observer of Orissa has correctly noted, "architecture was the ruling passion of Indian princes, not less than of European kings. . . . In both continents the national passion lavished itself not on the palaces of the monarchs, but on the temples of the gods."[44] In Orissa, this great activity in public works centered around Bhubaneswar. In all instances, the temples of Bhubaneswar were built with the help of royal patronage. The result of this prolific activity has been that the monuments of Bhubaneswar provide continuity to the history of the region. These temples represent the best of the north, the *nagara* style, and the south, the Dravidian style, and attest to the craftsmanship of local artisans in blending the two styles to produce distinctively Orissan art.

Not indigenous to Orissa, the Gangas, by permanently transferring their capital to Cuttack, by adopting local culture, and by supporting the Oriya language, succeeded in resurrecting the prehistoric Kalinga into a unified kingdom. The religious syncretism of their age came to bear its imprint on art, architecture, and literature. The great Sun temple at Konarak bears the stamp of this syncretism, its many sculptures celebrating Shiva, Jagannatha, and *Shakti* cults. Vedic Sun-worship, after a long period of oblivion, reappeared on the east coast. A nineteenth-century British Indologist provides a charming story of the construction of the Sun temple: "A son of Vishnu, having accidentally looked on one of his father's nymphs in her bath, was stricken with leprosy. The Indian Actaeon went forth into banishment; but, more fortunate than the grandson of Cadmus, while wandering on the lonely shores of Orissa, was cured by the divine rays of the sun. He raised a temple on the scene of the miracle, and to this day the Hindu believes that a leper who with a single mind worships the bright deity will be healed of his infirmity."[45]

Even the Lingaraja at Bhubaneswar came under the influence of the new religious creed of *Harihara*, representing both Shiva and Vishnu. An inscription in the *Jagamohana* (audience hall) of the Lingaraja records a grant by a Ganga for the maintenance of a perpetual lamp in the temple; and the Gangas are believed to have added two new chambers to the temple, the *natamandira* (dance hall) and the *bhogamandapa* (dining hall), and are believed to have introduced some other Vaishnavite features during renovation.[46] The *Ekamra Purana* recorded this syncretic sentiment: "There is no distinction between Vishnu and Siva. This is the eternal *Dharmma* [Hindu religious law] and the man who observes this *Dharmma* attains mukti [salvation]."[47] This was sound advice which, unfortunately, the Hindus were to ignore, making themselves vulnerable to Islamic invasions from the north. A reduced Orissa remained under Hindu rule until the middle of the sixteenth century, after which it yielded first to the Mughals, then to the Marathas, and finally to the British in the beginning of the nineteenth century. The end of Hindu rule in Orissa also brought an end to the period of temple building in Bhubaneswar.

Bhubaneswar was not to experience another great effort in public works until after independent India decided to build the new capital of Orissa next to the sacred town of Bhubaneswar. The decision to place the new capital city at Bhubaneswar represented the culmination of the Oriya regionalist movement, which harked back to the golden days of Kalinga when the people of the region lived under Hindu rule. Not since the Ganga period had the region known stable Hindu rule. Maharaja Gajapati Krishnachandra Narayanadeva of Paralakhemundi, a scion of the Gangas, in the twentieth century entered the Oriya struggle for the unification of Oriya-speaking areas under a single province, just as his anscestors had fought to bring Kalinga under one kingdom. This proved to be a long struggle in which the Oriyas were to remain divided from the Indian National Congress: the former viewing their struggle as an expression of Oriya nationalism, and the latter viewing it as an expression of regionalism.

·2·

THE NEW PROVINCE

On April 1, 1936, the new province of Orissa was created under Section 298 (i) (b) of the Government of India Act of 1935. The occasion marked the culmination of the Oriya movement for a separate province on a linguistic basis. Ever since the occupation of Orissa by the British in 1804, the administration of the province had been characterized by alternating rebellions and droughts and floods and famines. Soon after taking control of Orissa, the British had to deal with the first rebellion in 1817, which was followed by the rebellions of 1833 and 1847, and, in 1857, by the Great Rebellion that threatened the stability of British India and ended the East India Company's century-old rule in India. Crown rule, which took over the John Company's Indian possessions by Queen Victoria's Proclamation of November 1, 1858, was presented with the worst Orissa famine, that of 1866 in which over a million people perished, providing the Oriyas with their first political cause to rally around. "This catastrophe," Secretary of State Stafford Northcote embarassingly admitted in the House of Commons on August 2, 1867, "must remain a monument of our failure, a humiliation to the people of the country, to the Government of this country, and to those of our Indian Officials of whom we had been perhaps a little too proud. . . . [W]e must hope that we might derive from it lessons which might be of real value to ourselves, and that out of this deplorable evil good of no insignificant kind might ultimately arise." [1]

No real good came out of this evil. Instead, the British decision to uphold the dismemberment of Orissa for the sake of administrative convenience and efficiency, which had resulted in scattering the Oriya-speaking tracts in the neighboring administrative units of Bengal, Madras, and the Central Provinces, was to add to the hardship of the Oriyas. Having thus lost its political unity, Orissa languished in official neglect, and the city of Bhubaneswar, once populous and pulsating with pilgrims, fell into a long period of darkness. Andrew Stirling, a British Indologist, reported soon after the British occupation of Orissa that Bhubaneswar is "entirely neglected and deserted," and that the management of the city "is on a very small and inadequate scale."[2] R. L. Mitra, completing his voluminous *Antiquities of Orissa* in 1880, confirmed that Bhubaneswar had a "cheerless . . . lifeless look about it, which loudly proclaimed that the sun of its glory [had] long since set."[3]

Even before the advent of British rule, Orissa had already experienced political and geographic dismemberment under the Mughals and the Marathas. The Mughals amalgamated the Hooghly River and its ten dependencies with Bengal, and later subdivided the Cuttack, Bhadark, and Jaleswar divisions of Orissa for the convenience of revenue collection,[4] while the Marathas administered Orissa from their central Indian capital at Nagpur, never developing interest in the province beyond collecting annual tribute.[5] Orissa, nevertheless, managed to retain its cultural and linguistic identity under the Mughals and the Marathas.

The British administrative experiments in Orissa, on the other hand, resulted in stirring nationalistic feelings amongst the Oriyas, who came to view the British Raj as worse than the administrative tyranny and indifference suffered under the Mughal and Maratha governments. What was different about British rule was that it had broken the unity of the old land-controlling kin groups at the *pargana* (the lowest level of Mughal administration; coterminous with the highest level of kinship organization of Hindu kshatriyas, land controllers) level, and created new "intermediate classes" throughout the subcontinent.[6] After more than a century and quarter of administrative experiments in Orissa, R. A. Butler, undersecretary of state for India, assisted by John Austin Hubback, the newly appointed governor of Orissa, placed before the House of Commons the Order in Council for the constitution of Orissa as an independent unit, which, on advice from Parliament, was given imperial sovereign seal by King Edward VIII on March 3, 1936.[7] The royal order went into effect on April 1, 1936, on which occasion the British crown noted: "The long-cherished and natural desire of the Oriya people to be re-united after centuries of dependence upon other administrations is thus fulfilled. It is my hope and expectation that the new province will draw inspiration from the past and will prove worthy of the historic tradition of the land of Orissa."[8]

Coming in contact with Orissa in 1633, when the first British factory was established at Hariharpur, the British, "true to our national character," had transformed themselves from "merchants" into "rulers."[9] The British succeeded in establishing their interest in Orissa by defeating the Mughal army at Buxar in 1764, and by forcing the Mughal emperor Shah Alam to grant to the British the revenue of Bengal, Bihar, and Orissa. By granting the *diwani* (revenue) to the British, Shah Alam had lumped Orissa with Bengal and Bihar because the three provinces had been administered as a single unit under the Mughals. However, Orissa as granted to the British by Shah Alam constituted the single district of Midnapore, that is, only the territories in the north up to the river Suvarnarekha; beyond this to the south lay the mainland of Orissa under Maratha suzerainty.

Control of Orissa was viewed as strategically important in Fort William because the nearby presence of the Marathas represented a perpetual threat. Moreover, the Maratha occupation of Orissa territory beyond the border of Midnapore was considered an obstacle in the free communication between the East India Company's northern and southern territories. In addition, the frequent Maratha military incursions into Mughal territories to demand *chauth* (tribute) kept the British in a state of perpetual anxiety. For these considerations, Robert Clive dispatched Thomas Motte to Sambalpur in 1766 to persuade the Marathas to surrender control of Orissa. Clive failed to secure Orissa through negotiations, just as his two successors, Warren Hastings (1732–1818) and Lord Charles Cornwallis (1738–1805), were to fail in securing Orissa from the Marathas through negotiations.

It fell upon the Francophobic Lord Richard Colley Wellesley (1760–1842), who became the company's governor-general in 1798, and who was determined to secure the Indian subcontinent for British rule by "cleansing" all remaining pockets of native power that had become contaminated by French influence, to take full advantage of the selfish ambitions of the Maratha Pentarchy in the Second Maratha War, forcing Raghuji Bhonsle of Nagpur to cede to the company in perpetual sovereignty the province of Cuttack, including the Port and District of Balasore by the Treaty of Deogaon on December 17, 1803. In the final settlement, the British received control of the three districts of Balasore, Cuttack, and Puri in coastal Orissa and eighteen Feudatory States in the hill regions of west Orissa, constituting a total area of 23,907 square miles, of which 16,184 square miles were occupied by the Feudatory States.

Soon after occupying Orissa in 1804 the company set itself to the task of consolidation of land revenue administration, which was undertaken with the introduction of the British laws and regulations from Bengal. The Feudatory States were exempt from the British laws and regulations. Midnapore and the northern districts of Ganjam and Jeypore, which the company had acquired from Shah Alam in 1765, had been placed under the administrations of Calcutta and Madras, respectively. The eighteen Feudatory States in western Orissa were initially placed with different political divisions; however in 1862, they were transferred to the chief commissioner of the Central Provinces stationed at Nagpur. The British Orissa Division in the vast Presidency of Bengal thus constituted only the three coastal districts of Balasore, Cuttack, and Puri. The new division was placed under the joint commissionership of Colonel Harcourt and John Melville stationed at Cuttack, while James Hunter was sent to Puri as collector of revenue. Thus the immediate effect of company rule in Orissa was the systematic dismemberment of the province. The debate over where to place the headquarters of the Orissa Division was finally resolved in favor of Cuttack because of "the comparative fertileness of the land . . . the convenience of the Court of Circuit and the proportionately greater number of wealthy inhabitants in Cuttack."[10]

With revenue administration of Orissa placed firmly under the direct supervision of the Board of Revenue at Calcutta, the early years of company rule were spent in experimenting with various land revenue settlements. From 1803 to 1823, the company administrators tried a gamut of land settlements ranging from triennial to biannual to annual, none of them yielding satisfactory results, until a quinquennial settlement was adopted in 1823. The company's difficulties resulted from the fact that the Bengal Revenue Regulations were not enforceable in Orissa, mainly because Orissa, unlike Bengal, was not a permanently settled zone. As if to spite Oriya landowners and cultivators, the British disallowed the use of the local "cowry" currency in payment of revenue in 1812. By assuming a monopoly of salt the British added insult to Orissa's injury. The company's decision to import English-educated Bengalis from the neighboring state to fill the junior ranks in the local administration resulted in displacing Oriya *ameels* (revenue officers) and *sheristadars* (record keepers). The change in administrative personnel would not have been so disastrous for Orissa had Bengali officers not manipulated the unsuspecting Oriya landowners into surrendering their estates in default of revenue payment. From 1806 to 1816 as many as 1,011 estates out of a total of 2,340 were lost by Oriya landowners.[11]

The early English efforts in administrative experiments and social engineering resulted in alienating the Oriyas, who gave expression to their feelings, first, in a series of rebellions and, later, in the language movement that eventually grew to demand a separate province for the Oriya people. The Paik Rebellion of 1817 was the first expression of the Oriyas against the bankrupt British administration, when the landed militia in the Khurda region challenged the British for requisitioning their lands which they had occupied since the days of the Hindu kings. Jagabandhu Bidyadhar Mohapatra Bhramabar Ray, popularly known as Bakshi Jagabandhu, military commander of the Raja of Khurda, who harbored resentment against the British and the Bengali officer Krishna Chandra Singh for tricking him out of his estate in 1813, masterminded the alliance between the Khurda Paiks and the tribal Khonds from Ghumsar, a border estate in the Ganjam district of Madras Presidency. The Khonds had attacked British establishments in Khurda in retaliation for incarcerating Raja Dhananjaya Bhanja. Using Lord Jagannath as the symbol of Oriya unity, the Paik Rebellion spread throughout the southern and eastern parts of Orissa, but the British ruthlessly suppressed the rebellion before it could mature into a larger expression of a regional movement for independence. In consequence of the rebellion, the British instituted an inquiry into the conduct of their administration so as to prevent similar rebellions in the future. Orissa, however, was not prepared to accept the British Raj with equanimity and the aboriginal people in the Feudatory States continued to challenge the British throughout the first half of the nineteenth century.

Crushed and prevented from becoming a major expression of Oriya nationalism, the Paik Rebellion nonetheless became a symbol of Oriya unity on which Oriya nationalist sentiment would feed nearly half a century later. The changes that the British introduced in Orissa, although intended for survival and stability through consolidation of power and the introduction of English education, succeeded in accelerating the demand for a separate province by arming Orissa's new elite with the words in which to call for it.

Armed with the Charter Act of 1813 which had removed the company's blanket ban on missionary enterprise, the Christian missionaries opened the first English-medium charity school at Cuttack in 1823. The company was obliged to teach English to at least enough natives to facilitate and sustain effective administration of its territories; and so the company administration offered tuition wavers for the poor, scholarships for meritorious students, and encouraged vernacular language along with

English, making Cuttack into an important center for education.

By 1859 as many as thirty English-medium schools were operating throughout Orissa. Although insignificant in number compared to the number of English-medium schools in neighboring Bengal, English-educated Oriyas began to fill positions in the local British administration. Still, the economic and social development of Orissa languished because of political dismemberment; and the governments of Bengal, Madras, and the Central Provinces, which controlled large tracts of Oriya-speaking people, continued to emphasize the usage of Bengali, Telugu, and Hindi, respectively, in law courts, offices, and educational institutions of the three provinces.

The Oriyas remained handicapped by their own language in their native territory even under Crown rule that came into effect in 1858. Perhaps they would not have been so quick in articulating their resentment against the political and physical dismemberment of Orissa, and against the deliberate British neglect of the Oriya language, had the British official antipathy for the Oriyas' native land not been made to appear in an even worse light because of the great famine of 1866, which nearly devasted the province and demoralized the people. The main reason for the famine was the failure of the monsoon in 1865—monsoon rains which remain the lifeblood of Indian agriculture even today—but the disaster in human lives could have been contained had the free-trading British not exported the bumper crops of rice from the previous two years to Europe for huge profits.[12] The absence of reserve stocks resulted in hoarding and profiteering by the merchants, leading to abnormal rises in the price of rice. The poor, as always is the case in India, were worst hit because the price of rice regulated the wages of the unskilled laborers and artisans: The price of rice soared from fourteen seers (one Indian seer of weight is equal to 2.057 pounds—14 seers × 2.057 lbs. = 28.80 lbs.) for a rupee in 1865 to only nine seers (18.51 lbs.) in 1866, while the wages of laborers remained constant at the rate or two pice per day. Collector G. N. Barlow of Puri unsuccessfully tried to raise a relief fund from the leading local residents, just as he unsuccessfully tried to persuade the government of India to control rice prices.[13] "If I were to attempt [to control rice prices] I should consider myself no better than a dacoit or thief,"[14] declared the self-righteous Sir Cecil Beadon, lieutenant governor of Bengal, on his visit to Cuttack on February 13, 1866.

G. N. Barlow had also appealed to Commissioner T. E. Ravenshaw, the Orissa Division, to double the wages of laborers, claiming it was "preposterous in these days to be paying for the labour two pice per day." He added, "I do not think I am extravagant."[15] However, both the lieutenant governor and the commissioner remained sanguine about the situation, refusing to revise official policy to mitigate the hardship caused to the people by the famine. As if to provide cosmic proof of the British administrative incompetence and misplaced optimism, nature conspired to follow the 1865 drought with the 1866 floods, which washed away the early rice crop and completely submerged all available cultivatable land. The combination of drought and floods, the two natural disasters so endemic to India, ruined Orissa. The magnitude of human misery was so appallingly glaring that it generated a heated debate in the House of Commons in which Sir Stafford Northcote, secretary of state for India, found it increasingly difficult to defend the government of India's culpability in the Orissa famine disaster; and the Famine Inquiry Commission Report submitted by Northcote was rejected by practically every member who spoke on the House floor on the grounds that it "contained so much of censure and so little of excuse."[16]

The famine of 1866 had two lasting results: first, it forced the British to introduce some administrative reforms in Orissa; and second, it helped stimulate what has come to be viewed as the Oriya Renaissance but which may more accurately be viewed as seed time for modern Orissa's emergence, as yet microcosmically reflected in the mirror of Cuttack's trading urban society. For just as Bhubaneswar housed the temples and sacred water tanks of old Hindu glory and decline, Cuttack became the cradle of Oriya nationalism which was to charter a path separate from the national politics of Congress.

The *Calcutta Review* commented in the October 1866 issue that "the moral of the famine is the adoption [by] the Government of a policy of progress, and of moral and material improvement of Orissa."[17] The combination of moral imperative and the practical requirement of strengthening the administrative grip on Orissa, finally convinced the British to seriously consider the development of the province. Roads were built to link different parts of the province, and the East India Irrigation Company, which was started in 1862, dug a series of canals as a post-famine measure. The development of the railways, so far ignored in Orissa because of the high cost of bridging a number of rivers in the coastal region, was finally completed in 1899. The well-groomed but imperious Lord Curzon (1899–1905) traveled to Cuttack by train in 1900, becoming the first viceroy to visit Orissa. Progress was also made in education by upgrading the English-medium high school in Cuttack, established in 1841, to an intermediate college affiliated with Calcutta University in 1868. Madhusudan Das (1848–1934), who was destined to play a prominent role in Oriya nationalism, was among the first six graduating students of Cuttack College. Later, he went on to complete his baccalaureate, master's, and law degrees at Calcutta University in 1870, 1873, and 1878, respectively. Education for women, however, remained restricted to vernacular scholarship, and not until the end of the century did Cuttack College admit two Oriya girls.

The British Raj, administered from an imperial base thousands of miles away, provided the Indians with their earliest positive lessons in modern national consciousness. Moreover, the presence of the white Christian *sahib* in India served the dual purpose of reminding the Indians of their "native" differences—cultural, socioeconomic, and political—on the one hand, and an example of political and administrative unity achieved through the introduction of English education, modern technology, and mass communications, on the other. The Raj became the enduring example of the sublimation of personal interest and identity to the impersonal law and "higher" needs of national purpose, the lessons of which were not lost on educated Indians. The dichotomous role of the Raj in the growth of India's first nationalist movement can perhaps be measured by the fact that all the major nationalist leaders had received some English education. The spread of English education and the growth of railways, the postal service, and the press, both native and English, helped spawn the early national consciousness in the presidency towns of Calcutta, Bombay, and Madras. Since at least the 1830s, Calcutta had set the pace for Indian national consciousness, and what was written in Calcutta-based papers or debated in public places by the city's intellectual elite (*bhadralok*) was carefully reviewed throughout India, including in neighboring Orissa.

Christian missionaries first introduced the printing press in Cuttack in 1838 for propagating religious ideas, and it became a major vehicle in Orissa for spreading national consciousness in the second half of the nineteenth century. Orissa experienced a proliferation of papers and journals in the second half of the nineteenth century as well; the most notable among them being the *Utkal Dipika*, published and edited by Gaurishankar Ray, a prominent social reformer. The *Utkal Dipika* and other papers provided the forum for the Oriya elite at Cuttack, the headquarters of the Orissa Division, for debating social and cultural issues. The energy generated by public debates contributed to the creation of several organizations devoted to improving the lot of the Oriya people. The Mutual Improvement Society was the first to be started, in 1859, when leading local residents and some Englishmen residing in Cuttack met in that city to discuss sociocultural issues. Although this organization disappeared in the course of time without leaving any information about its accomplishments, Orissa experienced a proliferation of associations after the famine of 1866. Among the many associations to emerge in Orissa, the Utkal Sabha became the most powerful in 1882, and later it would merge with the Utkal Union Conference to fight for a separate province for Orissa.

Oriya associations remained preoccupied with the problems of Orissa, the most important of them being the amalgamation of the Oriya-speaking tracts under a single administration. Orissa's ambivalence with national issues was conspicuous by her absence at the first annual meeting of the Indian National Congress at Bombay on December 28, 1885, convened under the presidency of Womesh C. Bonnerjee, a Calcutta barrister, and attended by seventy-three elder Indian statesmen from different provinces of British India. However, meeting on March 3, 1886, at Cuttack the leading Oriya men discussed the resolutions adopted by Congress in its first session[18]—resolutions which, while proclaiming loyalty to the Crown, called for providing more opportunities to the Indians in the administration and various government councils, and the reduction of military expenditures in favor of internal economic development. There was nothing in the resolutions with which the Oriyas could identify; still, seven Oriya representatives—four from the Utkal Sabha and three from the National Society of Balasore—attended the second session of the Indian National Congress held in the last week of December 1886. Madhusudan Das and Gaurishankar Ray represented the Utkal Sabha to present before Congress the problems of Orissa. It would be a while before the Congress leadership would agree to support the Oriya cause, albeit reluctantly; but the two Oriya leaders were to learn from Congress the liberal language in which to articulate the demand for a separate Orissa.

Long before the Oriyas pressed the government of India for the creation of a separate state, the government itself felt the necessity of restructuring the administration of Orissa as a result of the 1866 famine. Moved by the Famine Commission Report, Sir Stafford Northcote, secretary of state for India, as early as 1867 had requested Sir John Lawrance, viceroy of

India, to consider reducing the spread of the Calcutta Presidency by formulating Orissa and Assam into a separate commissionership.[19] Northcote's idea was supported by Major Chesney, a prominent English officer, who wrote that "Cuttack would indeed make but a small independent province. . . . The people speak a different language from the Bengalees and the river system of the country, which takes its origin in Central India, tends to separate it from the delta of the Ganges." Arguing that this isolation, and especially the difference of language, make for a separate administration of Cuttack a positive attraction, he recommended that parts of Orissa attached to the Central Provinces "might be rejoined" with Cuttack. He further recommended that "a very appropriate addition to such a province would be the northern portions of the Ganjam district on the Madras coast adjacent to Cuttack which are peopled by the same Oriya-speaking race and are very inconveniently placed for communication with and supervision by the distant Government of Madras. The Oriya portion of the Midnapore district of Bengal would also with propriety be transferred to the new administration."[20] Doubting the practicability of the idea on financial grounds,[21] both Sir Lawrance and Cecil Beadon, lieutenant governor of Bengal, eventually decided to constitute Assam and some neighboring districts into a separate commissionership in 1875, leaving Orissa under the Bengal Presidency administration until 1912.

The government of India's decision not to implement Northcote's suggestion probably would have passed as no more than a footnote in the history of Orissa had a few patriots not decided to make political capital of the situation to arouse political consciousness among the Oriyas. The guardians of the Oriya language saw in Northcote's suggestion the hope of not only safeguarding their language against the onslaught of Bengali but also of protecting local administrative jobs from slipping to the English-educated *babus*. Having its origins in linguistic passions, Oriya nationalism in one sense was directed more against the Bengalis, Telugus, and Hindi-speaking Hindus who displaced the Oriyas in jobs which—in the Oriya view—rightfully belonged to the people of Orissa. So in 1895, when the chief commissioner of the Central Provinces decided to abolish the Oriya language from official use in the predominently Oriya-populated Sambalpur district, he in effect provided a fertile cause to the Oriyas to launch a language movement for the amalgamation of Oriya-speaking tracts scattered in Bengal, Madras, and the Central Provinces.

Acutely sensitive to their inferior status under British rule, the Oriyas had always displayed some measure of xenophobia, particularly against the influx of the Bengalis from neighboring Bengal. Bengalis had been migrating to Orissa in search of economic opportunities and a better life even before the British decided to import English-educated *babus* to fill junior ranks in the administration. The Mughals and the Marathas had used Bengali officials in their administrations, and Orissa had appeared as a refuge to the Bengalis ever since their king fled to Orissa in 1203 A.D. Bengalis in Orissa had mostly assimilated the local culture, and some of them were even to participate in the Oriya Language Movement in later years. But the Bengalis who migrated to Orissa under British sponsorship not only displaced the Oriyas from jobs but also maneuvered to suppress the Oriya language in schools and government agencies. As a result Bengali soon replaced Oriya in schools, forcing Oriya children to study in the Bengali medium in their own province. Exacerbating the situation was the absence of Oriya textbooks and a paucity of Oriya teachers,[22] which provided the atmosphere for the Bengali language to prosper in Orissa.

Whatever benefit and administrative convenience there might have accrued to the government of India in attaching Orissa to Bengal, the prominent local newspaper the *Utkal Dipika* lamented as early as 1868, has been "a positive hinderance in the way of the rise of the natives of the soil." Arguing that there were colleges in Bengal while not even a high school existed in Orissa until recently, and that the government continued to support compulsory teaching of Bengali to Oriya children, and that the government continued to fill any lucrative vacancy by people from Bengal, "except in so far as posts of 10 [rupees] or 20 [rupees] were concerned for which nobody would care to come down . . . from Calcutta," and that so long as "the District and Provincial authorities . . . do not gradually appoint people under them to higher posts," the *Utkal Dipika* concluded that "it is futile to expect any improvement in the status of the people of Orissa."[23]

"There will really be no good done to Orissa if Bengalee is made compulsory here for all and Oriya abolished from schools"[24] because, warned the *Utkal Dipika*, "[l]ocal people will never give up Oriya."[25] Appealing to Divisional Commissioner T. E. Ravenshaw to consider the matter "carefully" and "sympathetically," and encouraging him to persuade the government to retain the Oriya language in Orissa schools, the *Utkal Dipika* made four recommendations for the improvement and cultivation of the Oriya language:

1. Abolish Bengali altogether from all government aided schools.
2. Entrust the selection of text-books to a committee of two or three prominent Oriya gentlemen instead of leaving it to the inspector of schools.
3. Encourage scholars to prepare Oriya textbooks through government assistance.
4. Publish all educational notices and circulars in local newspapers and periodicals for a wide circulation among the public.[26]

The *Utkal Dipika*'s campaign to promote the Oriya language helped in formulating public opinion among the Oriyas, who wrote numerous letters to newspapers and journals, as well as to the government of India, in support of the Oriya language. Moved by public opinion, Commissioner Ravenshaw publicly expressed the government's intention to support the Oriya language at a prize distribution ceremony at Cuttack High School in 1868, when he declared for the first time that the Bengalis should learn Oriya and that the earlier difficulty of teaching the language because of the lack of Oriya textbooks had been removed with the introduction of the vernacular press.[27] This was a bold change in his position from the previous year when he had favored a bilingual curriculum in the Bengali and Oriya languages. He was later instrumental in starting a medical school in Cuttack and in upgrading Cuttack High School to the level of an intermediate college, named after him in 1879.[28] To meet the demand for trained teachers for Orissa schools, the government started Normal Teacher Training School at Cuttack in January 1869 and also sanctioned a budget of 1,100 rupees for annual expenditure. Meanwhile, the Oriyas pooled their resources to start the Cuttack School Book Company for the publication of Oriya textbooks. The Raja of Mayurbhanj, encouraged by the government and private efforts to promote Oriya, donated 20,000 rupees to Ravenshaw College in 1879.

Commissioner Ravenshaw's liberal measures in promoting Oriya resulted in polarizing the Bengalis and the Oriyas in Orissa. Sensitive to their alien status in Orissa, and perceiving the new government measures as a threat to their privileged economic and social status, the Bengalis appealed to the Education Department against introducing Oriya as the medium of instruction in schools because it would have disastrous consequences for the large Bengali population of Orissa. The *Utkal*

Hitaisni, a history periodical started by the expatriate Bengalis in 1869, argued in favor of the Bengalis by pointing out that Orissa owed her development in religion, culture, language, administration, and social practices to Bengal. It was a polemical argument carefully constructed by assigning the disputed origin of the Gangas, the last Hindu dynasty to rule Orissa, to Bengal. The opposing Oriya view was articulated in the *Utkal Dipika*, a sociocultural journal started in 1866 by Gaurishankar Ray, himself an expatriate Bengali, who castigated the three governments of Bengal, Madras, and the Central Provinces under whom the Oriyas were prevented from fulfilling their "natural" aspirations.

Raw linguistic passions were further inflamed on both sides when Dr. Rajendra Lal Mitra, a Bengali archaeologist who had volunteered his services in 1868 to the government of India for the restoration and documentation of the neglected ancient monuments of Orissa,[29] tactlessly remarked in Cuttack that as long as the Oriya language was not abolished there could be no progress in Orissa.[30] A year later, taking advantage of his position as the government-appointed archaeologist, he reiterated his argument on the Oriya language issue in a scholarly gathering of the Royal Asiatic Society of Calcutta, where he declared that "the fusion of the Oriya language into [Bengali was not] at all impracticable. The experiment has already been tried in [Midnapore] and found completely successful."[31]

To the satisfaction of the Oriyas, Mitra's thesis was challenged at the same scholarly meeting by Collector John Beams, a member of the prestigious Indian Civil Service stationed at Balasore, who in his paper "On the Relations of Oriya to Other Modern Indian Languages" argued that the Oriya language was not only older but more developed than Bengali and that Oriya could not be considered a dialect of Bengali.[32]

In the Madras Presidency, T. J. Maltby, another member of the Indian Civil Service, provided a new fillip to the Oriya language agitation with the publication in 1873 of his book *A Practical Handbook of the Oriya Language*, which strongly advocated the introduction of Oriya in the law courts and schools. The successful campaign against imposing Bengali in the three coastal districts of Orissa stimulated the Sambalpur Oriyas to demand the abolition of Hindi from the courts and schools of that zone. The leadership for the Sambalpur language agitation was provided by Shri Basudeva Sudhala Dev (1850–1903), Shri Sachidananda Tribhuvan Dev (1873–1916), Shri Jalandhara Dev (1867–1952), and Shri Badakumar

Balbhadra Dev (1877–1937), all members of the royal house of the Gangas. Raja Viramitrodaya Singh Deo of Sonepur state also decided to support strongly the language agitation.[33]

The language agitation in Orissa stirred nascent nationalistic sentiments (some might prefer the term "regionalistic"), which eventually culminated in a demand for amalgamating the Oriya-speaking tracts into a separate province at the turn of the century. The process was facilitated by the proliferation of the vernacular press and sociocultural associations in the second half of the nineteenth century. Paradoxically, the catalyst for this incipient change had been the introduction of English education, which proved at best a mixed blessing to British rule. Mountstuart Elphinstone, as shrewd a young Scot as ever to be sent by Dundas to India, knew how dangerous a two-edged sword Western education would prove to be and called it "our highroad back to Europe." By the time Lord Ripon, a Liberal convert to Catholicism who became British India's most popular viceroy during his brief tenure (1880–84) in that high office as a result of the fall of the Disraeli government, introduced the new scheme of local self-government in India in 1882, political consciousness had sufficiently matured in India. Ripon had hoped that by creating municipal and district government boards, he would be tapping into the rapidly growing class of intelligent and public spirited men in India; and he had hoped in this way to restore Indian confidence in British rule, while giving the Indians the chance to guide and govern themselves; and although in practice officialdom invariably exercised its influence on all local boards, these local boards, rural and urban, were to turn into training schools for the Indian nationalist leadership in the future.

The significance of Ripon's legislative measure of local self-government was not lost on Orissa. On June 30, 1882, prominent Oriyas gathered in Cuttack to celebrate the new government measure. Madhusudan Das, Madhusudan Rao, Bipin Behari Mitra, Priyanath Chatterjee, and other leaders delivered eloquent speeches, pointing to the potential powers of local bodies for the people. Six weeks later, the rally in support of Ripon's measure was repeated at Puri. The *Utkal Dipika* confidently reported that the people of Orissa were "ready" to shoulder their responsibilities to the local bodies for effective and efficient government.[34]

That same year the Utkal Sabha was constituted in Cuttack to provide political direction to the Oriya people. Apparently having its origin in the earlier Orissa Association that met for the first time under the presidency of Oriya literateur Radhanath Ray in January 1878, the Sabha, as it came to be called, was to undergo yet another mutation to become the Utkal Union Conference at the beginning of the twentieth century, and was to become the driving force for amalgamating the scattered Oriya-speaking tracts. The first meeting of the Sabha was convened on August 16, 1882, in the premises of the Cuttack Printing Company. The meeting had been called by Chaudhury Kasinath Das, a *zamindar* from Bhingarpur, Madhusudan Das, a Calcutta-trained lawyer who converted to Christianity, and Gaurishankar Ray, the publisher and editor of the Cuttack-based *Utkal Dipika*, the three Oriya notables taking the office of president, vice-president, and secretary, respectively.

Initially instituted to serve as the forum for literary, cultural, and socoal discussions by educated Oriya men, the Sabha quickly became involved with the question of amalgamating the Oriya-speaking tracts under one government. On May 21, 1883, the Sabha committed its first political act by endorsing the Criminal Jurisdiction Bill[35] which had been authored by Ripon's new law member, Sir Courtney Ilbert, to remove racial inequities enacted in 1872 that made it impossible for Indians in the British Judicial Service to try cases involving Europeans, even for minor offenses. The Liberal Ripon agreed with his law member that there should be no such bias in the British legal system, and no member of the Governor General's Executive Council in Calcutta anticipated any opposition against a measure whose object was "simply the effectual and impartial administration of justice," as Sir Courtney put it when he presented the bill to the Legislative Council in February 1883.

Calcutta's nongovernmental European community's response to Sir Courtney's bill was so overwhelmingly negative that it could only be passed in a thoroughly emasculated form, permitting Europeans to demand a jury at least half European in complexion in courts presided over by Indian judges. The effectiveness of organized protest through public pressure—attacking the government, running newspaper campaigns, signing petitions, and arguing in public forums—proved extremely powerful in making the government of India yield and the viceroy capitulate, the lessons of which were not lost on India's intelligentsia. Out of this awareness emerged the Indian National Congress, the brainchild of a retired English civil servant, Allan Octavian Hume (1829–1912). Lord Dufferin, who had replaced Ripon and who was so eager to ascertain the "real wishes" of the Indian people through a "responsible" national organization, gave his official approval to Congress. Although Congress cooperated with the Sabha in 1886 in petitioning the government for the introduction of liberal reforms which would reconstitute the legislative councils so as to allow real representatives of the Indian people into those bodies,[36] the programs of Congress and the Sabha were to run on parallel paths: Congress would endeavor to espouse national causes, while the energy and enthusiasm of the Oriya leadership would remain focused on problems at home that would keep Oriya nationalism out of the national mainstream for more than two decades.

At the core of the Oriya political consciousness was the concern for amalgamating the Oriya-speaking tracts under one administrative unit or, if possible, into a separate province. The earliest Oriya proposal for integrating the scattered Oriya-speaking tracts under a single administration was made by Raja Baikunth Nath De of Balasore and Bichitrananda Patnaik in a memorandum to the government in Calcutta in 1876.[37] Drawing its inspiration from the 1868 recommendations of Sir Stafford Northcote for the creation of two separate commissionerships for Orissa and Assam, and more specifically from the separation of Assam from Bengal achieved in 1875, the Oriya memorandum was to remain unheeded by the government. Twelve years later the Oriyas once again pleaded their case before the unsympathetic Sir Stewart Colvin Bayley, lieutenant governor of Bengal, on his visit to Cuttack in November 1888.[38] The Oriya question, as the demand for amalgamating the Oriya-speaking tracts came to be called, remained dormant until John Woodburn, chief commissioner of the Central Provinces, passed the order in 1895 abolishing Oriya from official use and replacing it with Hindi in the district of Sambalpur. The new executive order was to go into effect on January 1, 1896. That decision radicalized the political situation throughout Orissa, and that decision came to be equated with "the worst form of gagging . . . unknown even in the most despotic form of Government."[39]

Sambalpur in the nineteenth century had undergone several administrative changes. After the collapse of Maratha power in 1818 it came under British protection, which allowed the continuation of local monarchical rule. No longer willing to put up with political instability resulting from protracted succession disputes, the British took over direct control of Sambalpur by applying the Doctrine of Lapse when Raja Narayan Singh died childless in 1849. But because the British decided not to include Sambalpur in the Orissa Division, it remained attached to the Southwest Frontier Agency with its headquarters at Ranchi. In 1860, Sambalpur was temporarily transferred to the Orissa Division of the

Bengal government; but two years later on April 30, 1862, it was transferred to the newly constituted Central Provinces.

Sambalpur's predominantly Oriya-speaking population, however, presented a problem in the Hindi-speaking Central Provinces. Recognizing this unnatural arrangement, H. G. Cooke, commissioner of the Orissa Division, had recommended in his annual administrative report in 1895 the extension of divisional boundaries so as to include the Oriya-speaking areas. Maintaining that "any portion of the race that is forced into an unwilling combination with distinct races incures the danger of having the national characteristics and aspirations sacrificed to those of the predominating portion of the population in the administration under which it is forced to live,"[40] Cooke requested the amalgamation of the Sambalpur district with its tributary states of Patna, Sonepur, Rairakhol, Bamra, Kalanandi, and the whole or part of the Ganjam district with the states of Kimidi and Ghumsur into the Orissa Division. Once again, the government of India failed to respond.

The language agitation thus sparked in Sambalpur was articulated by the *Sambalpur Hitaisini*, a weekly journal founded in 1889. The journal raised the question that if the government found it difficult to administer an Oriya district in a Hindi-speaking province, what stood in the way of transferring it to Orissa? Would that be more harmful than sacrificing the people's mother tongue? The Utkal Sabha sent a memorandum in June 1895 to Viceroy Elgin protesting the arbitary abolition of Oriya in Sambalpur. But none of these efforts proved strong enough to move the inert bureaucratic machine of the government of India.

The arrival of George Nathaniel Curzon as the new viceroy in 1899 changed the political climate in India. Educated at Eton and Balliol and having groomed himself for the viceroyalty through world travel, study, and service in Whitehall as undersecretary of state both in the India Office and in the Foreign Office, Curzon was to prove himself as not only one of the best-informed and most hardworking of viceroys but equally intolerant of the "stately" and "slow" bureaucratic machine. Soon after assuming his new position, he visited Orissa in 1900 and was struck by the natural beauty and art of that province. The political climate also appeared to improve for the Oriyas with the advent of the chief commissionership of Sir Andrew Fraser in the Central Provinces. More sympathetic to the Oriya language question than his predecessor, and agreeing with the Oriyas on the awkward position of Sambalpur in the predominantly Hindi-speaking Central Provinces, he recommended to the government of India in 1901 the transfer of Sambalpur to the Orissa Division.[41] Meanwhile, Madhusudan Das and other Oriya leaders pleaded their case before Lord Curzon. Lord Curzon, while miscalculating the passions of the Oriyas for their language, did restore the use of the Oriya language in Sambalpur in January 1903, but chose not to transfer the district to Orissa. His familiarity with India notwithstanding, Curzon never fully grasped the extent of the linguistic passions of the people—passions which were to reassert themselves in neighboring Bengal two years later when he would commit the mistake of partitioning that province, providing yet another example to the Indians of the British government's preference for bureaucratic efficiency over human considerations—and certainly over native considerations.

The Oriya response to Curzon's decision was predictable. Equating the loss of Sambalpur to "a limb separated from the body," hundreds of Oriyas signed a petition to the viceroy, urging him to unite the people of Orissa by placing the districts of Ganjam and Sambalpur and the Orissa Division "under the Government of Bengal or any one government and one University."[42] Raja Baikunth Nath De of Balasore sent a similar petition to Curzon, requesting him to create a separate administrative unit out of all Oriya-speaking territories or to keep them integrated under one provincial administration of either Bengal, Madras, or the Central Provinces.[43]

Meanwhile, the Oriyas found an unexpected ally for their cause in Secretary H. H. Risley, government of India, who wrote on December 3, 1903, to the chief secretary of the Bengal government, urging him to place all Oriya-speaking territories under one administration. After examining the cases of the governments of Bengal, Madras, and the Central Provinces, he concluded the Oriya-speaking territories would be better off under the Bengal government. This arrangement would have two advantages: first, it would put an end to the protracted language agitation by the Oriyas; and second, the governments of Madras and the Central Provinces would get rid of the troublesome Oriya districts of Ganjam and Sambalpur, respectively. But the Risley proposal was not without a caveat: He proposed to Lord Curzon to partition Bengal to relieve the excessive administrative burden resulting from the new arrangement so as to create a new lieutenant governorship for East Bengal and Assam, and to compensate Bengal for the loss by adding the Oriya areas.[44]

The British scheme, under which Bengal was partitioned in 1905 into two new provinces along a line drawn down its midsection just east of

Calcutta and the Hooghly, was undertaken without consulting or considering Indian opinion; and instead of solving either the Oriya question or relieving the pressure on the populous province of Bengal (about 85 million), the official scheme succeeded in satisfying none of the parties involved. However, the new administrative arrangement produced two separate responses in Bengal and Orissa. For the Bengali-speaking Hindu majority of Calcutta's *bhadralok* (elite), the new arrangement meant a minority status in the new province of Eastern Bengal and Assam, in which there would be a Muslim majority of approximately six million. While the rest of West Bengal retained a Hindu majority, it included so many Bihari- and Oriya-speaking neighbors of the Bengalis that it ended up with a non-Bengali-speaking majority. Thus for the Calcutta-based Bangali *babu* the British scheme was a flagrant example of divide and rule.

In Orissa, on the other hand, the spontaneous response of the people to the Risley report was one of gratitude and overwhelming emotion. Both the Oriya press and leadership congratulated the government and expressed publicly the indebtedness of the Oriyas for its "considerate" decision.[45] Still, the new administrative arrangement did not fully satisfy the aspirations of the Oriyas. Disappointing the Oriyas was the retention of Ganjam and Vaizagpatam by the Madras Presidency, ostensibly sustained on the insistence of Sir Andrew Fraser, who had been promoted to the lieutenant governorship of Bengal in 1904. The Oriyas were equally disappointed to see Sambalpur transferred to Bengal without the Oriya-speaking tracts of Phuljhar and Chandrapur-Padampur. As a result of the new arrangement, the Orissa Division came to acquire twenty-four states, becoming part of the Bengal government. Seraikella and Kharsuan states were added to the Orissa Division in 1916, and the boundary of the newly constituted Orissa was to remain unchanged until April 1, 1936, when a separate Orissa was created by the British. Orissa and Bihar, however, were separated from Bengal in 1912 when Lord Hardinge annulled the partition of Bengal.

In the midst of these administrative changes, a small group of enthusiastic Oriyas assembled at Cuttack on December 30, 1903. This was the first official meeting of the *Utkal Sammilani* or the Utkal Union Conference, which spearheaded the Oriya movement until the formation of Orissa as a separate province in 1936. The gathering was a stately affair, presided over by Maharaja Sir Ramchandra Bhanj Deo of Mayurbhanj, with Raja Rajendra Narayan Bhanj Deo of Kanika serving as the chairman of the reception committee and Madhusudan Das as the secretary. Pointing to the social, cultural, and political problems of the Oriyas, Conference declared its primary goal of achieving a separate province for Orissa, a goal which Conference reiterated annually, and which kept Conference and Congress at odds until 1920.

Conference's efforts notwithstanding, the Oriya question remained moribund until the viceroyalty of Lord Hardinge, who in a letter dated August 25, 1911, suggested to the secretary of state for India the annulment of the partition of Bengal, the creation of a new province of Bihar and Orissa, and the formation of a separate chief commissionership for Assam. The viceroy reasoned that, because the Oriyas and the Biharis have little in common with the Bengalis, this arrangement would receive the enthusiastic support of both the Oriyas and the Biharis. Once again, the British government had neglected to consider public opinion, and the Oriyas overwhelmingly rejected the proposal. Madhusudan Das articulated public sentiment at the Berhampur session of Conference on April 6, 1912: "I suppose there is no people under the British Government who have been treated more unjustly and unkindly than the people of Orissa who have done nothing to deserve such treatment."[46] The Oriya sentiment reverberated in the sleepy chambers of the House of Lords in June 1912, when Lord Curzon noted that "the interests of the Oriyas have been sacrificed without compunction" simply because they "are a non-agitating people."[47]

The government of India pushed through the decision in the face of Oriya opposition, and the creation of the new province of Bihar and Orissa was announced by King George V on December 12, 1911, at his coronation *durbar* in Delhi. Sir Charles Stuart Bailey became the first lieutenant governor of the new province, and his executive council, constituted on August 1, 1912, originally consisted of three members. The Orissa Division included the districts of Angul, Balasore, Cuttack, Puri, and Sambalpur; the total area of the division was 13,736 square miles, and its population was estimated at 4,968,873 in the 1921 census. Ranchi served as the capital of the new province until 1919, when Patna became the capital city, although Ranchi remained the summer capital of the government.

The debate on Orissa was kept alive by Oriya members of the Bengal Legislative Council, which had been expanded as a result of the Indian Council Act of 1892. Madhusudan Das was elected three times to the Bengal Legislative Council, in 1896, 1900, and 1909. The parliamentary training acquired in that body proved useful for the Oriyas in the Bihar and Orissa Legislative Council for demanding better educational facilities, improved economic development through expansion of existing and introduction of modern industries, establishment of law and medical schools, and inclusion of women in educational and social reforms of the new province.

The popular perception prevailing among the Oriyas was that their backwardness and economic suffering could be removed only by the creation of a separate Orissa province, for which cooperation with the British Crown and its government in India was considered necessary by the Utkal Union Conference. Madhusudan Das, the chief architect of Conference, strongly believed that Orissa had much to lose by confronting the government of India. That realization had two consequences. First, Conference adopted a policy of appeasement towards the government, reflected in the glowing tributes to the British Crown made in all sessions. Cooperation with the government of India also helped Conference in improving relations with the feudatory chiefs of Orissa, since their titles were protected by the British; and many feudatory chiefs became active members of Conference, calling for the support of the Conference program as an act of patriotism.

Second, cooperation with the British prevented cooperation with the Indian National Congress. The Congress resolution of 1903 opposing the Risley report was viewed by the Conference leadership as being inimical to Orissa. Moreover, the prepondrance of Bengalis in Congress made that organization appear hostile to Conference. The break between the two organizations had occurred as early as 1902, when Madhusudan Das had refused to attend the annual Congress session that year. Soilabala Das, the adopted daughter of Madhusudan Das, recalled her father's decision in her poignant biography of her father:

> . . . in 1902, my late father and [the] late Sir Surendra Nath Banerjee had a great discussion about the difficult problems of Orissa, in the Grand Hotel, Calcutta. . . . My father wanted that the Indian National Congress should take up the question of Orissa, that the Oriya speaking tracts should be amalgamated as a Province. But Surendra Nath was not in favour of taking up [the] provincial question in Congress and so my father parted from the [Indian] National Congress.[48]

The government of India's latest scheme of annulling the partition of Bengal had not resulted in a separate province for Orissa. That had radicalized a section of the otherwise pliant Conference leadership, demanding a shift in the Conference program from cultural to political. But since conversion of Conference into a political body would have meant that government officials and feudatory chiefs could no longer participate in its sessions, an annonymous suggestion was made to split Conference into two branches: one political and the other sociocultural.[49] That suggestion was never carried out, but Conference in its 1913 session at Puri for the first time publicly addressed the question of amalgamating the Oriya tracts; and by December 1916, the Conference leaders were openly demanding a separate province for Orissa. In addition, the Conference leaders were demanding that Jeypore Agency in Madras be turned into a separate district and the Oriya language be introduced there, as well as in Patna University and in the courts in Singhbhum and Ganjam. Two years later presiding over the special session of Conference, Madhusudan Das, who had built his reputation as a private persuader and an astute politician, publicly castigated the government of India for ignoring the Oriyas in the creation of Bihar and Orissa Province, which, he claimed, was consistent with the British policy of administrative expediency at the cost of human considerations. He emphasized that "Orissa will not yield to the Biharis the position of an intermediary ruling race," and warned the government that "If the present position is not improved, there will be friction, which is not desirable in the interests of both Bihar and Orissa."[50]

Turning seventy in the spring of 1918, Madhusudan Das was beginning to show signs of physical exhaustion in the autumn of his life, and by the end of that year he declared his retirement from Conference, which he had helped found, and from the editorship of the *Oriya*, which he had used for advocating the Oriya demands. The new and younger leadership of Conference was becoming increasingly restless with the organization's old policy of appeasement with and loyalty to His Majesty's Government in India. Although Madhusudan Das was to remain active on the political scene of Orissa as an elder statesman until his death in 1934, his withdrawal from Conference created a vacuum which was filled by Gopabandhu Das (1877–1928), the new rising star of Orissa who had been elected to the Bihar and Orissa Legislative Council in 1917.

The Bihar and Orissa Legislative Council, created under the Indian Council Act of 1909, the brainchild of John Morley (1838–1923), the brilliant secretary of state for India who had been retained to head Indian affairs in Whitehall with the electoral victory of the Liberal Party under Campbell-Bannerman in 1906, was not designed to be a responsible legislative body. Consisting of twenty-one elected members, nineteen nominated members, and three executive councillors, the Council's first session was held on January 20, 1913. Five Oriyas attended the session, three of whom were elected and two nominated. Madhusudan Das and Maharaja Baikunth Nath Deo were the nominated members. The franchise was limited and excluded the common man from the Council, and there were no political parties to contest elections on the basis of platform or ideology. The outbreak of war in 1914 produced such an overwhelmingly loyalist and supportive response from Indian nationalist politicians of all parties, as well as from princes, that the Oriya question was relegated to the background, however.

Not until Edwin Montagu, who had replaced Sir Austen Chamberlain as the secretary of state for India after the latter had resigned for his inept handling of the Indian troops in Iraq, arrived in India in 1917, becoming the first secretary of state to do so while in office (he had travelled to India once before in 1913 as undersecretary of state), did the Oriya question again receive the attention of His Majesty's Government in India. Before embarking for India, Montagu had announced on August 20, 1917, in the British parliament that "the policy of His Majesty's Government, with which the Government of India are in complete accord, is that of the increasing association of Indians in every branch of the administration and the gradual development of self-governing institutions with a view to the progressive realization of responsible government in India as an integral part of the British Empire."[51] Calling himself "an Oriental" because of his Jewish birth, he met the waiting Oriya delegation upon his arrival in Calcutta in December 1917. The Utkal Union Committee, a constituent wing of the Utkal Union Conference created just a year earlier in December 1916, and consisting of such Oriya stalwarts as Madhusudan Das, Raja Rajendra Narayan Bhanj Deo of Kanika, Hari Hara Panda, Brajasundar Das, Gopabandhu Das, Sudamcharam Naik, and the Raja of Seragada (Ganjam), pleaded to the secretary of state that Orissa should have "wider representation in the councils, both Local and Imperial, and in the University . . . in a manner that would admit of the proposed united Orissa being granted an equal status with Bihar, in order to avoid the risk of the Oriyas being relegated to a subordinate position which has been their lot in the past."[52]

Soon after he returned home in 1918, Montagu hammered out his "Report on Indian Constitutional Reform," which embodied the principle of increasing "popular control" at both local and provincial levels of government; the Imperial Legislative Council was also enlarged and made more representative, although Montagu was careful to leave executive authority untouched at the center. But he aimed at deliberate obfuscation of the Oriya question by recommending the establishment of a subprovince at a very early date, while agreeing to the soundness and desireability of linguistic distribution of areas.

The Oriya response to the secretary of state's report was predictable. In a special session held at Cuttack in September 1918 the Utkal Union Conference passed a resolution, declaring the "deep disappointment" of the Oriya people "in finding no definite provision in the Report for the amalgamation of the Oriya-speaking tracts under one administration." Further, the resolution expressed its concern that, without the "desired amalgamation" preceding or accompanying the constitutional reform, "the Oriyas will not only be deprived of the benefits of the scheme itself but will also be placed under serious disadvantages" as a consequence of "their being in the minority under several existing administrations." In another resolution Conference rejected the proposal for constituting a subprovince for Orissa, reiterating the Oriya position "that unless a separate province under Governor-in-Council and a legislative assembly with an elected non-official majority be given to the united Oriya-speaking tracts, the proper solution to the question cannot be satisfactorily reached and the legitimate aspirations of the [Oriya] people . . . cannot be fulfilled."[53]

Montagu's constitutional reforms were finally implemented in the Government of India Act of 1919; but the Act of 1919 was followed by harsh, repressive recommendations made by the Rowlatt Committee, which had been appointed by the government of India to investigate "seditious conspiracy" and the possible need for peacetime legislation along lines of the martial law Defence of India Act that had been passed as a wartime emergency measure in 1915. The repressive Rowlatt Acts were driven through India's Imperial Legislative Council at high speed, over the universal opposition of elected members, who found their passage to be yet another rude reminder of their helpless position as British subjects in India.

The Rowlatt Acts were accompanied by the most catastrophic influenza epidemic that India has witnessed, taking a toll of twelve million lives in 1918–19. Mohandas Karamchand Gandhi (1869–1948), who had returned to India to enter politics after his twenty-year exile in South Africa, and who, because of his sensitive spirit and spiritual soul, must have viewed the aftermath of the world war as nothing less than proof of the failure of British rule, called the Rowlatt Acts "symptoms" of "a deep-seated disease" in the government. In protest of the Rowlatt Acts he called upon all Indians to observe a nationwide strike during the first week of April 1919 as a prelude to the launching of a national noncooperation campaign. Whatever goodwill the British might have had left on their side was destroyed by Brigadier R. E. H. Dyer when his Gurkha and Baluchi infantry poured 1,650 rounds of live ammunition into some ten thousand men, women, and children gathered on a Sunday afternoon in April in Amritsar's Jallianwala Bagh (garden) to celebrate the Hindu Festival of Baisakhi. By sunset on that holocaust Sunday some four hundred Indians were dead and twelve hundred wounded, bringing to end India's era of late-Victorian liberal cooperation and Edwardian politeness and ushering in the era of Gandhian noncooperation.

Already feeling neglect by the government of India and fighting the famine of 1919 in the province, Orissa was radicalized by the turbulent national events of the last two years. It was in such a climate that the Imperial Legislative Council in February 1920 passed a resolution introduced by Sir Sachidananda Sinha, a Bihari by birth and soon to become the first Indian governor of a province, which directed the governments of Bihar and Orissa, Bengal, Madras, and the Central Provinces to provide relevent statistics on Oriya population and the areas where Oriya was spoken on the basis of the census data. The resolution also called for the creation of a mixed committee of governmental and civilian members with the responsibility of developing a scheme for the amalgamation of the Oriya-speaking tracts scattered under different governments.[54] Sinha reasoned that the Biharis would be neutral on the question of amalgamating the Oriya-speaking tracts either under the government of Bihar and Orissa or under a separate province of Orissa.[55]

Meanwhile, Sir Sachidananda Sinha had taken over the governorship of Bihar and Orissa Province on December 29, 1920. The next day the Utkal Union Conference in its sixteenth session at Chakradharpur passed the historic resolution accepting the Congress creed as one of its objectives. Congress success was due mainly because it had finally adopted the principle of linguistic nationalism in the forming of Indian provinces, recognizing Orissa's right for a separate province. Gandhi's visit to Orissa in March of the following year to examine the famine damage strengthened the position of Congress and the nationalists. Still, Congress and Conference ran into a conflict when the latter decided to contest elections to the Bihar and Orissa Council against the general boycott of the elections to the provincial councils called by Congress. Responding to the Congress call, Gopabandhu Das and other nationalists did not enter the contest. Those who were elected mostly represented the propertied classes and belonged to the Utkal Union Conference. Among the new Oriya nationalists to come in contact with Gandhi and Congress was the young Harekrushna Mahtab, destined to play an important role in the creation of Orissa Province and the construction of the new capital city at Bhubaneswar. However, the struggle between the regionalists, who viewed the plight of the Oriyas and amalgamation of the Oriya-speaking tracts as the main problem of Orissa separate from the national politics, and the nationalists, who viewed the Oriya question as part of the larger national struggle for independence, continued in Orissa.

Disagreement between Congress and Conference leaderships helped the government in delaying making a decision on the question. Moreover, preventing the government from making a decision was the shifting Oriya position that ranged from amalgamating the Oriya-speaking tracts under one government to placing the Oriyas under a separate province of Orissa. In the absence of any official survey, it was also not clear whether the outlying Oriya-speaking tracts under the Central Provinces, Bengal, and Madras did really wish to be united under a single administrative unit—either of the Bihar and Orissa government or of a separate Orissa government.[56] H. LeMesurier, vice-president of the Executive Council, explained the government's position before the newly elected Legislative Council of Bihar and Orissa:

> A question . . . arises owing to the fact that the movers of [various] resolutions have suggested two different ways of carrying out [the amalgamation of the Oriya tracts]. Two of the movers asked that the Oriya-speaking tracts should be united and formed into a separate province under a separate administration, while the other three ask that the tracts may be amalgamated and placed under one Government. . . . The [Government of Bihar and Orissa's present] position is that a letter has been prepared for submission to the Government of India and in it Government have asked for further information regarding the attitude towards the proposals, either or both, which are embodied in the present resolution of the inhabitants of the tracts which, though claimed to be properly Oriya, are at present under other Governments. These include a portion of the Midnapur District in the Presidency of Bengal,

a portion of the Ganjam District and the Feudatory States of Madras, and also certain zamindaris in the Central Provinces, regarding which the local Government have very little information of any kind.[57]

In addition, LeMesurier explained that the government felt there might be some serious "administrative difficulties" in transferring the Oriya-speaking tracts from their present administrations. Included in these difficulties was a possible objection by the Madras government to the transfer of Ganjam because of the presence of a profitable salt manufacture in that district. Next, the land revenue and village administrations in the Oriya tracts under Madras, Bengal, and the Central Provinces were "different" from that prevailing in Bihar and Orissa. Also, an officer who might be "transferred" with the territory would have to master a new system for which his training had not prepared him.[58] "Government have not hitherto considered separately the suggestion of creating an entirely new administration for the Oriya-speaking tracts alone," explained LeMesurier. "It is doubtful whether in area and population this will equal the major provinces of India or whether the people would be willing to accept less than a fully developed Governor's province with the consequently expensive system of administration. But at present this question hardly arises, as the first matter to be decided will be whether the outlying tracts do in fact wish to be re-united with those comprised in Bihar and Orissa."[59]

The Oriya members of the Bihar and Orissa Council rebutted the government's arguments, claiming that these were not the reasons "which should outweigh the united wish of the Oriya population" for amalgamating the Oriya-speaking territories.[60] However, the Oriya ambivalence on whether to amalgamate the Oriya-speaking territories under any one government or create a new province of Orissa was reflected in Babu Bishwanath Kar's speech in the council: "We want to be amalgamated first of all under one government. If possible, we would like to have a separate Government." But apparently Kar, who had originally introduced in the council the motion of amalgamating the Oriya-speaking territories under one government, and who had sought the permission of the council president to present his case in his native Oriya rather than in English, was not certain how the government would respond. Not wanting to confront the government, he added that the question is not "for us to decide," and that "It would be decided by the commission to be appointed for the purpose." He nevertheless did emphasize that the

Oriyas "want one Government." He added: "It may be a separate Government, or it may be the Government of Bihar and Orissa, or it may be the Government of Bengal, or it may be the Government of Madras, or the Central Provinces; but to our mind it is most probable that the minor portions will come to the major portion in which case it would be placed under the Bihar Government."[61]

Their ambivalence about what should be the future form of the Oriya-speaking territories notwithstanding, the Oriyas were increasingly becoming alienated with His Majesty's Government in India. Most of this alienation was rooted in the linguistic nationalism of the Oriyas. Babu Rebati Kanta Gosh, an Oriya member elected to the council from South Cuttack put it thus:

> We are in minority everywhere. We suffer politically, materially, linguistically, socially all round. In fact the very existence of the language and race is threatened. It is a wonder that His Majesty's Government and the British people that went into the War to guard the independence and integrity of small nationalities should stand aside and see a small race being gradually effaced from the face of the earth in their own dominions through administrative blunders. In the case of the Oriyas equity, justice and fairness have been in discount. Persistency in error and a dogged obstinacy have always been in evidence in people responsible for the good government and well-being of the Oriya people.[62]

To provide a rational justification for the creation of a new province three questions had to be addressed: 1) whether the new province would have a viable area; 2) whether the new province would have a viable population; and, 3) whether the new province would have a viable financial base. Armed with the 1911 census data and economic figures compiled by the Utkal Union Conference, the Oriya leadership made a strong case for constituting a separate Orissa province. That data revealed that if the Oriya-speaking tracts under four governments—Bengal, Madras, Bihar and Orissa, and the Central Provinces—were to be united together and the Feudatory States of Orissa attached to them, the new province would cover "an area of 89,029 square miles (British: 42,325; non-British: 46,704) with a population of fifteen million two hundred and fifty thousand one hundred and fifty eight (15,250,158) of which the Oriya population will be ten million." These figures indicated that "In population and area the amalgamated Oriya province will be almost equal to that of the Central Provinces, Berar and Burma [area: 99,823 square miles; population: 13,916,308] taken separately and much larger than Assam [area: 53,015 square miles; population: 6,713,635]. And the approximate revenue may come up to a crore and thirty lakhs [rupees]." Compared to the revenue of 16,840,863 rupees in the case of the Central Provinces and 12,800,000 rupees in the case of Assam, the financial condition of Orissa appeared favorable.[63] (One crore equals 10,000,000; one lakh equals 100,000.) The following table will clarify the situation:

	Area (*Sq. Mil.*)	Population	Revenue (*in Rupees*)
United Orissa	89,029	15,250,158	13,018,270
C.P. & Berar	99,823	13,916,308	16,840,863
Assam	53,015	6,713,635	12,800,000

Source: *Proceedings of the Legislative Council of the Governor of Bihar & Orissa*, Nov. 25, 1921. India Office Library & Records, London.

The position of the governments of Bihar and Orissa, Bengal, Madras, and the Central Provinces on Oriya unification varied. Bengal, which included the Oriya-speaking district of Midnapore, opposed the transfer of territory to Orissa on the grounds that the Oriyas in Bengal showed no enthusiasm for the proposed new province. The government of the Central Provinces, while admitting to the presence of a language movement in Phuljhar estate of the Raipur district, opposed the transfer of the Oriya-speaking territory on the grounds that such a transfer of territory would have a negative impact on the non-Oriya population of that area. The Madras government was opposed to the transfer of the Ganjam district, although it would be willing to allow an inquiry commission decide the transfer of the other Oriya-speaking areas under its control. The government of Bihar and Orissa, while expressing some reservations about the transfer of Ganjam and Koraput (in the Vizagpatam district), was the only one to go along with a new subprovince of Orissa if public opinion favored such a decision.[64]

Meanwhile, the Utkal Union Conference after a hiatus of two years met at Berhampur on the last day of March 1923 and reiterated the demand for amalgamating the Oriya-speaking tracts under one government. Conference also passed a resolution supporting the use of *swadeshi* cloth in deference to Congress, which had built considerable support in Orissa as a result of Gandhi's visit to that province. The same year Sir Malcolm Hailey and C. W. Gwynne replaced Sir William Vincent and A. Mcleod as home member and joint secretary in the government, respectively. Sympathetic to Oriya sentiment, they realized that the Oriya question could not be resolved without first ascertaining the wishes of the Oriyas living in the Ganjam district. Accordingly, C. L. Philip, political agent, Orissa Feudatory States, and A. C. Duff, collector, Bellary (in Madras), were appointed in late 1924 to inquire into "the attitude of the Oriya inhabitants of the Madras Presidency towards the question of amalgamation of the tracts" with Orissa.[65]

The appointment of the Philip-Duff Commission produced an immediate response from the Oriyas and the Telugus: the Oriyas launched a strong campaign for the amalgamation of the Oriya-speaking tracts and the Telugus launched a strong antiamalgamation campaign. The Philip-Duff Inquiry Report, which cost the government Rs. 12,441, was submitted on December 26, 1924. Concluding that "there is a genuine longstanding and deep-seated desire on the part of the educated Oriya classes of the Oriya-speaking tracts of Madras for amalgamation of these tracts with Orissa under one administration,"[66] the two veteran administrators recommended in the report the transfer of the Oriya-speaking tracts in the Madras presidency to Orissa. But the Madras government's strong opposition to the report resulted in the government of India's postponing a decision.

Oriya indecision itself contributed to the postponment of the government's decision. Congressman Nilakantha Das in the Legislative Council of India argued for a separate Orissa Province. He was supported by the Bihari Muslims, who viewed the amalgamation of the Hindu Oriya-speaking tracts with Bihar and Orissa as reducing the Muslims to even greater minority status in the province. Some members of Conference thought that Orissa as a separate province could not survive financially, and therefore argued in favor of amalgamating the Oriya-speaking tracts with Bihar and Orissa. The Telugus in the Legislative Council of India opposed the transfer of the Oriya-speaking tracts. Consequently, Orissa's fate remained undecided until the arrival of Sir John Simon in India in early 1928.

Sir John Simon arrived in India at the head of a seven-man Indian Statutory Commission to evaluate the success of the Montagu-Chelmsford Reforms and to formulate what would be the "next stage" of Indian constitutional reforms. The absence of even a single Indian representative on that parliamentary commission sent a wave of consternation throughout India, and the commission was greeted by angry mobs waving black flags and shouting "Simon, go back!" In Orissa, Conference decided to ignore Congress's call for a nationwide strike, and greeted the commission upon its arrival in Patna, the capital of Bihar and Orissa, with signs stating "Orissa welcomes, Simon!" Hoping to enlist the support of the commission, Conference presented a memorandum to Simon and his seven men that read: "Sirs, we the members of the Utkal Union Committee, on behalf of the Oriya people, accord you a most hearty welcome to the ancient city of Pataliputra, the capital of the Province of Bihar and Orissa."[67] After noisy and positively hostile receptions throughout India, Simon was only too happy to admit to his hosts in Patna that "We are greatful for what you have been kind enough to say about our welcome."[68]

The government of Bihar and Orissa informed the visiting commission that, while it supported the amalgamation of the Oriya-speaking tracts under one government, it was not in a position to undertake the additional financial burden that would result from transferring the Oriya tracts from Madras to Bihar and Orissa.[69] But the government would be willing to support the amalgamation if the government of India would be willing to make up "the anticipated deficit."[70] However, the government of India was not willing to undertake any "new financial liability."[71]

The Statutory Commission Report, published on June 7, 1930, concluded that the present provincial boundaries separated areas and populations who ought to have been "united," and that the province of Bihar and Orissa appeared to them a "glaring" instance of "artificial union," as both the constituents differed from each other not only in physical features but also in racial, linguistic, and cultural characteristics.[72] Reasoning that people speaking one language, if united under one administration, would form a "compact and self-contained area," the Statutory Commission recommended that any distribution of territories for provincial individuality must take into consideration the use of "a common language, race, religion, economic interests, geographical contiguity, a due balance between country and town, and between coast line and interior" as "relevant factors." Further, any redistribution of territory must reflect "the largest possible measure of general agreement on the changes proposed, both on the side of the area that is gaining, and on the side of the area that is losing territory."[73]

Based on these guidelines, which were to become the basis of reorganization of states in postindependence India as well, the Statutory Commission recommended the creation of a separate Orissa province. The new province was to be built around the Orissa Division by adding Angul, the Feudatory States, Khariar, and the northern part of the Ganjam district, predominantly populated by a tribal people. Excluded from the proposed Orissa province were Singhbhum, Phuljhar, Padampur, and the estate of Jeypore in Vizagpatam Agency; the Mohanpur and Gopiballabhpur Oriya tracts in Bengal were also recommended for inclusion in Orissa. Finally, the Statutory Commission recommended to the government of India the creation of a boundary commission headed by an impartial chairman to investigate the main cases of provinces in which readjustment was called for.[74]

Congress's open opposition to the Statutory Commission's work in India resulted in alienating the Oriyas. The Oriyas were further bruised by the Nehru Committee's Report (1928), authored by the aristocratic Congressman Motilal Nehru, which, while agreeing to the possible redistribution of provincial boundaries "on a linguistic basis" in accordance with the Nagpur resolution of Congress in 1920, made no special provision for any minority membership in the proposed "Commonwealth of India." When Subhas Chandra Bose, an Oriya-born and -educated Bengali nationalist and a member of the Nehru Committee, proposed that the creation of a separate Orissa be made contingent on financial viability, the Oriyas in Congress demanded an amendment to the Nehru Report. The whole episode once again brought into focus the sharp differences between Congress, which was demanding *swaraj*, and the Oriyas, who were demanding a separate Orissa and were content to have a separate province within the British Raj. Rapprochement was achieved by the skillful Harekrushna Mahtab, destined to play a prominent role in the provincial Congress party in Orissa, when his resolution for the creation of a separate Orissa was adopted by Congress at Cuttack in 1931. A committee was constituted with Congressman Nilakantha Das as the chair to present the Oriya case before the proposed boundary commission.

Acting on the Statutory Commission's recommendation, Viceroy Irwin announced on September 1, 1930, the decision to set up two boundary commissions—one for Sind and the other for Orissa—and in a letter to the secretary of state for India "asked for the expeditious appointment of a Boundary Commission" to satisfy the natural desire of the Oriyas.[75] Later in November, His Majesty's Government convened the first Round Table Conference on Constitutional Reforms in London. Congress boycotted the conference, which was attended by Indian princes, *zamindars*, *taluqdars*, industrialists, liberals, and Muslims and other minority community leaders. Raja Sreekrishnachandra Gajapati Naryan Deb of Parlakimedi, who had a tenuous residency claim in Orissa,[76] and who was later to form non-Congress ministeries twice in Orissa, represented Orissa at the Round Table Conference.

The Round Table Conference ended, however, with little accomplished. The question of a separate Orissa province was not specifically discussed at the conference, nor was the Statutory Commission's recommendation for constituting a boundary commission challenged. So in September 1931, the government of India appointed Sir Samuel O'Donnell the chairman of the Orissa Boundary Commission with the approval of Whitehall "to examine and report on the administrative, financial and other consequences of setting up a separate administration of the Oriya-speaking people, and to make recommendations regarding its boundaries in the event of separation." Two other "impartial" men were to serve on the O'Donnell Commission, and assisting them would be three associate members drawn from "the areas most interested."[77] Thus, the three impartial men on the Orissa Boundary Commission consisted of Sir Samuel O'Donnell (chairman), H. M. Mehta, member of the Council of State, and T. R. Phookun, member of the Central Legislative Assembly; the Raja of Parlakimedi, Sir Sachidananda Sinha, and Narasinha Raju were appointed associate members to protect the interests of the Oriyas, Biharis, and Telugus, respectively. B. C. Mukherjee, an Indian civil servant, was appointed the secretary of the commission, while R. D. Balvally from the Accountant General's Office was appointed the financial advisor. The O'Donnell Commission, as it popularly came to be called, was to report on 1) the boundary arrangements of the new province, 2) the administrative, financial, and other consequences of the new province, and 3) the administrative and financial impact of the new province on the neighboring territories of British India.[78]

O'Donnell and his commission completed their report in early January 1932, despite the rumors that the governments of Bengal, Madras, Bihar and Orissa, and the Central Provinces, which were to be affected by the new province, had manipulated census statistics to oppose the transfer of Midnapore, Ganjam, Singhbhum, and Phuljhar, respectively. The impartial men on the commission proposed that the new province of Orissa should include "the Orissa Division, Angul, Khariar *zamindari* of the Raipur district, and the greater part of the Ganjam district and the

Vizagpatam Agency tracts."[79] The new province was to have an area of approximately 33,000 square miles and a population of about 8,277,000.

The O'Donnell Commission recommended against setting up a high court, a university, and a provincial penitentiary in Orissa so as to minimize costs generally associated with the creation of a separate province. New Orissa was to share these services with Bihar for a specified fee. The new province was also to be without its own cadre of provincial civil servants. Such severe measures of administrative austerity notwithstanding, the new province was expected to have a deficit of Rs. 3,521,000, in the first year, and in the next fifteen years the deficit was projected to reach a staggering figure of Rs. 4,093,000.[80] Not even new taxes were expected to help the new province balance its budget, and Orissa was expected to depend on the central government to remain solvent. Later, financial implications were to play an important part in the decision for the construction of the provincial capital city.

O'Donnell's report produced protest movements throughout Orissa because certain Oriya-speaking territories had been excluded from the new province. Rising from its languid state, the Utkal Union Conference passed a resolution in August 1932 demanding the inclusion of Midnapore (in Bengal), Singhbhum (in Bihar), and Parlakimedi (in Madras) in the new province—a resolution which the Raja of Parlakimedi presented to the Conservative Willingdon, who had replaced Lord Irwin as the new viceroy of India.[81] O'Donnell's report was also criticized by the Utkal Provincial Congress Committee on the grounds that "A province without a High Court and a University and with a heavy deficit could neither satisfy the intelligentsia nor the common man, who were already unable to bear the existing burden of taxation."[82]

Expressing dissatisfaction for their own reasons with O'Donnell's report were the governments of Bengal, Bihar and Orissa, Madras, and the Central Provinces. Bengal feared that a financially weak new province would add to the burden of the rest of the provinces in British India—a fear that was shared by the other three provinces to be directly affected by the new province. The government of the Central Provinces was willing to agree to the transfer of Padampur to Orissa, but it strongly objected to the transfer of Khariar on the grounds of historical association and geographical contiguity. The Madras government's position was most complex. Madras was willing to transfer the northern parts of Ganjam to Orissa, but was unwilling to surrender Parlakimedi, whose fate had been left undecided by O'Donnell and his commission because ethnically and linguistically it was a Telugu majority area but ruled by a raja who held close family ties with Orissa. Madras was also opposed to the transfer of Jeypore, where the Oriya-speaking population was in the majority but whose rulers had expressed conflicting sentiments on the question of being transferred to Orissa: Raja Ramchandra Deb IV (reigned 1920–31) was opposed to the transfer, but his successor Vikram Deb IV (reigned 1931–51) was in favor of the transfer to Orissa.

Meanwhile, in London the Second Round Table Conference had produced no tangible results, and the effects of Depression politics in Britain were to have their influence on the government of India. It was in such an atmosphere that Willingdon's government decided to try a tougher line, once again showing inclination of the machine to act on considerations of administrative efficiency rather than on human considerations. On the grounds of financial prudence, Willingdon decided to go against O'Donnell's report by recommending the retention of Vizagpatam Agency and Parlakimedi by Madras. The proposed province under the Willingdon scheme was to be substantially smaller than originally envisaged in the O'Donnell report, ostensibly in the interest of financial and administrative considerations.

The Oriya response was predictable. The situation in the rest of India was also radicalized by Sir Ramsay MacDonald's announcement of his Communal Award in mid-August 1932, prompting Congress to launch the second Civil Disobedience campaign. Impervious to the Indian scene, the machinery of the Raj continued its constitutional "reforms" with a Third Round Table Conference held in November 1932. Secretary of State for India Sir Samuel Hoare by his announcement on Christmas Eve the same year had made it official that a separate Orissa Province would be formed in the new constitutional setup for India being considered, and that it would be headed by a governor like the other ten provinces in British India. Publication of the government's White Paper the following year produced nearly universal criticism in India. The Oriyas were particularly disappointed. Nevertheless, following the ritual of three readings in both Houses and the subsequent consent from the Crown, the White Paper was finally transmuted into the Government of India Act of 1935, India's last British-made constitution.

The Oriya disappointment resulted from the substantially reduced size of Orissa as envisaged in the White Paper. Excluded from the new province were Vizagpatam Agency, Jalantar *maliahs* (tribal hilly areas), and Parlakimedi. In total size, Orissa was reduced to 21,545 square miles from the 33,000 square miles recommended by O'Donnell. The "boundary demarcated for the new Orissa Province is highly disappointing in as much as it does not include even the areas unanimously recommended by the Orissa Boundary Committee and also excludes the Parlakimedi estate proposed by the majority of the said Committee,"[83] declared Rai Bahadur Loknath Misra in the Bihar and Orissa Legislative Council. Rajas of Parlakimedi and Jeypore were equally critical of the White Paper.

Faced by widespread opposition to the White Paper, Sir Samuel Hoare referred the Orissa boundary question to a subcommittee of the Joint Parliamentary Committee. Chaired by Secretary of State for India Hoare, the other members of the subcommittee included Lords Zetland, Derby, and Lothian, Major Clement R. Attlee, and R. A. Butler; and three Indian delegates: Sir Pheroze Sethna, Sir N. N. Sircar, and Zafrullah Khan. Samuel O'Donnell was invited to attend the proceedings as an observer. To get different opinions from all the concerned parties, the views of the viceroy and of the Madras government were also invited.[84] The Oriya delegation was led by the Raja of Parlakimedi.

The collective wisdom of the subcommittee seemed to have been in favor of transferring Jeypore and some other Oriya-speaking areas in Madras to Orissa, while retaining Parlakimedi in the Madras Presidency. Thinking that such an arrangement would not be acceptable to either the Telugus or the Oriyas, the government of India requested the subcommittee to reconsider the arrangement.[85] Meanwhile, to overcome the Telugu opposition to the transfer of Parlakimedi to Orissa, the Raja of Parlakimedi decided to divide his estate between Madras and Orissa, taking with him the town of Parlakimedi to Orissa. However, Viceroy Willingdon was opposed to any division of the Parlakimedi estate to satisfy the personal considerations of the ruler. Fearing opposition from the Madras government, the viceroy was also opposed to the transfer of Jeypore to Orissa.

Indeed, the whole Orissa boundary question appeared insoluble in the early 1930s. As if to make a trial of strength with the government of India, the Utkal Union Conference declared that it would "oppose by all legitimate, peaceful and constitutional means the working of the Province if . . . (1) Jeypore, (2) [the northern and eastern parts of the Parlakimedi estate, (3) Parlakimedi *maliahs*, (4) [the] western portions of Mandasa and Jalantar estate, and (5) the entire *zamindari* of Budharsingh" were not included in the new province of Orissa.[86]

Following a protracted period of negotiations, the Joint Parliamentary

Committee on Indian Constitutional Reform submitted its report in November 1934. The report contained the recommendations of the subcommittee on the Orissa boundary question. According to the report, the new province of Orissa was to receive (a) that portion of Jeypore estate which the O'Donnell Commission had recommended for transfer to Orissa in 1932, (b) the Parlakimedi and Jalantar *maliahs*, and (c) a small portion of the Parlakimedi estate, including the town of Parlakimedi. Orissa thus constituted would comprise an area of 32,695 square miles as opposed to 21,545 square miles recommended in the White Paper, and would have a population of 8,043,681.[87] Considering that the joint government of Bihar and Orissa was struggling with extra financial problems resulting from a recent earthquake, the government of India offered to make up the deficit of the new province.

Created as a governor's province separate from Bihar under the Government of India Act of 1935,[88] Orissa was "perhaps the most homogenous province in the whole of British India, both racially and linguistically," the Joint Parliamentary Committee Report proudly noted. In Orissa "the communal difficulty is practically nonexistent; and its claim appears to have the sympathy and support of all parties in India."[89] Consent from the Crown for the new province was obtained on March 3, 1936; and on March 28 the Joint Legislative Council of Bihar and Orissa met for the last time in Patna, when the Bihari members of the council offered warmest wishes for success to their departing Oriya brothers. On April 1, 1936, the government of India promulgated the Constitution of Orissa Order, heralding the birth of Orissa as the eleventh province of British India. It would take another ten long years of protracted debate, however, before the new government of Orissa would decide where to place its capital city.

·3·

THE CAPITAL SITE

At the close of the third session of the Round Table Conference in London on June 24, 1933, Secretary of State for India Sir Samuel Hoare announced the intention of His Majesty's Government to create a committee to enquire into the administrative problems incidental to the creation of the new province of Orissa. Two considerations occupied the minds of senior officials in the government of India for implementing the decision to create the new province of Orissa. The first of these considerations was to keep the administrative expenses to a minimum in the creation of the new province; and the second was to find a qualified administrator for the new provincial government. The government of India's decision to underwrite the deficit of the new province had cleared the last financial hurdle for Orissa. But government officials lacked unanimity as to the appointment of a chief administrator who could organize the departments, assign responsibilities, and establish administrative procedures. There was also no unanimity as to whether the rank of the chief administrator should be deputy governor, lieutenant governor, or governor. The self-serving suggestion by Sir James Sifton, governor of Bihar and Orissa, that a lieutenant governor or a deputy governor be appointed in Orissa proved constitutionally impossible to implement because the Act of 1919 made no provision for a lieutenant governor's province.[1]

The government of India decided to request of the Home government the selection of the new governor for Orissa. The Home government selected career administrator Sir John Austin Hubback as the new governor of Orissa. Sir John Hubback's London shopping spree before embarking for India stands in stark contrast to the impoverished Orissa to which he was appointed. "It was indeed a thrill to be spending the considerable sum supplied by the Government of India on objects which we could expect to use and enjoy for the next five years," he exultingly recalled later.[2] Included among the items purchased by the new governor for his India assignment were "a Daimler and a Humber, together with a station wagon," a mahogany dining room set, "Parker Knoll chairs" for the drawing room, a grandfather clock, a billiard table, linen, a combination gramophone and radio set, and an assortment of "long playing records, comprising works by Mozart, Haydn . . . Handel, along with much of Gilbert and Sullivan." The governor later lamentably recalled that "A record of Gracie Fields unhappily succumbed early on when an A.D.C. escaped his own notice sitting on it."[3] The Raj spared no expense to make the daily life of the new governor as comfortable as possible in a state where existence alternated between droughts and floods, the two scourges of India.

Upon his arrival in Orissa, Sir John Hubback assumed the chairmanship of the Orissa Administration Committee that had been created on orders from Secretary of State for India Hoare to look into the administrative problems of the new province. Eight other members served on the committee: 1) Rai Bahadur Lakshmidhar Mahanti, 2) Rai Bahadur Loknath Misra, 3) Babu Birabar Narayan Chandra Dhir Narendra, 4) Madhusudan Das, 5) Rao Sahib N. Ramamurti Naidu, 6) W. O. Newsam, 7) N. Senapati, and 8) Sri G. C. Debo Mahasayo (zamindar of Chikati). V. Ramaswami from the Indian Civil Service (ICS) cadre was appointed secretary of the committee.[4]

The paramount problem facing the Orissa Administration Committee (1933) was where to place the capital city of the new province. The O'Donnell Commission (1931) had assumed in its report that Cuttack would be the capital. However, in the absence of any scientific survey of the city and with no assessment of the needs of the new administration, the government of India had not made any definite decision on where to locate the capital. Consequently, the Orissa Administration Committee was asked to recommend a suitable site for the headquarters of the new province, providing complete details of the site, approximate cost of building "the Government House, Secretariat, Council Chamber and residences for senior officials posted at headquarters and of any provisional accommodation that may be necessary before permanent buildings are ready." In addition, the committee was requested to explore the possibility of sharing "the High Court, University with its constituent Colleges, Medical, Science, Veterinary, Engineering, etc., and any other institutions" with "one or more of the adjoining provinces" to keep the expenditure to the new province at a minimum. For the same reason, the committee was also requested to explore whether Orissa was to have its own administrative cadre or "officers from outside should be deputed for limited periods and entitled to exchange." Finally, the committee was asked to recommend "territorial charges and their headquarters"—"in particular the question whether the Khondmals should be amalgamated with the Khond areas in Ganjam and whether Angul should be made a Sub-division of the Cuttack district."[5]

Competing with Cuttack for the capital city status were Berhampur (with Gopalpur as a summer resort), Puri, and Angul. The Orissa Administration Committee issued a general questionnaire to selected officials, civilians, and public bodies, inviting them to send their responses to the question of the capital site. A special questionnaire was also sent to heads of departments and other special officers in Bihar. Assisting the committee with technical and financial details for the new capital was Chief Engineer H.A. Gubbay and his Public Works Department (PWD) staff.

Competition from other cities notwithstanding, Cuttack apparently enjoyed popular support for consideration as the capital city. While acknowledging the joint claim of Berhampur and Gopalpur for the capital city for reasons of "equable climate and possibilities of town development," their geographic location which offered relative safety against "flood" and "epidemics," availability of cheap labor in the area, and lower construction costs, the Orissa Administration Committee concluded that the twin cities did not possess any historically unifying force and therefore popular sentiment did "not view their claim with favour."[6]

Angul was considered for the capital city because of its "central geographic position," its location on high ground that allowed for good drainage, and because no land acquisition cost would be necessary since "all the land belonged to Government." However, considering that Angul was physically separated from the coastal districts and Sambalpur by a belt of Feudatory States that could not be depended on for the maintenance of the roads, which could jeopardize the free and regular flow of communications, and also considering that Angul was fourteen miles from the nearest railway station—a railway station that was situated on a branch line and not on the main line—and realizing that there was no immediate "prospect of early improvement of railway communications," that city was eventually disqualified from becoming the capital.[7]

Puri, a devoutly Hindu city, a city which had served as the capital of the region under the Gangas in the fourteenth century, and a city with an equable climate and a reputation for being a health resort and the coolest place from March to June in the region, was the strongest rival to Cuttack as a choice for the capital—a rivalry which was to prevent a final decision for almost a decade. Moreover, the supporters of Puri argued that there already existed a government house at Puri, the land on the sea front was owned by the government, the nearly completed water works in the area assured an adequate supply of drinking water, and, the influx of pilgrims to Puri notwithstanding, the city had successfully improved sanitary conditions which had abated cholera in the area, substantially bringing down the mortality statistics compared with many other towns of Bihar and Orissa.[8]

Not everyone agreed, however. Those opposing Puri for a capital city argued that there were inherent disadvantages in "making an all-India centre of pilgrimage the seat of a provincial Government." Moreover, Puri, like Angul, was not on the main railway line, there were no educational institutions in the city, and the climate of the area was "enervating" for an extended stay because of the long rainy season during which "the sea breeze, on which comfort at Puri depends, is replaced by a land breeze."[9]

Historically, Cuttack had the strongest claim to becoming the capital, even though its exact origin remains obscure. Lying on longitude of 85 degrees and 50 minutes, East, and latitude 20 degrees and 29 minutes, North, Cuttack is situated at the bifurcation of the Mahanadi River and its main branch, the Katjori. Because of its location between the two rivers, Cuttack was originally known as *Abhinava* (new) *Baranasi Kataka*, a possible imitation of the older Hindu city of Baranasi (Varanasi), which is also situated between the rivers Barna and Asi.[10] The word "kataka" etymologically means military cantonment, and also capital city.

Growing out of five villages in the area, and surrounded in the north, west, and south by forested hills, Cuttack started as a cantonment city because of its impregnable location—a strength which was later to be considered as its weakness for becoming a capital city by its detractors. However, because Cuttack commanded the high road running from the north to the south of India along the eastern coast, invaders, pilgrims, merchants, and travelers had no alternative but to cross the Mahanadi and the Katjori near the city, which was rapidly transformed from a cantonment township into a metropolis. Moreover, the high roads from central India also ran along the Mahanadi Valley, terminating at

Cuttack; and the Mahanadi itself offered an efficient waterway for commerce and communication with the hinterland. Cuttack is also believed to have been connected through both road and waterway with the great international medieval ports of Chelitalo (Puri), Palura (Dantapura, the ancient capital of Kalinga), and Tamralipti (Tamluk in West Bengal).[11] Cuttack therefore must have evolved into a thriving trading center, which is attested to by the many old structures, narrow lanes, and historic temples, mosques, churches, and other medieval monuments which fill the city.

The early history of Cuttack is linked with the Kesari dynasty in the tenth century, and it might have been the seat of the royal court. The importance of Cuttack rapidly increased after the occupation of Orissa by Chodaganga Deva early in the twelfth century, when he allegedly transferred his capital from Kalinganagara to Cuttack because of its central location. However that may be, Cuttack was certainly the capital at the opening of the sixteenth century under the Gajapati dynasty which succeeded the Ganga rulers of Orissa; and Cuttack was also the capital of Mukund Deva, the last Hindu king of Orissa, who is believed to have fortified the city against the invading Afghan army by enlarging the great fort of Barabati on the southern bank of the Mahanadi. Abul Fazal Allami in his *Ain-i-Akbari* refers to Cuttack as a flourishing capital city during Mukund Deva's reign.[12]

The Afghans, however, were not destined to rule Orissa, which was finally annexed by the Mughal emperor Akbar in 1592. Cuttack became the headquarters of the Mughal *subedars* (governors) in the sixteenth and seventeenth centuries, a mention of which is made in the *Ain-i-Akbari*. It was in Cuttack "that the first Englishmen to visit Orissa, Ralph Cartwright and his companions, were received in 1663 by the representative of Shah Jehan, and granted leave to trade freely and to establish a factory."[13]

By 1747, Orissa had practically come under the Maratha occupation, and Cuttack greatly prospered as a center of trade, serving as the clearing house for goods brought by the Marathas of Nagpur and the English merchants in Bengal and the Northern Sircar. The long line of the Maratha stables, which are currently in use as quarters for the military police, indicate Cuttack's position as the military stronghold of the Marathas. The city also witnessed some other developments, with the Marathas building some temples and otherwise taking measures to beautify the city, as well as fortifying it by strengthening the Barabati fort.

Following the British occupation of Orissa in 1804, Cuttack became the center of local administration "not only for the British districts of the Orissa Division but also for the Feudatory States for well over a hundred years."[14] In 1876, the Cuttack municipality was constituted with thirty members, of whom twenty four were elected, four ex-officio, and two nominated by the government. The municipality board became responsible for improving the city, providing electricity, drinking water, medical facilities, and primary education. In an attempt to further modernize the city and provide for better communications, new roads were built and other public works projects undertaken, albeit under financial restrictions.[15]

Taking into account Cuttack's rich historical past and place as the administrative center, the Orissa Administration Committee in its report concluded that the "selection of Cuttack as the capital of the new province would be a graceful tribute to past history and popular sentiment."[16] Other factors in favor of Cuttack were its bulging population of 65,263 (1931 Census) compared with Berhampur's population of 37,750 and Puri's 37,568; its situation on the main east coast line of the Bengal-Nagpur Railway; its easy accessibility from the Ganjam, Puri, and Balasore districts; its short distance both by rail and road from Angul; and its year-round accessibility from Sambalpur within twelve hours.[17]

Cuttack was also the main market for the surplus produce of the Orissa States and the principal commercial and industrial town of the new province. The presence of several educational institutions in Cuttack, including Ravenshaw College, most of which had been founded during the British administration, had transformed the city into a modern intellectual center, and the city had become the focus of the Orissa nationalist movement.[18]

Still, Cuttack was not without its faults. The dry heat from March through May, and the high humidity that sets in after the rains, made for a "much less relaxing" climate in Cuttack. Cuttack was also exposed to the threat of flooding by the Mahanadi, although stone embankments had kept the town safe for centuries. Therefore, the Orissa Administration Committee cautiously declared that the "position of Cuttack at the head of the Mahanadi delta makes it eminently fitted as the centre of operations against the periodic floods, whose prevention and relief will certainly form one of the principal preoccupations of the new Government."[19]

In its final statement, the Orissa Administration Committee unanimously supported the selection of Cuttack as the capital city, but not before making proper arrangements for imperial comfort. Puri, popular for its mild summers, was designated the summer headquarters for the months of April, May, and June when the climate of Cuttack was at its worst. Only the governor and his immediate staff, made up mostly of British officers, were to move to Puri, not necessarily the whole secretariat. The concept was not new since there already existed the practice by which the government of India using public funds escaped the heat in New Delhi by moving to Simla for the summer; and in the Bombay Presidency the government moved from Bombay to Mahableshwar for the summer and later to Pune (Poona) for the monsoon season.

In Orissa, however, rail and road communications had yet to be improved between Cuttack and Puri before the safe and speedy movement of the governor and his staff could take place between the two cities; and a decision was taken to establish a telephone trunk line between Cuttack and Puri at a capital cost of Rs. 48,000 which would make the governor's absence from Cuttack less conspicuous. The recurring cost of Rs. 11,500 for this service was to be defrayed by the receipts from the Puri telephone exchange and the trunk line.[20]

But apparently such measures were not enough to provide sufficient relief from the great ranges of diurnal temperature of Cuttack for the officialdom, for whom escape from the scorching sun was as much a matter of good health as it was part of imperial tradition. Considering there was no place within the new province which could "provide the advantages of a change from the Cuttack climate," a scheme was devised to establish a summer camp at Mahendragiri in Mandasa estate, "an unoccupied hill nearly 5,000 feet high less than 20 miles from the sea, and within a distance of 5 or 6 miles from the proposed southern boundary of [Orissa]."Acting on behalf of the Orissa government, the Madras government was to secure the permission from the proprietor of the hill for leasing "a part of it for the erection of the necessary buildings and for the provision of water." The whole exercise of setting up the summer camp would cost the financially weak province Rs. 75,000.[21] The committee also felt that, considering there were no adequate residential quarters for the governor in the remote Ganjam district, it was "reasonable" to expend a sum of Rs. 50,000 for constructing a circuit house at Gopalpur. The new circuit house would also facilitate greater contact between the imperial officials and the poor people of Ganjam district.

Not everyone on the committee agreed with the idea of building a summer camp at Mahendragiri, and the idea of building a circuit house at

Gopalpur received at best a reluctant acceptance. The dissenting view was articulated by Rao Sahib N. Ramamurti Naidu, whose presence on the committee as the representative of the Tamils and Andhras made it obligatory on his part to note that the "construction of a summer camp on [Mahendragiri] will encourage the Oriyas to agitate further for inclusion of more Andhra area in the new Province, and will prove the thin end of the wedge for penetrating into the Andhra country still further." He added, "By making such a suggestion the Committee would unwittingly be lending their authority for the fomentation of such an agitation, and transgressing in spirit the instructions in terms of reference which lay down that 'considerations of the selection of boundaries will lie wholly outside the Committee's purview.'"[22] Naidu was equally unhappy about building a circuit house at Gopalpur since the Ganjam district was originally taken from Andhra and amalgamated with Orissa, but in the end he gave his grudging approval.

In addition to selecting the capital site, the Orissa Administration Committee provided details for the capitol complex and for the administrative and university buildings. The capitol complex was to consist of the Government House (the official residence of the governor), the Secretariat, and the Council Chamber. Five sites were identified for the capitol complex: 1) the fort area with its surrounding open spaces; 2) Chaudwar, a Cuttack suburb near the Nirgundi station 3) Chauliaganj to the east of the town; 4) the low hills area two miles west of Barang, about six miles south of Cuttack; and 5) a site in the neighborhood of Chauhatta ghat to the west of the town, enclosed by the embankment which protects Cuttack from the Mahanadi and the Katjori floods.[23]

The first four sites were ruled out for one reason or another. The fort area was thought to be too small to accommodate all the government buildings. Moreover, the construction of the government buildings so close to the fort would be in conflict with the fort as a historical monument, as well as impinging on the recreational amenities which the public derive from the open space. "The area to the east of the fort on the banks of the Mahanadi could not be utilized without closing and diverting a public road," the committee concluded. Since the ground was used for an annual religious fair in November, and since there was a temple on the bank which, with the ghat alongside, was used for daily worship and bathing presented additional obstacles.[24]

The Chaudwar site was ruled out because it was separated from the town by the Mahanadi, and a road bridge over the Mahanadi would have cost far more than the whole capital would otherwise cost. A ferry service could not be considered because at some seasons of the year it would be dangerous. For the same reasons Barang was ruled out. So also was ruled out Chauliaganj because that was the only direction in which the college could develop if it were to grow into a university. Moreover, much of the site was low-lying, making drainage exceedingly difficult.

The Chauhatta ghat site was considered the most suitable for the capitol complex because reports from the Public Works Department (PWD) indicated that it was less prone to local flooding than many other residential parts of Cuttack. The entire site was securely protected against river floods by embankment and, with the improvement of drainage, was likely to remain dry in all but quite abnormal conditions. Moreover, the high ground on the south side provided a panoramic view of the circle of hills to the north. The presence of a small *basti* (residential colony) and the army rifle range on the site were not considered hurdles for construction because the *basti* could be easily relocated and the Army Department was willing to surrender the rifle range. Whatever doubts that might have existed about this site were removed by messrs. E. R. Smitth, Sims, and Gubbay of PWD who concluded in their report that the site was suitable for multistoried buildings, that the site was desirable from a health and sanitary point of view, and that the provision of drinking water and electricity would not be expensive.[25] Accordingly, the committee recommended that in addition to the Government House, the Secretariat, and the Council Chamber, residences for government officers should also be built on the proposed site.

To estimate the residential requirements for the new administrative staff, the Orissa Administration Committee made a detailed analysis. A similar analysis had been prepared earlier by the O'Donnell Commission in which it was assumed that the Orissa Feudatory States would be under the "supervision" of the governor of Orissa, and that Orissa would include the Vizagapatam Agency tracts. Discounting the two assumptions, the Orissa Administration Committee provided a chief secretary (of commissioner's standing) for the new province assisted by an undersecretary and a whole hierarchy of staff below them, ranging from state attorney general to divisional forest officer. Similarly, the new province was to have an inspector general of police, with a hierarchy of staff below him. Provisions were made for senior staff in the areas of public health, education, and public works. A provision was made for a deputy chief engineer to assist the chief engineer in completing construction of the capitol buildings "with expedition and economy."[26]

Senior officials so named for the new province were to be housed in Cuttack either by using existing residences or by building or acquiring new ones or by encouraging them to find their own accommodation. Considering that the last option could lead to inflated rents since Cuttack had only a few suitable houses, and considering that it would not be fair to

	Rs.
Government House	700
Chief Justice	50
Chief Secretary	45
Revenue Commissioner	00
Chief Engineer	00
Deputy Secretary	35
Inspector General, Medical/Jails	35
Inspector General of Police	00
Director of Public Instruction	35
Under Secretary	25
Assistant Secretary	20
Registrar of Secretariat	15
Asst. to Inspector General of Police	00
Asst. Superintendent of Police	20
Deputy Director of Public Instruction	25
Government Advocate	00
Secretary to the Legislative Council	00
Personal Assistant (Excise)	20
Personal Assistant (Registration)	00
Personal Assistant (Public Health)	00
Personal Assistant (Jails)	20
Sergeant Major	10
Police Barracks	16
	1071

Source: *Orissa Administration Committee Report* (1933).
NB: Where there was no provision made the officer in that position was to receive housing from the existing stock of homes in Cuttack. (All figures are in thousands.)

burden officers required to work in a "trying" climate, and also considering that acquisition of houses in Cuttack would be as "dilatory and costly" as building them, the committee strongly recommended construction of new homes "for all officers who are not already provided for, or who cannot be provided for from the stock of existing Government residences."[27] Accordingly, the housing cost for the governor and other officials of the new provincial government was estimated at Rs. 1,071,000 distributed as shown on page 73.

In the absence of any hard data or clear guidelines for estimating housing requirements for the ministers of the new government and a legislature of sixty members drawn from all parts of the new province, the Orissa Administration Committee provided Rs. 70,000 for house accommodation for ministers and Rs. 100,000 for building quarters capable of housing twenty members of the legislature. If more quarters were to be required, the Orissa government was expected to provide them. In addition to clerks already employed in the divisional offices, a total of fifty clerical staff members was recommended to serve the Secretariat at Cuttack. The total cost for the various buildings, furniture, and layout were estimated at Rs. 3,187,000 distributed as following:

	Rs.
Land acquisition	350
Government House	700
Residence for Officials	371
Secretariat and Council Chamber	760
Furniture: Government House	100
Furniture: Secretariat/Council Chamber	100
Two Houses for Ministers	70
Quarters for Legislative Members	100
Quarters for 40 ministerial officers	170
Water supply for the capital site	126
Electric Installation	40
General Layout: drainage, roads, fillings, etc.	300
	3187

Source: *Orissa Administration Committee Report* (1933).
NB: All figures are given in thousands.

During the time the capitol complex was under construction, the temporary headquarters of the new province was to be at Puri, where the existing Government House could serve as the interim residence for the governor, albeit after remodeling the residence at an estimated cost of Rs. 158,000 to make it suitable and comfortable for the imperial dignity of His Majesty's representative in India. The remodeling of the Government House was to include replacement of the electrical system and the plumbing, structural additions and alterations to provide more living space, new furniture, and creation of a garden as being necessary in order to make the place "even tolerable for a period of some three years" during which the capital was to be completed and so the house could serve as a residence for a period of some three months every year thereafter. Similarly, the adjoining Circuit House was to receive electrical improvements and an updated plumbing system. That the bulk of the Oriyas lived in abject poverty without even the basic amenities was not considered important enough while calculating the expenses necessary for imperial comfort. Provision for a billiard room, a card room, three dressing rooms, a boudoir, and extra bedrooms were considered just as necessary for the governor as the improved provisions for electricity and drinking water. Accordingly, the remodeling cost for Government House at Puri was distributed as following:

Government House:	Rs.
Additional accommodation	35,000
Additional verandah	16,000
Electrical fittings	7,000
New generators	38,000
Water supply	4,000
Furniture	25,000
Garden	25,000
Circuit House:	
Electrical fittings	4,000
Water supply	4,000
	158,000

Source: *Orissa Administration Committee Report* (1933).

What could not be denied for imperial comfort was achieved by cutting back the area of public services. The O'Donnell Commission had recommended against setting up a high court, a university, and a provincial penitentiary in Orissa to minimize cost generally associated with the creation of a separate province. New Orissa was to share these institutions with either Bihar or another neighboring state for a specified fee. O'Donnell had also opposed Orissa's own cadre of provincial civil service in the interest of economy.

Calcutta and Madras proved unwilling to share services in the matter of the high court. The Madras government outrightly rejected the idea of affiliation with any part of new Orissa, and the Calcutta government would only consider the proposal if Orissa was willing to pay the salaries of two judges of the high court and the salary of a registrar of the grade of district and sessions judges. In addition, Calcutta would not approve judges of the Calcutta High Court's coming to Orissa on circuit. The Patna High Court was not opposed to affiliation since under the existing circuit system two judges of the court already came on circuit to Cuttack three or four times a year. However, the existing arrangement was considered unsatisfactory, and the Orissa Administration Committee felt that constitutionally provincial autonomy was impossible without a separate and independent high court.

The suggestion that Orissa be assigned a chief court with one or two judicial commissioners was rejected by the committee on the grounds that such a court would not substitute for a high court, nor would the province have judicial autonomy because, in the event of a difference of opinion between judicial commissioners, "either the opinion of the senior judicial Commissioner must prevail or the right of appeal must be waived or the matter must be referred to the High Court of another province." So the idea of affiliation with a High Court of another province with three full judges was rejected because such an arrangement would not only be expensive but also impracticable.[28]

Although recognizing that any judicial system for Orissa must be consistent with the special circumstances of the new province—circumstances that included limited financial resources, small and simple nature of litigation resulting from poverty and racial homogeneity of the region, and the tractable and patriotic character of the Oriyas[29]—the Orissa Administration Committee unanimously voted for the creation of a separate high court as soon as Orissa was inaugurated as the newest province of British India.[30]

The Orissa High Court was to consist of a chief justice and three puisne judges. To save administrative costs, the committee proposed to abolish district and sessions judges in Orissa; and judges of the high court were to do the work of district and sessions judges, while a bench of two or more judges would exercise the appellate jurisdiction of a high court. "This is," the committee reasoned, "a reversion to the English model as exemplified in the judicial administration of the Presidency towns in India."[31] The whole scheme was to have an annual budget of Rs. 261,129 and a suitable residence for the chief justice was to be constructed at an estimated cost of Rs. 50,000.[32]

In the matter of the university, the prevailing popular sentiment was "that in the last resort [the Oriyas] would prefer a separate University to a separate province." The committee was quick to grasp that the Oriyas would be "gravely disappointed" were they to win provincial autonomy and racial unity but be "denied a University for their own."[33] There already existed an estimate for Rs. 250,000 in capital costs and Rs. 70,000 in recurring annual expenditures prepared by the office of the director of public instruction, Bihar and Orissa, for a separate university with basic facilities. But the committee came up with a more ambitious scheme of Rs. 2,000,000 for covering the construction costs and providing interest for the recurring charges, arguing that "it should not be impossible to raise an endowment fund of something like that sum [within] a few years, especially if the Ruling Chiefs continue to show the interest they have displayed in the past in higher education for the Oriyas as a whole."[34] Until a separate university could be constructed, the committee recommended that the Ganjam district should continue to be affiliated with Andhra University and the rest of Orissa with Patna University—but not without expressing its grave objections to dual affiliation on a permanent basis. As for the medical, engineering, and veterinary colleges, the committee recommended the status quo, that is, their continued affiliation with Bihar. Orissa was also urged to enter into an agreement with the Bihar government for the training of candidates for the police and excise departments, and to leave its railway police under the Bihar government, as Bengal did, for a proportionate fee.

Anticipating objections from the Bihar government concerning the accepting of prisoners from Orissa owing to want of accommodation, the committee provided for a separate penitentiary for Orissa at a cost of Rs. 300,000 in capital expenditures and annual recurring charges of Rs. 19,000. The government of India was expected to build the penitentiary, while the Orissa government was expected to find sources for meeting the recurring charges. Orissa was expected to continue sharing services with several institutions in Bihar, prominent among them being Reformatory School at Hazaribagh, Indian Mental Hospital, Ranchi Mental Hospital for Europeans, Bacteriological Laboratory, Pasteur Institute, and Gulzarbagh Survey Office and Traverse Establishment. An audit of accounts, however, was to be entrusted to the accountant general of Bengal since that office was larger and nearer to Cuttack than the accountant general of Bihar and Orissa at Ranchi.[35] It was hoped that such an arrangement would require no temporary or permanent residences and that the Circuit House and a few rooms in the Secretariat could provide the space needed during the budget preparation period.

Orissa was also to be affected by the territorial changes recommended in the Orissa Administration Committee report. The first of these proposed territorial changes was the assimilation of the Khondmals tracts with the Ganjam district on the basis of racial similarity between the Khonds of Madras and Ganjam, and administered by the collector and agent of the governor in Ganjam.[36] The other proposed change was to make Angul a subdivision of the Cuttack district, although the people of Angul wanted to keep Angul separate because of the concessions in the assessment of land revenue they received on the basis of their economically depressed status. But maintaining that an area of 881 square miles with a population of 148,459 was economically not viable as an administrative unit, and considering that Angul was only sixty miles from Cuttack, the Orissa Administration Committee reasoned that in the long run the people of Angul would be much happier being a part of Cuttack rather than a subdivision of Sambalpur. "There is really no reason to fear," the committee reassured the people of Angul, "that with the abolition of the district [as an independent identity], the Government will not display the same solicitude for the uplift of the depressed classes as at present."[37]

In addition, the Cuttack district was also to retain the town of Banki, twenty-seven miles from Cuttack, although there had been a suggestion for transferring it to Puri in order to lighten the responsibility of the district officer of Cuttack. However, the Orissa Administration Committee recommended that Khariar, with an area of 1,489 square miles and a population of 160,892 and an annual revenue of Rs. 80,000, be converted into a new subdivision of the Sambalpur district. Such an arrangement would require new buildings to accommodate the subdivisional officer and his staff, the capital cost for which was estimated at Rs. 57,000.[38]

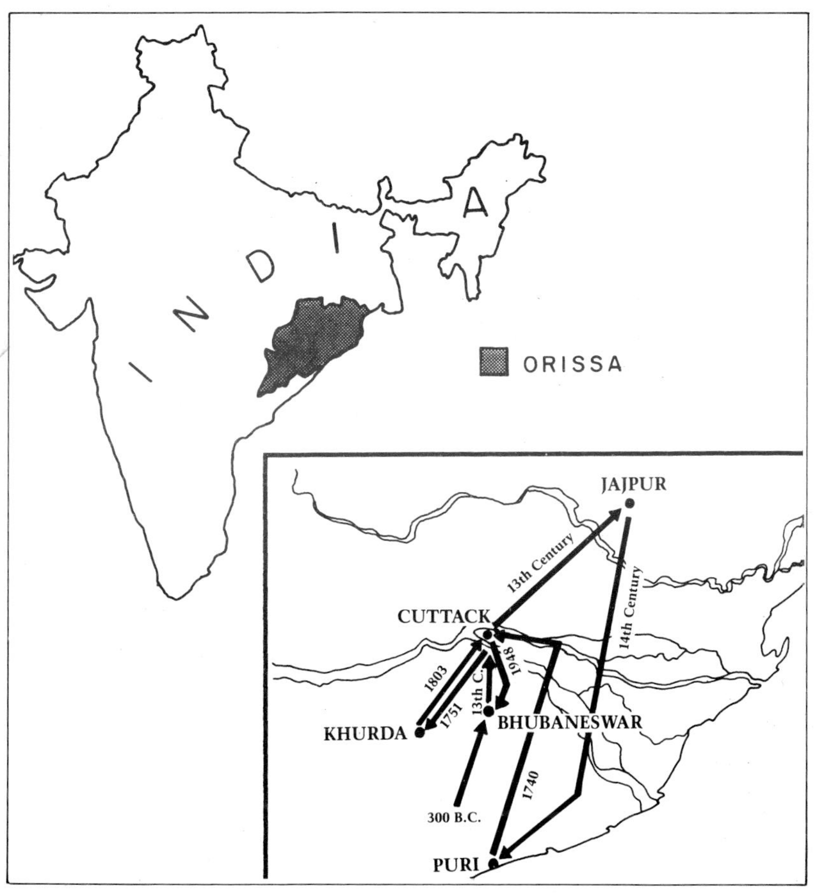

1. *Map of India showing Orissa.*

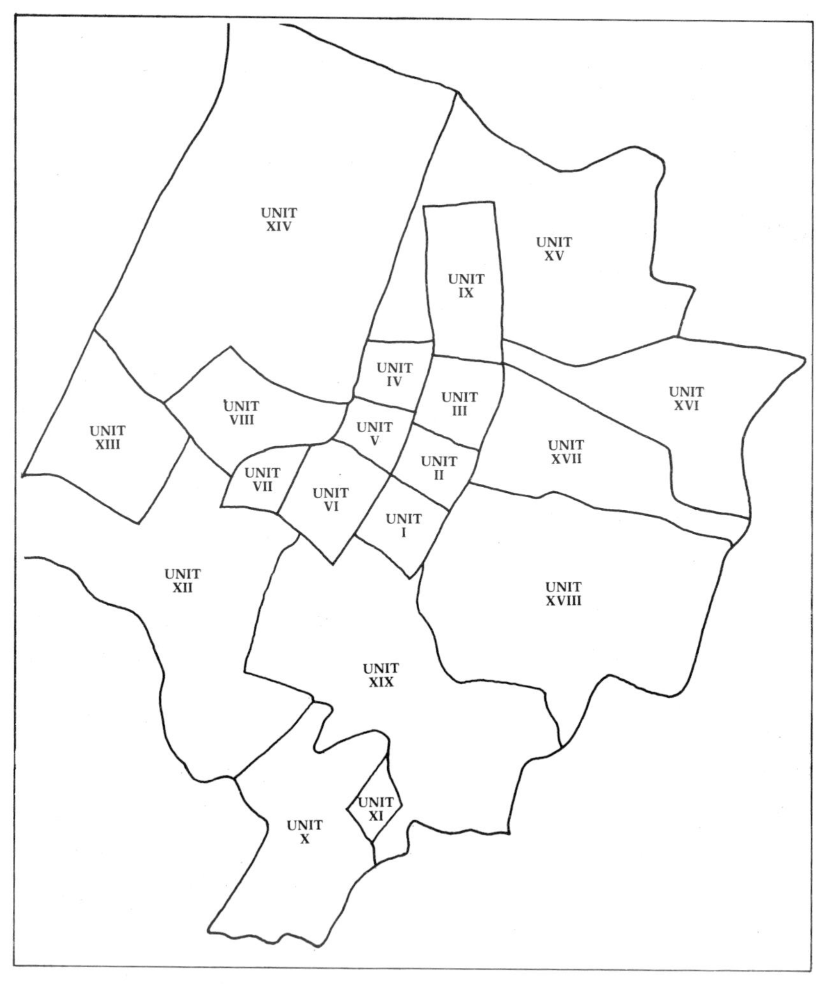

2. Bhubaneswar City and its functional areas.

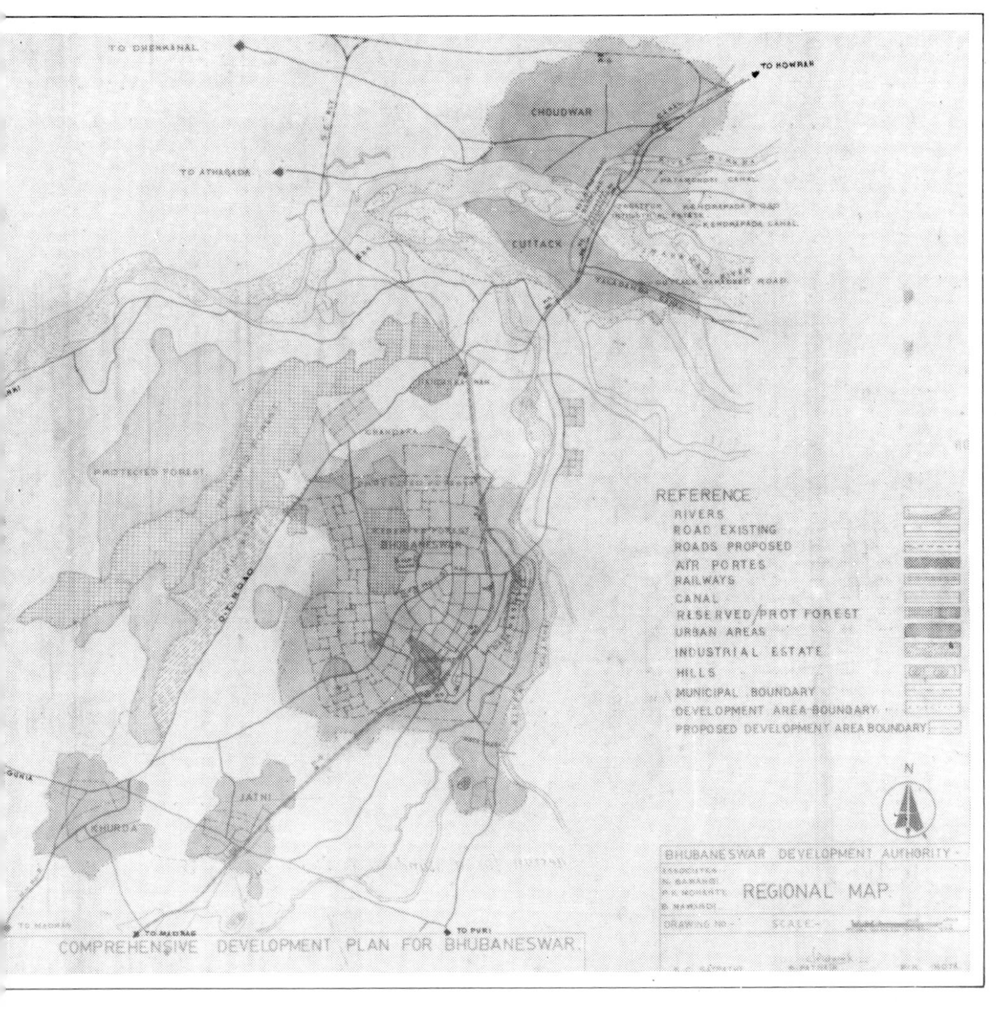

3. Regional map of Bhubaneswar.

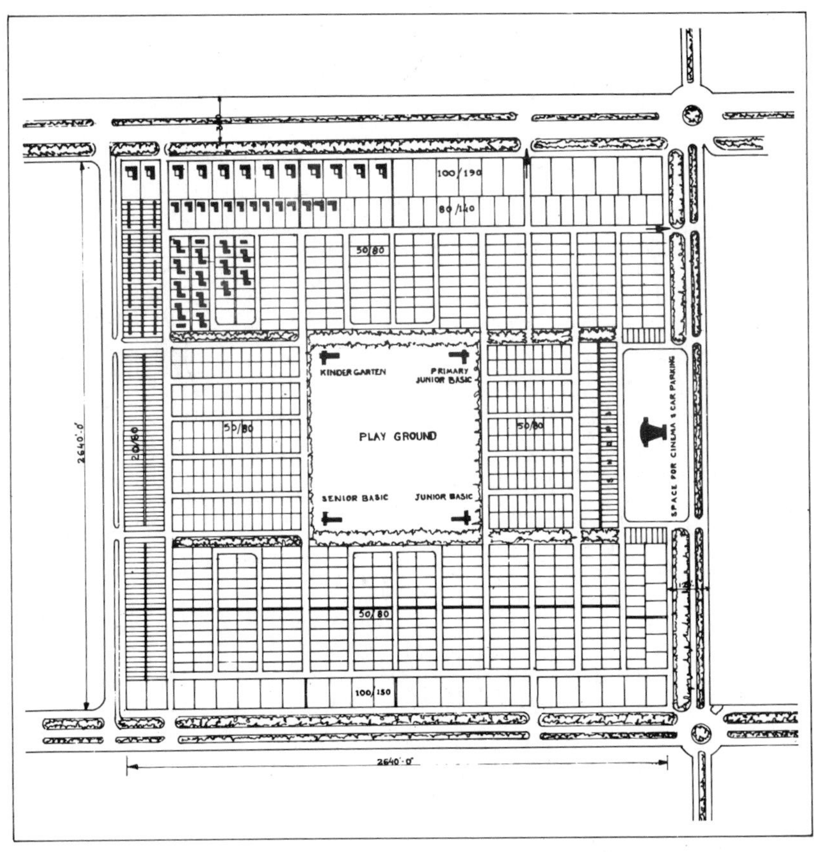

4. Otto Koenigsberger's design for a standard neighborhood unit.

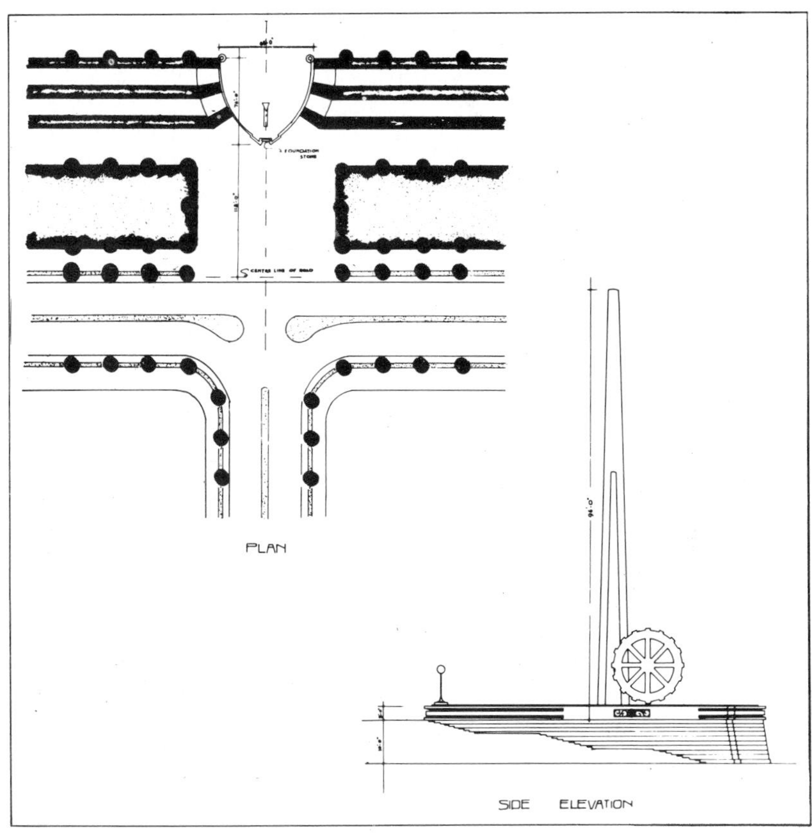

5. Otto Koenigsberger's plan for the Gandhi Memorial which was to be placed in the Assembly complex. The Orissa government vetoed the plan, and instead built statues of local leaders Gopabandhu Das, Madhusudan Das, and national leader Gandhi.

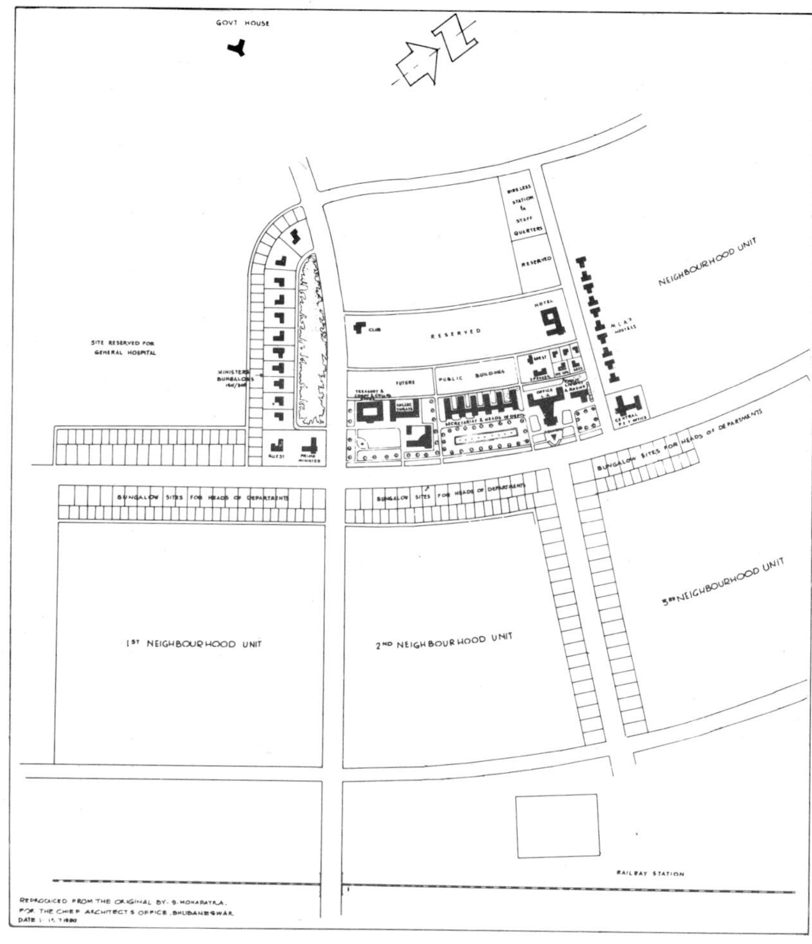

6. Design for the Administrative Center by Otto Koenigsberger.

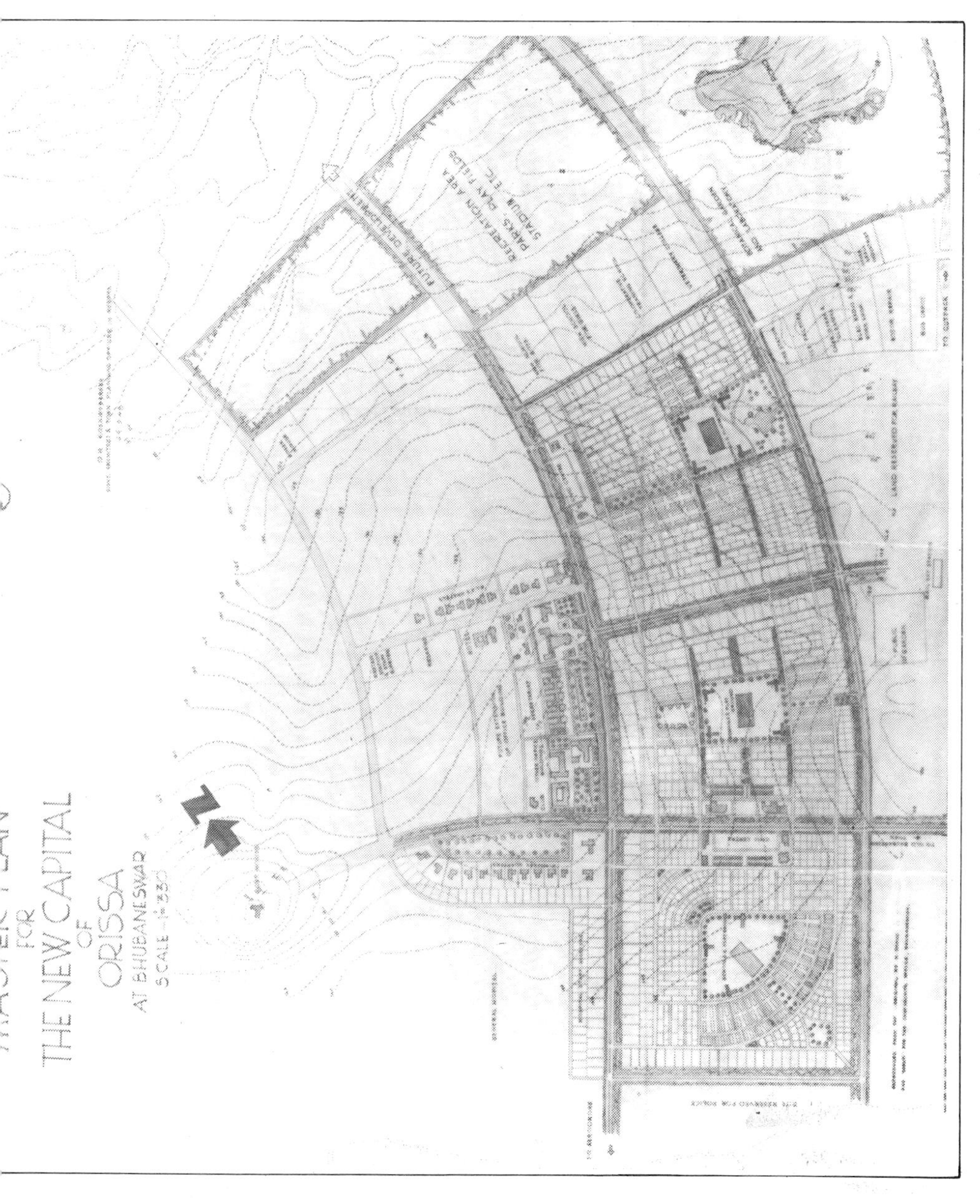

7. Otto Koenigsberger's master plan for Bhubaneswar.

1. Lingaraja temple, old Bhubaneswar. This and all other photographs by the author, unless noted otherwise.

2. *Santi Stupa (Buddhist) on top of Dhauli Hills. It was built with Japanese financial assistance.*

3. Top: *A statue of national leader Gandhi* and bottom: *local leaders Gopabandhu Das and Madhusudan Das on the Assembly grounds.*

4. *The capital city is home to several religious shrines. This is the Church of Christ in Unit 4.*

5. *Slums such as this have sprung up in different parts of new Bhubaneswar.*

6. Affluent two-story private residence in Unit 7. Architect: R. K. Behera.

7. Middle Income Group flats.

8. Social Sciences Building, Utkal University.

9. Raj Bhavan (Governor's House) has a rectangular plan and raised floor. The two-story house is entered through a colonnaded portico, which functions as a porte cochere.

10. The Foundation Stone with Nehru's inscription, near the Secretariat, in Unit 5.

11. The Secretariat in Unit 5. Architect: J. L. Vaz. The building stretches 880 feet in length, and the entrance is approached by a lofty marble-paved palm court containing the reception office and waiting hall.

12. The Assembly in Unit 5. Architect: J. L. Vaz.

13. Rabindra Mandap in Unit 4. Architect: J. L. Vaz. Notice the stupa-inspired roof.

14. *Street view of the Jan Path (People's Road).*

15. *Raj Path (Royal Road) leading to the Raj Bhavan (Governor's House).*

16. City Center (main) Market. This market covers parts of Units 1 and 2. Architect: J. L. Vaz. Notice the low-rise buildings embellished with temple-inspired turrets.

17. Santi Stupa (Buddhist) and Shiva temple coexisting on top of Dhauli Hills.

18. Ancient caves in Khandagiri Hills (Elephant Caves).

19. Otto H. Koenigsberger, the first planner of Bhubaneswar (Capital City). Photograph courtesy of Otto H. Koenigsberger.

Noting that a self-contained cadre of civil servants was impossible for Orissa because of financial reasons, and that service in Orissa was "unpopular with officers of all ranks and races" because of the climate, the committee endorsed the O'Donnell Commission's recommendation of a joint cadre with Bihar. There was one slight modification, however. Whereas the O'Donnell Commission had proposed twenty-five posts for the Indian Civil Service (ICS) and fifteen for the Indian Police Service (IPS), the Orissa Administration Committee proposed to reduce the ICS posts and slightly increase the IPS posts. The length of tenure in Orissa for each officer was to be such that it would allow him to become familiar with the province but not so long as to minimize his suitability for further service in Bihar. Accordingly, a period of four years was recommended for deputation. For the Ganjam district, however, the Committee felt that "it will be necessary for some years to borrow two . . . ICS [officers] with experience of the District and of Madras land tenures." A police officer with local experience was also considered an asset, as was an officer of the Indian Forest Service from the Madras cadre.[39]

The comprehensive report provided by the Orissa Administration Committee cost the government of India Rs. 16,000. The various recommendations relating to the construction of capital city and other administrative changes made by the committee added up to a sum of Rs. 3,875,000 distributed as following:

	Rs.
Cuttack	3,187,000
Puri	158,000
Gopalpur	50,000
Mahendragiri	75,000
Khariar (subdivisional buildings)	57,000
Berhampur (Central Jail)	300,000
Cuttack-Puri telephone line	48,000
	3,875,000

Source: *Orissa Administration Committee Report* (1933).

That the Orissa Administration Committee had recommended Cuttack for the capital city even before the new province of Orissa was officially inaugurated on April 1, 1936, did not prevent a heated debate from developing over the question of the capital site. Soon after the inauguration of the new province, the question of where to locate the capital turned up in the Orissa Legislative Assembly and was not to be settled until a decade later. At the heart of the controversy was the stark fact that all recommendations for the capital city had been made by the government-appointed committees, and the process did not involve the participation of either the people or their representatives. Failure to involve the people in the capital site selection process resulted in the failure to build a popular consensus in favor of Cuttack and kept all construction work at a standstill. With the inauguration of the assembly, however, the representatives of the people of Orissa felt that it was "for them to select a proper and suitable site for their capital." Reminding his colleagues in the assembly that in making such a decision they had to keep in view "the past . . . the present [and] the possibilities of the future," Assemblyman Biswanath Das emphasized that in the selection of the capital "the Government . . . will [have to] follow the directions that the Assembly gives on this question."[40]

If there were members in the Orissa Assembly who were willing to speak strongly and eloquently in support of Cuttack, there were also members in the assembly who strongly supported the selection of Puri. The old Cuttack-Puri rivalry resurfaced, forcing the government to delay the construction work. Assemblyman Bichitrananda Das articulated the popular sentiment when he declared "that in this vital matter . . . we could not be unanimous."[41]

Considering that throughout the history of India the capital cities have occupied a position of primacy among all cities—the wealth and well-being of a kingdom being measured by the scale and grandeur of its capital city—each leader viewed the selection of the capital as an opportunity to bolster his own position by placing the capital in his constituency. Moreover, construction of the new capital was expected to generate economic activity, and each leader wanted the benefits to flow to his constituents. In a poor province like Orissa the rivalry for the capital site was bound to become intense, although relatively affluent Punjab was also to go through the same conflict in the selection of a capital site before agreeing on Chandigarh.

Preventing unanimity among the Oriyas over the capital site were not only sentimental reasons but also real rupees involved in the construction cost. The government's own indecision in implementing the Orissa Administration Committee's recommendation allowed for the capital site controversy to intensify. Cuttack had been recommended by the committee in view of the requirements of a province which was two-thirds of the extent of the province actually formed in 1936; and had the government implemented the decision, the capital site issue would have become a settled fact and the Oriyas would have been forced to reconcile themselves to the situation. As it were, Governor John Hubback sought relief from the popular agitation over the capital site by referring the issue to the Orissa Advisory Council, which decision was immediately challenged by several prominent Oriyas on constitutional grounds. Raja Bahadur of Khallikote eloquently explained the problem in the Orissa Assembly:

> The first fly in the ointment . . . came from [the] disparity in the size of the Province . . . as was in the imagination of the Orissa Administration Committee when they recommended Cuttack [in 1933] and the Province as was actually announced to be formed about the end of 1934 by the Joint Parliamentary Committee.
>
> This addition in the area altered the geographic centre of the Province. People living in the Malkangiri area of Jeypore right on the banks of the Godavari would naturally desire a shifting of the capital as far south of Cuttack as possible. The estimates prepared by the Orissa Administration Committee for the Secretariat and other buildings necessary could not hold good for a Province with a more extensive area. . . . [The] Orissa Budget eventually provided for a staff of 40 per cent of the size of Bihar and Orissa staff, while before the Orissa Administration Committee sat it had been estimated that the size would be only 10 or 15 per cent of the size of Bihar and Orissa. . . . what was considered adequate by the Orissa Administration Committee could not be actually adequate for the Province.[42]

Perhaps it was in recognition of this disparity that Governor Hubback had referred the whole question of capital to the Orissa Advisory Council. Meanwhile, the government of India had forwarded Rs. 2,400,000 to Orissa out of a total grant of Rs. 4,250,000 for the construction of the capital, with the instructions that the money be spent by the Central Public Works Department. The Central Public Works Department instituted its own team of experts headed by Superintending Engineer F. T. Jones and assisted by Consulting Government Architect Russell to select the capital site. The Jones Committee in its report in 1936 concluded that the capital should be placed at Rangailunda, near Berhampur. While acknowledging the historical significance of Cuttack, the Jones Committee made the most serious indictment of Cuttack by declaring it to be "isolated and cramped with rigorous natural barriers, which allow no room for present needs or future expansion." Further, Jones and his men added that the prospect of Cuttack as a capital city "depended on the possibility of bridging the rivers [Mahanadi and Katjori], a very expensive undertaking."[43]

The fact that the recommendations of the Orissa Administration Committee and the Jones Committee were at variance with each other only contributed to the capital city controversy. What made the situation even more grievous was that the Orissa government had spent nearly Rs. 1,200,000 of the grant on buildings at Koraput and Nawapara—buildings which were not part of the actual capital outlay—thereby making the financing of the new capital difficult.

So when the Orissa government appointed Financial Commissioner Dain to prepare a feasibility report on the construction of the capital, the government was immediately accused of deliberate procrastination. The task of the Dain Committee was limited to the four government proposed sites: Cuttack, Barang, Chaudwar, and Puri. Failure to include Rangailunda and Khurda in the feasibility study resulted in creating suspicions against the government. The Dain report supported Puri for the capital city, arguing that construction costs at Cuttack would be much higher. However, the report concluded that these "recommendations are made within the restricted terms of the choices before us" and that "a site better than any of these could be found."[44] Such a conclusion only put the provincial government in a compromising position.

Those supporting Rangailunda for the capital city argued that it was located in the geographic center of the new province, that it had a salubrious climate and comfortable sea breeze, that it had plenty of land available for future expansion in any desired direction, that it had an excellent drinking water supply and drainage, and that it could be well connected by land, water, and air, since nearby Gopalpur was soon expected to develop "into a port and a naval base."[45] Moreover, cheap labor and building materials were available near the site.

Considering the economic and political benefits which accrue from a capital city, each political leader of the new province looked at the question of the capital site from the vantage point of his constituency. There is a distinct political advantage to be gained from a capital city: "It is there that the laws . . . are conceived and legislated; it is there that chief executive of the state is located; and it is to capital cities that people . . .

look for inspiration, for economic development, and for political favors." Also, "any political, cultural, or social movement seeking national attention," such as the Oriya movement, "directs its efforts to the capital city."[46] As one Oriya leader pointedly said: "If members from Ganjam want Rangailunda, members from Cuttack want Cuttack, Balasore people want Chandipur, and as a member from Jajpur I want Jajpur to be capital, there will be no end to these wranglings, and we can never come to a decision."[47]

Troubling the decision makers in selecting the capital site was also the presence of minorities of Muslims and Christians in the predominantly Hindu state. For that reason Puri was considered unsuitable because "Muhammadan and Christian officers will be put to inconvenience if they are to live in rented houses [in the Hindu city]."[48] The sentiment was powerfully articulated by Maulavi Adbus Sobhan Khan on behalf of the Muslims, when he declared in the Orissa Assembly that "So far as politics is concerned, so far as religion is concerned, so far as expenses are concerned, except a few lakhs this side or that, Cuttack has the best chance from the Muslim point of view. Representing my community, my cause, I should say that Puri is not the fit place for the capital and religion must be separated from politics."[49]

Some secular-minded Hindu leaders were equally opposed to having the capital at a religious site. Arguing that "nowhere in India or elsewhere has the capital of a province been located at a religious centre," they pointed to the one exception that was made in the case of Allahabad in Uttar Pradesh, which the British ultimately were forced to replace with Lucknow.[50] When it was pointed out that the Dain report was written by non-Hindus supporting Puri, that Calcutta, the capital of Bengal, was a place of pilgrimage because of the presence of the Kali temple, that Calcutta drew more pilgrims than Puri,[51] and that Rome was an example of a capital city,[52] the opponents of Puri pointed to the 1921 census which declared the entire district of Puri as having "the highest proportion of insane persons in the Province. Puri district is much afflicted with leprosy. Dr. Santhru, the leprosy expert, described Puri as 'one of the most leprous districts in the Province of Bihar and Orissa.'"[53]

After a long acrimonious debate that nearly sent the whole question of the capital city back for another round of expert reports, the Orissa Assembly late into the night on September 24, 1937, approved Babu Girija Bhusan Das' motion of placing the capital at Cuttack-Chaudwar, a Cuttack suburb on the north bank of the Mahanadi. However, that decision was never implemented as much for the lack of political commitment as for the lack of sufficient funds. "We have to realize," lamented Biswanath Das in the assembly, "that a country with floods on the one side, and famine staring on the other, with our helplessness, with the minimum possible capacity for taxation and hence the minimum amount of expenditure on record can hardly expect to invest more money than what is available to-day for a capital construction."[54]

What was available to the new province for the entire capital project was a total amount of Rs. 4,250,000, out of which some money had already been spent, leaving the balance which was far below the projected cost. Meanwhile, the outbreak of World War II provided a convenient reason for postponing the entire project. Not until Orissa's first elected postwar ministry was formed under the leadership of Harekrushna Mahtab did the capital city question once again resurface in the assembly.

The congested character of Cuttack was only one reason against converting that city into a capital. Cuttack, despite its history as the political headquarters of Orissa, provided no more than a small-town atmosphere. A city with a collection of small to medium size businesses located along narrow meandering streets, a city made up of neighborhoods segregated along caste and class lines, and a city which never developed into a pilgrimage site despite its many temples, Cuttack was reminiscent more of the rural Orissa than of the urban-secular center to which the new province aspired. "In whichever place we may construct our capital," Biswanath Das correctly assessed the situation in the assembly, "municipalities are not in a position to come to our aid as we find in the major provinces like Bombay and Madras. If Cuttack is poor, Puri is poorer and so on."[55]

Meanwhile, the postwar Reconstruction Department as early as January 1945 had suggested that "if it were contemplated to construct the new [provincial] headquarters buildings in Cuttack town then as a result of the postwar reconstruction plans it would now be necessary to include in Cuttack considerably more than double the original amount of accommodation that was projected for the new capital buildings." Estimating the floor space that would be needed for the buildings, residences, and offices, the Reconstruction Department concluded that "whatever chances there might have been of squeezing the [government] headquarters machinery in the existing town of Cuttack before the plan of reconstruction [arose] it has now become a physical impossibility unless the place is to be completely built over even apart from other considerations such as the desirability of business and industrial expansion in Cuttack itself."[56]

Reasoning that "residences and offices for the postwar reconstruction schemes will have to be constructed as soon [as] the war situation permits the release of materials," the report strongly urged that "a decision has . . . to be taken where these buildings are to be constructed which in turn renders a decision as to the location of the [provincial] headquarters buildings a matter which cannot be postponed very much longer and the question arises whether these buildings should be located at Bhubaneswar or Chowdwar [Cuttack] or some other place." Reprovingly, the Reconstruction Department added: "it is not the desire of [the] Reconstruction [Department] to embarrass [the provincial government] by requesting an early order on a point which has already been the cause of sufficient acrimony, but it is clear that construction planning will suffer . . . if a decision is not made available in the fairly near future."[57]

Apparently, Bhubaneswar along with Bowdar were first considered by the Reconstruction Department for placing some government buildings since Cuttack was proving to be too crowded to accommodate all the new buildings. Bhubaneswar was attractive as a capital city not only because it was a pilgrimage center and a symbol of Orissa's past pride, but also because it was close to Cuttack and contained large tracts of open spaces. The Reconstruction Department was willing to build semipermanent buildings in Cuttack until a permanent decision on the capital site was reached by the Orissa government, but it warned Governor Howthorne Lewis' caretaker government that such a decision would not result in a systematic planning of the capital.[58]

The Maharstrian-Brahman B. K. Gokhale, who was serving as a special advisor to Governor Howthorne Lewis, quickly capitalized on the Reconstruction Department's idea of possibly placing some government buildings in Bhubaneswar. He saw Cuttack remaining the principal commercial center, Chowdwar, a Cuttack suburb on the north bank of the Mahanadi, developing into an industrial complex, and Bhubaneswar, about twenty miles south of Cuttack, becoming the capital city as well as the chief cultural-educational center of the new province.

This was the first time—and so far possibly the last—that the capital city project was viewed in a larger regional context, with proper emphasis on economic, cultural, and educational considerations. Not everyone shared Gokhale's urban vision, however. Residents of Cuttack felt that they would lose substantially if the capital were moved to Bhubaneswar.

Moreover, the Muslims and Christians in the province viewed Bhubaneswar with the same suspicion with which they had earlier viewed Puri. The old capital city controversy would have once again flared up had the Public Works Department on April 14, 1945, not reported that "expansion of Cuttack . . . does not [appear] very promising . . . and it appears that going to Bhubaneswar for further expansion may be the best solution." The report added:

> [In Bhubaneswar] there is plenty of land available right along the railway lines on both sides of it from Bhubaneswar right up to Mancheswar. If the buildings extend in this area this will not really mean creating 2 separate towns but really one continuous Metropolies [*sic*] from Charbatia to Bhubaneswar with the Military Headquarters in the vicinity of Charbatia and the University at the other end of Bhubaneswar. This [has] already been done without any serious difficulty in Bihar where the town extends from about 2 miles of the East of the Patna city to Dinapur which is well over 15 miles.
>
> The only difficulty anticipated at Bhubaneswar is likely to be . . . water supplies which may not be so easy as compared to supplies at Cuttack. But a superficial examination of Bhubaneswar and the vicinity so far indicates that this should not be an impracticably serious obstacle. Borings by the [Agriculture] Dept. have been ordered by the [General Administration] and it is understood that [the] Development Dept. are taking action.
>
> P.W.D. do not consider that in these days of high rates there would be any justification for spending money on semi-permanent buildings. . . . In any case, considering the scrapping of the temporary buildings, construction of permanent buildings straightway [*sic*] would be substantial savings. A decision on siting of the Capital buildings should, it is considered, be now taken without which detailed planning is difficult.[59]

The report by the Public Works Department was just the kind of supporting document that Gokhale needed to sell his urban vision to the idiosyncratic Oriya leadership, many among whom were serving prison terms for having participated in the Gandhian *satyagraha*. Congressman Harekrushna Mahtab was among those still in prison when Gokhale met him with his idea of converting Bhubaneswar into the capital of Orissa. Belonging to the entrepreneurial Khatri family from Punjab, which had migrated to Orissa a few generations earlier possibly in search of better economic opportunities, Mahtab had become closely associated through the nationalist movement with the Cambridge-educated Jawaharlal Nehru and through the community development program with the American Quaker missionary Horace Alexander, who had been Mahtab's house guest in 1927 when he first visited Orissa in connection with flood relief work.[60] Coming under the influence of the two men, Mahtab combined in himself as much passion for industrialization as for improving village life through simple and cheap inventions recommended under the community development program.

Sensitive to Mahtab's dual instincts and aware of Mahtab's rapidly growing political influence which was soon to place him (Mahtab) in the leadership role in Orissa's first elected postwar ministry, Gokhale found no reason to waste time in contacting Mahtab while he (Mahtab) was still serving his sentence in Poona (modern Pune) prison. Mahtab, eager to see Orissa prosper under his own leadership, was quick in grasping the merits of Bhubaneswar as a site superior to crowded and river-bound Cuttack.

Becoming premier (after independence in 1947 the designation was changed to chief minister, and provinces were renamed states) of Orissa in 1946, Mahtab however did not find full support for Bhubaneswar in the Orissa Assembly. Fortunately for Mahtab, on September 2, 1946, Congress under Jawaharlal Nehru took over the interim government on Viceroy Archibald Wavell's (1943–47) invitation, changing the political picture in India. Uncertain about the future and not knowing what position the new government might take toward the question of the capital city, the Orissa governor C. M. Trivedi wrote Mahtab: "The question of the location of the capital of the province is becoming an urgent one. I believe our intention is to obtain the approval of the Assembly to the choice of Greater Cuttack or Bhubaneswar as the capital of Orissa." He speculatively added, "As for the name, might I suggest the name 'New Cuttack' following the analogy of New Delhi? This is merely a suggestion . . . what happens to the name Bhubaneswar? I suppose we must preserve the separate name of Bhubaneswar."[61]

By the end of September 1946, Mahtab had won the assembly's approval in favor of Bhubaneswar by persuading his colleagues that, after the amalgamation of twenty-six princely states with Orissa and in order to push for various developmental projects, the large Orissa administration could not be accommodated comfortably in Cuttack. As a concession, Cuttack was to retain the High Court and Utkal University, thus assuring Cuttack's primacy as the cultural center of Orissa after the construction of the capital at Bhubaneswar. Cuttack was to remain the premier city of Orissa, and Bhubaneswar was to be no more than an administrative colony, patterned roughly after New Delhi. As one Oriya leader later eloquently remarked: "Bhubaneswar will be a sort of Washington of Orissa, but Cuttack will always remain its New York."[62] However, that expectation was to prove unrealistic for the financially strapped new province, and what Bhubaneswar eventually developed into contained neither some of the better features of New Delhi nor of Washington.

Within a matter of weeks of making the decision to place the capital at Bhubaneswar, the Orissa government put the government of India on notice that the preliminary investigation of the area revealed that the site would require "considerably more work than was previously contemplated."[63] The new site was almost uninhabited and situated between Mancheswar and Bhubaneswar about eighteen to twenty miles south of Cuttack. Having mainly laterite soil and mostly covered with tangled masses of tropical vegetation, the Bhubaneswar site was undulating to a degree and varied in level from 100 to 125 feet above mean sea level, the higher end being towards the west. The proposed construction area was expected to encompass approximately twelve square miles, of which ten square miles lay in the Puri district and two square miles to the north of the area in the Cuttack district. Considering that only 1.5 square miles (12.50 per cent) of the total area was tenanted, it was estimated that compensation to tenants for acquired land will not exceed a total sum of Rs. 560.000. To take full advantage of low land acquisition cost, Orissa government proposed to acquire the entire area of twelve square miles in "the first instance," although for the original layout not more than nine square miles was to be built over, reserving the remaining area of three square miles for a green belt round the city. At completion, the new capital city was to have a population of 12,000, which was expected to rise to an estimated 15,000 people in about five years, made up mostly of bureaucrats but also with a sprinkling of police and military personnel, school, bank, and postal employees, small businessmen, and service people.[64]

The Military Engineering Service was to clear the forested area and level the site for a sum of Rs. 700,000. Another Rs. 50,000 were earmarked by the Orissa government for developing survey maps of the area, while Rs. 2,800,000 were expected to be spent on roads, drainage, and trees. For a total population of 15,000, the Public Works Department estimated 45 miles of main roads and an equal length of subsidiary or grid roads. The main road was to have a width of 45 feet and a metaled carriageway of 30 feet with a tar macadamized surface, built at an estimated cost of Rs. 45,000 per mile; and the grid road was to have a width of 24 feet with a 12-foot metaled surface, built at an estimated cost of Rs. 18,000 per mile.[65]

Although experiencing financial difficulties, and planning a capital city on the eve of India's imminent independence, the provincial government was unable to rid itself of the imperial vision in detailing the various government buildings. The main building of the Government House (governor's residence) was to be an imposing double storied structure, covering an area of approximately 25,000 square feet and costing about Rs. 24 per square foot or a total of Rs. 600,000. Another Rs. 650,000 were to be expended on plumbing and electricity fittings, staff and servant quarters, landscaping and garden, and furniture—bringing the total cost for the Government House to Rs. 1,250,000.[66]

The Secretariat and the various departmental buildings were also to be constructed to fit with the imperial vision[67] and were to have such comforting features as air conditioning, large offices for gazetted officers (a gazetted officer was assigned 250 square feet in office space whereas a clerk received only 75 square feet for his office space), private garages, landscaped and manicured lawns, altogether costing a total sum of Rs. 2,400,000.

In the tradition of imperial architecture that became so pervasive after the Great Rebellion of 1857 but which never fit in with the realities of India, the Legislative Assembly was to be "a very high building" of two stories, covering an area of 6,000 square feet. Other features of the building included verandahs, staircases, balconies, lawns and gardens, air conditioning, private garages, and so on, pushing the total cost of the building and residences for legislative members to Rs. 560,000. Further, the government proposed to provide residential accommodation for all government employees "on a 100 per cent basis" at Bhubaneswar, the cost of which was estimated at Rs. 9,600,000. An additional amount of Rs. 1,530,000 was allocated for such other institutions and buildings as hospitals, schools (separate high schools for boys and girls and mixed primary schools), police station, Circuit House, and so on.[68]

The Orissa government itself was to set up and operate the power house instead of leaving the transmission of electrical power to a licensee. The Daya River waters were to be used for generating power, just as the river was to provide drinking water for the city. It was hoped that the sandy bed of the river during the dry season could be drilled with short-length tube wells to provide drinking water. According to calculations, 40 gallons of water was expected to be consumed per head per day. Bhubaneswar was to have two markets for daily shopping needs of the residents. In sum, the capital city was to be built at a total cost of Rs. 28,510,000 distributed as following:

	Estimated costs in lakhs of rupees
Land acquisition	5.6
Jungle clearing and leveling	7.0
Contour survey of site	0.5
Roads	28.0
Government House	12.5
Secretariat and Departments	24.0
Assembly and M.L.A. Quarters	5.6
Residences and Quarters	96.0
Institutions and local offices	15.3
Electrification	18.4
Water supply	20.0
Sanitation/Drainage	21.0
Markets/shops	1.2
Tools/plant (est. expenses)	30.0
	285.1

Source: Public Works Department Estimate, Bhubaneswar, Dec. 20, 1946. NB: 1 lakh = 100,000.

The projected cost of Rs. 28,510,000 for constructing the capital at Bhubaneswar was substantially more than Rs. 3,875,000 estimated earlier by the Orissa Administration Committee in 1933. The Orissa government already had in hand Rs. 3,600,000 from an earlier government of India grant, leaving a deficit of about Rs. 25,000,000. Arguing that construction of the new capital was "a matter of great urgency," indicating the problem of scattered provincial government offices because of the scarcity of both public and private space in Cuttack, and fearing a major administrative crisis unless additional floor space did not become quickly available for the rapidly expanding bureaucracy, the Orissa government appealed to the government of India for financial assistance. Expecting to raise Rs. 5,000,000 locally, the Orissa government requested the government of India "to make a grant . . . of at least Rs. 2 crores to enable this [government] to take up" construction of the capital (1 crore = 10 million).[69]

Soon after deciding to place the capital at Bhubaneswar, the Orissa government contracted with V. C. Mehta, chief engineer and town planner, Kanpur Development Board in Uttar Pradesh, to inspect the site. Assisted by the Orissa government architect Julius Vaz, Mehta, who was considered "an expert in Indian type of city building,"[70] submitted his report on June 21, 1947, approving the site at Bhubaneswar and maintaining that communications and water supply should not be a problem because of the close approximation of the Kuakhai River and the proposed development of National Highway No. 5. He, however, recommended that "the capital should be built on one side of the railway line in order to avoid the use of too many railway level crossings."[71] Considering that Orissa's population was expected to rise from 8.7 million to 14 million after the amalgamation of the princely states of Orissa was completed, Mehta suggested that planning should be done for fifty years ahead and actual construction should be done for the next twenty-five to thirty years.[72]

But limited financial resources of the new province of Orissa remained a major obstacle in starting construction work on the capital. As early as August 1946, a full month before the Orissa Assembly was to give its formal approval to Bhubaneswar, Governor C.M. Trivedi explained the financial constraints of the new province to Sir Eric Coates, finance member of the Viceroy's Executive Council: ". . . The amount of Rs. 40 lakhs for the capital is of course quite inadequate, not only because of the existing ruling prices, which so far as one can see, are bound to continue for some years, but also on account of the expansion of our administrative staff which has come to stay. We shall in due course make an official reference for the increase of this grant to about treble the figure, but I am writing this letter personally to you to let you know what is coming."[73]

What Governor Trivedi was attempting to do was to make a strong case for special consideration of Orissa in light of that state's long neglect, first under the government of Bengal and then under that of Bihar. Having learned the idiom of the paternalistic imperial government, what better way to make a claim for financial assistance from the central government than by declaring Orissa to be the "poorest" child of British India? "I appeal to you to help this child of your creation," pleaded Governor Trivedi to Sir Eric, "not only because of the paternal interest which you should feel in its fortunes, but also because I happen to be for the time being in the capacity of one whose duty it is to do the best he can for the all-round development of your child."[74]

Meanwhile, with the formation of the interim government in early September 1946 by Congress, the financial future of Orissa once again became uncertain. Governor Trivedi wrote Premier Mahtab: ". . . I am very anxious that we should continue to reinforce our requests by demi-official correspondence at the Member level in the Interim Government. I feel this is essential if we are to keep Orissa in the picture and get for it what it not only needs but in my opinion deserves."[75]

While the Orissa government was still negotiating with the government of India for financial assistance for the capital city project, political agitation broke out in the province over the construction of Hirakud Dam, a government of India-sponsored Mahanadi Valley project, partly inspired by the Tennessee Valley Project in the United States. The agitation resulted from the fact that the construction of Hirakud Dam required displacement of 200 villages. The agitation by itself was a source of political embarrassment to the government; but when the five villages from Bhubaneswar that were designated for displacement in the construction of the capital decided to join the larger agitation, construction work at Bhubaneswar had to be stopped.[76] Also delaying progress on the capital construction was the agitation by princely rulers of Orissa, who were opposing amalgamation with the Union.[77] Meanwhile, the outbreak of the Civil War of Succession, which turned the final years of British rule into an orgy of communal violence, terror, and slaughter, only created further delays in the capital project, even though "the Muslim population" of Orissa was "hardly" significant.[78] Moreover, there were still unsettled territorial disputes between Orissa and her neighbors, Madras, Andhra, Bengal, and the Central Provinces, all of whom were hoping that with the end of British rule they might be able to regain some of the territories lost to Orissa in 1936.[79]

It was in such a sociopolitical flux that Governor Trivedi reported to Premier Mahtab the response of the government of India on the question of financial assistance for the new capital: "I have had some news about the fate of our request to the Government of India for a grant of Rs. 2 crores for the construction of our new capital, and I am sorry to inform you that the orders will be that though the obligation of the Centre to help Orissa in building up her new capital is being accepted, the project should not be pushed through at the present time, when inflationary conditions have not completely disappeared, and the scarcity of building materials also has not been entirely relieved." Cautiously admitting that he did "not know what prospects there are of the reconsideration of this decision," Trivedi nevertheless positively indicated that he was "prepared to do whatever I can to get the decision reconsidered."[80]

Apparently, the government of India's response was as much conditioned by the prevailing inflationary conditions as by the problems of transfer of power and the influx of Hindu and Sikh refugees, who had already started to pour into Punjab and Bengal, and Orissa was not one of the states that was directly affected by the Civil War. While the interim government was still in place, Governor Trivedi kept his promise by writing Finance Minister Liaquat Ali Khan, on March 12, 1947:

> . . . My Ministers and I have received [the Government of India] communication with much disappointment. The very early construction of the new capital is a matter of exorable necessity for us. It is not one of the works which can be postponed. There is literally no accommodation, either office or residential [,] in Cuttack at a time when our staffs are expanding, and grave inconvenience is being experienced at present. Even our Secretariat is housed in temporary military buildings which we acquired from the Defence Department, and which are not likely to last for more than three or four years. Moreover, there is very little, if any, room for constructing temporary accommodation. The buildings in which our Secretariat is housed at present actually stand on the Maidan [field] which is the only open [land] for the whole of the town. . . . The immediate object of this letter is not to request you to reconsider the decision. It is almost certain that we shall ask for its reconsideration, and address the Government of India officially about it. . . . The actual object of this letter is to let you know that we are greatly disappointed with the decision. In fact, I may say without exaggeration that it has come as a shock both to my Prime Minister and myself.[81]

As a Muslim League member in the Hindu-Congress dominated interim government, Liaquat Ali Khan had built himself the reputation of obstructing the effective functioning of every department and discouraging every project by arresting funds, proving by his noncooperative tactics (dictated by Mohammed Ali Jinnah) that a unified Indian government along secular lines was simply impossible after the British left. Meanwhile, the Oriyas lost a good supporter in Lord Wavell in New Delhi, who was replaced by Lord Louis Mountbatten (1900–1979), Queen Victoria's great-grandson and the dashing wartime commander of all Allied forces in Southeast Asia, in March 1947 to implement the transfer of power. Before leaving India, Lord Wavell wrote Governor Trivedi promising to tell his "successor to keep an eye on [Orissa's] welfare," and assuring the Orissa government that "he will mention to Liaquat Ali Khan [the Oriya] disappointment at the fate of [their] request for a grant of Rs. 2 crores for [their] new capital."[82]

Political parleys produced a more conciliatory response from Liaquat Ali Khan, who reassured Governor Trivedi that he had "every sympathy for Orissa's problem of finding suitable accommodation for its expanding . . . administration," and that he was prepared to give his "sympathetic consideration" to "any fresh point of view brought out by [the Orissa] Government."[83] Governor Trivedi's response of April 1, 1947, to Liaquat Ali Khan was long:

> It has been urged that the capital project is unproductive. It is certainly unproductive in the ordinary sense of the term, but our point is that we cannot function adequately as a province without a new capital. . . . one of our biggest difficulties at present is to find accommodation, both office and residential, for our administrative staffs which continue to grow and must grow if development is to take place. . . . The Government of India are faced with the same difficulty at New Delhi and are, I understand, now undertaking schemes for provision of additional accommodation involving heavy outlay. . . . We have shifted our Secretariat to the temporary military buildings, and have had to give the old Secretariat to heads of departments. The military buildings are very hot indeed, and it is quite impossible for the staff to work there in the afternoons, and one of the results of the shifting of the Secretariat has been the introduction of morning offices during April, May and June. Work will undoubtedly suffer. . . . There are several officers who have either no accommodation or in some cases, most unsuitable accommodation. We have located certain offices at Puri, and will probably locate others at Berhampur, but at both these places there is acute scarcity of accommodation, and the scattering of the staff is of course not conducive to maximum efficiency at a time when administration is becoming complex necessitating frequent personal discussions and when there is pressing need for urgent disposal of business. The office of the Comptroller, Orissa, has for long been located in Ranchi [Bihar]. This has been another source of delay with resultant

inefficiency, but it is not possible to bring the office to Cuttack. We have no Assembly buildings, the sessions being held in the Ravenshaw College, when the College itself badly needs all the accommodation it has. . . . it is not possible to construct temporary buildings in Cuttack. There is no suitable land available for expansion. . . . If we do not start the construction of our new capital immediately, I am afraid our difficulties, acute though they are at present, will become progressively more acute, and we will have to place a ban on all expansion. The effect of such a ban on the Provincial Government's development plans and what is equally important, the psychology of the people, will, in my view, be disastrous. . . . In its wide implications and its broad effects the [capital] project is productive, not in money, but in development. . . . The delay over our new capital is very largely due to causes beyond our control. The province has now been in existence for 11 years, and out of these, six years have been years of war. During the earlier years there was vehement controversy over the location of the capital. . . . The present ministry lost no time in . . . [obtaining] a verdict of the Assembly in favour of Bhubaneswar last September.

. . . No one, certainly not myself, can foretell the trend of prices. Some say that depression may come about sooner than we anticipate. If it does, well and good. In any case, prices will not be stabilized at the pre-war level. Very likely stabilization may take place at anything from 50 to 75 per cent above that level, and we should be getting the benefit of the stabilization from the second or third to the fifth year during which the bulk of the expenditure would be incurred. . . . I wanted only to emphasise that we have not estimated the cost at the present prevailing level of prices, but at a level of 100 per cent above the pre-war level.

The responsibility for giving the province a new capital rests with the Central Government. This was implicit in the creation of the province, and the grant made at the time. . . . The sole aim of this [project] is to improve the lot of the common man in Orissa. (As you know, Orissa is the poorest, the most backward and the most undeveloped part of India.) . . . This is the only way of successfully countering the propaganda of the Communists, the Socialists and the Forward Bloc.[84]

Later that month in April, Governor Trivedi met Liaquat Ali Khan in New Delhi and was able to get some commitment for the capital project based on "a mutual understanding." On the strength of that meeting

Governor Trivedi wrote Premier Mahtab that "we should probably be getting an additional sum varying from Rs. 1 crore to Rs. 1.5 crores."[85] After some more protracted negotiations, in mid-May 1947 the government of India indicated the amount it was prepared to offer Orissa for the capital project. Orissa did not receive Rs. 2 crores as originally requested, but the amount was substantially more than seemed possible at a time when India was facing the pressing problem of refugees from West and East Pakistan. "We would naturally have liked to have a grant of Rs. 2 crores as asked for in the official correspondence," Governor Trivedi wrote Liaquat Ali Khan. He graciously added, "We however accept with many thanks your decision to give us a grant of Rs. 132 lakhs [Rs. 1.32 crores]. . . . We agree that this is a generous settlement, and, personally, I am under a deep debt of gratitude to you. . . ."[86]

The sum of Rs. 132 lakhs was in addition to Rs. 36 lakhs left over from the previous grant of Rs. 40 lakhs made to Orissa, and it was to cover cost of such items as buildings, land, the layout of the town, roads, water supply, drainage, and electricity. Orissa was expected to finance the cost of "the extra residential accommodation necessitated by expansion and one-half of the cost of water supply, drainage and electrification." It was reasoned that "all these items will, to a degree, be revenue-earning and might very reasonably be financed from borrowed funds. The burden on Orissa's revenue will then be reduced to the minimum."[87]

In light of the new grant, the Orissa government decided to reduce the area of development of the new capital from nine to about six square miles "with a view to cut down the cost of jungle clearance and preparation of site as also the cost of roads, water supply, drainage and transmission of electrical energy."[88] However, the debate over the location of the capital at Bhubaneswar was to continue to simmer into the 1950s. With the departure of Mahtab from Orissa to join the central government cabinet, there remained no strong advocate for Bhubaneswar in Orissa. Governor Trivedi had been replaced by Dr. K. N. Katju; and while Dr. Katju was supportive of Bhubaneswar, his involvement with Orissa's future was more academic than emotional. Meanwhile, Nabakrushna Choudhury's government took office in May 1950, and Governor Katju was replaced by Asaf Ali. The new government's commitment to Bhubaneswar was at best indifferent, and two of its members, Biswanath Das and Finance Minister Radhanath Rath openly opposed the construction of the capital at Bhubaneswar. Governor Asaf Ali reintroduced the religious controversy by arguing that the capital of a secular state "should not be located at a religious center" such as Bhubaneswar.[89]

Clearly the record shows that, despite the bold confidence with which the Oriyas had put their dream forward, many of the Oriya leaders were privately to remain far from sure that the grand scheme of the capital city was right. It was exactly this doubt born out of conflicting interests and narrow considerations that was most often urged as a conclusive proof for thinking the scheme was bound to fail and the scheme might have failed had Harekrushna Mahtab not returned to Orissa in October 1956 to form the second Congress government, putting an end to the capital city controversy and providing the full support of the government for the construction of the capital at Bhubaneswar.

·4·
THE ARCHITECT

Bhubaneswar was thus to be a continuing story of an always mounting hymn of thanksgiving for prosperity, of the appearance of multistoried administrative buildings as reincarnated temples of old. Such was the dream which began to form itself in the minds of Oriya leaders; and such was the program which, once the dream was conceived, they set themselves, with characteristic Oriya hyperbole, to realize. "Let us in developing [the capital city] and fashioning it," declared Assemblyman Vysyaraju Kasiviswanadham Raju, "be inspired by art and architecture and show to the world that the new capital of Orissa is not merely a copy of a Western town but a town which has grown out of the culture of the Orissan people and that it is an artistic and architectural symbol of Orissan culture."[1]

What went with this, again, was a lush flowering of the old local patriotism and particularism native to Orissa, which, from the beginning, had been responsible in shaping this dream. Such a dream, once conceived, was accepted by both its sponsors and the public—in this country so long trained to believe what it wanted to believe—as being practically realized.

But the logic of circumstances plainly required that the inspired impulse for building the capital be intelligently matched with proper resources and building skills, both visibly absent in a province struggling to stand on its own feet. Unless the capital is built properly, Assemblyman Babu Girija Bhusan Dutta cautioned as early as 1937, ". . . a hundred years hence the capital site will be a buried city, like Nineveh of Babylon and Orissologists will [have to] make [an] expedition to unearth the civilization buried there."[2]

There were some other sober voices in the Orissa Assembly that sounded a note of caution against building the city on a grand scale. "If we compare our budget with the budgets of other Provinces," warned Babu Godavaris Misra, "it will be clear that ours is a Province which requires great economy. Whereas Madras has receipt of about Rs. 17 crores, and Bombay [of] Rs. 14 crores, this Province has a revenue of about Rs. 1.5 crores." (One crore is equal to ten million.) Citing the examples of Patna and New Delhi, he argued that in Patna the original estimate of Rs. 2 crores actually rose to Rs. 7 crores, and in New Delhi the original estimate of Rs. 6 crores rose to Rs. 20 crores. "But in our Province, we cannot afford to have such disproportionate expenditure on the construction of [our] capital."[3]

Construction work on the site also languished because of the shortage of technical staff. Lamenting about fatigue resulting from long working hours, Chief Engineer A. Karim wrote Premier Harekrushna Mahtab that unless the government quickly appointed a second chief engineer, construction work will "fall in arrears and suffer in efficiency."[4] The same shortage of technical staff had forced the Orissa government to contract with the Army for the clearing of the site; but bad weather had resulted in delays. Delays were also caused when the Military Engineering Service (MES) branch of the Army was slow in providing the estimates for clearing the site.[5]

Moreover, between 1946 and 1948 Orissa underwent a quick succession of three governors, which only added to the political uncertainties of the new province. Such uncertainties prompted Premier Mahtab to request of Prime Minister Nehru in the summer of 1948 a governor who would last and be sympathetic to Orissa. Governor Hawthorne Lewis (April 1, 1941–March 31, 1946) had been sympathetic to the Oriya people, although the decision to place the capital at Bhubaneswar was taken under the governorship of Sir C. M. Trivedi (April 1, 1946–August 14, 1947). Governor Trivedi had played an important role in securing funding for the capital from the government of India—and he was later to use his experience in Bhubaneswar effectively in the development of Chandigarh for Punjab—but his transfer to Punjab was viewed as a loss in Orissa. His successor, Dr. Kailash Nath Katju (August 15, 1947–June 20, 1948), a Kashmiri Brahman, had a natural interest in the Hindu antiquity of Bhubaneswar. But his tenure in Orissa turned out to be too short, and he was replaced by the Muslim M. Asaf Ali in the government of India's secular efforts to encourage greater interaction between Hindus and Muslims.

But in Orissa, Governor Asaf Ali's appointment was viewed with suspicion—a suspicion born out of the Hindu-Muslim feud that engulfed India in the early days of independence, and a suspicion which has continued to create conflict between the two communities to this day. Moreover, the memory of difficulties in securing funding for Bhubaneswar from Finance Minister Liaquat Ali Khan in the government of India was still fresh in the minds of Oriya leaders. Not surprisingly, therefore, Mahtab wrote Nehru: "If Dr. [K. N.] Katju has to go to Bengal, would it be possible for Mr. Pakwasa to come over here from [the Central Provinces]?" He pointedly added: ". . . I have the confidence to manage with any Governor who may be sent here; but we prefer Mr. Pakwasa or Mr. Sriprakas to any other gentleman whom you may select as Governor of Orissa."[6] Nevertheless, the government of India confirmed the appointment of Asaf Ali, who remained in office from June 21, 1948, to June 6, 1952.

The controversy over the appointment of a "sympathetic" governor acquired a special significance because of the inherent Oriya suspicion of outsiders. The appointment of outsiders as provincial governors under the Raj was introduced by the British as a measure of checks and balances, and the Congress government carried over the practice of appointing outsiders as state governors under the Swaraj. But apparently the fears of Oriya leaders of an unsympathetic governor had less credibility than was warranted by the appointment of Asaf Ali as the governor of Orissa. Asaf Ali's predecessor, Governor Trivedi, who was perhaps the strongest supporter of economic development in Orissa, during his brief tenure had several times chided the indolent Orissa administration, and had launched an administrative efficiency campaign in the province as early as the spring of 1946.[7] Governor Trivedi particularly targeted the Public Works Department for its inefficiency in a public speech. Public Works Minister R. K. Biswasroy naturally complained to Governor Trivedi about his unsympathetic remarks, and as an expression of his resentment abstained from an important cabinet meeting on April 23, 1947. Governor Trivedi explained his position: ". . . all of us, including yourself, have been trying our best to improve the PWD, and . . . there has been some improvement. The rate of improvement is, however . . . not rapid enough . . . ." He added: "The PWD is not the only department which stands in need of improvement. The whole of our administrative machinery is very weak and all of us . . . are trying to strengthen it." Governor Trivedi, however, attempted to mollify the minister by inviting him to Puri as his guest "for a day or two, if not longer."[8]

In the absence of technically trained manpower, Governor Trivedi's concern with the performance of the Public Works Department was legitimate. For the new province to construct its capital and to implement many a developmental scheme, a large number of technical personnel were needed. Postindependence India was woefully inexperienced in technical areas. "Architectural schools were virtually nonexistent, indigenous architectural tradition had practically faded, and local craft skills were visibly on the decline."[9] The situation in Orissa was worse, since that province, having been created recently, depended on neighboring provinces for many of its educational and administrative needs.

Unable to rely completely on its own resources and forced to bring in outsiders, Orissa's old antipathy to outsiders was naturally aroused. The Oriyas were especially uncomfortable with the influx of the aggressive Punjabi contractors in search of economic opportunities, and who came to be viewed by the Oriyas as being no better than the Bengalis who had earlier stolen jobs from them. In such a situation the prospect of hiring a Western planner appeared far more appealing than hiring a northerner, who might decide to stay permanently in Orissa. But the poor economic condition of the country had created a shortage of American dollars, thus ruling out the possibility of hiring Western planners and architects for the construction of the capital city. "Another aspect of the economic situation, and a most vital aspect, is the lack of [American] dollars," wrote Prime Minister Nehru to Premier Mahtab. He added, "This lack of dollars is chiefly due to food imports."[10] In fact, the foreign exchange situation was so severe in the country that the Union Finance Ministry had advised Prime Minister Nehru to issue instructions to provincial governments against spending any dollars overseas. "It is . . . extremely necessary to check as a matter of urgency the tendency on the part of the Provincial Governments to operate on their own in the international capital goods market"[11]—advice that Prime Minister Nehru quickly passed on to all the provinces in the Indian Union, including Orissa.

With the option of hiring a Western town planner ruled out because of the shortage of American dollars, the Orissa government arranged with V. C. Mehta, chief engineer and town planner, Kanpur Development Board, to visit Bhubaneswar. Mehta's initial visit to Bhubaneswar was exploratory and without a firm commitment. Accompanied by Under Secretary A. Pujari, PWD, Government Architect Julius L. Vaz, and Superintending Engineer M. L. Bahl, Central Circle, Mehta visited the site on the morning of June 21, 1947. In his preliminary report, Mehta described Bhubaneswar as a "suitable" site for the capital. He also reported that communications and water supply were going to be the two primary needs of the new capital, and he thought the water needs of the city could be met by the Kuakhai River, and the communications of the city could be improved by realigning the proposed National Highway No. 5 to serve the capital.[12]

To avoid too many railway crossings, Mehta recommended the capital be built on one side of the railway line. To accomplish that objective, he recommended the National Highway No. 5 be shifted west of the proposed Kuakhai bridge, thereby providing better accessibility to the capital from Cuttack. He also correctly advised the Orissa government to provide sufficient room for future expansion, especially since the impending amalgamation of princely states with Orissa was expected to raise the province's population from 8.7 million to 14 million. But Chief Engineer Karim disagreed with Mehta, arguing that amalgamation of princely states with Orissa was not likely to affect the administrative character of Bhubaneswar. Moreover, the government was not allowing any "private buildings within the capital"; private citizens were to be given separate sites outside the capital. Also, Utkal University, the High Court, and the Chamber of Commerce were to be located at Cuttack—a decision which was expected to prevent any overcrowding of Bhubaneswar.[13]

Mehta nevertheless insisted that overall planning of Bhubaneswar should be for the next 50 years, and that construction of new buildings should be able to accommodate needs for "the next 25 to 30 years." He expressed his concern that old Bhubaneswar was already witnessing "uncontrolled" developments, which were likely to influence the capital city. So far, the government's measures for regulating construction in old Bhubaneswar had not been very successful.[14]

There was also no agreement as to whether the Assembly, the Secretariat, and the offices of heads of departments should be combined into one bloc, as had been done at Lucknow, or to follow the example of Patna, where the Assembly had been placed in a separate building. Architect Vaz favored the Patna example, while some others in the government preferred the Lucknow example. There was also disagreement over whether to use laterite or brick for buildings. Apparently, Mehta favored the use of laterite because bricks were more expensive; however, Karim felt that the use of laterite would give the capital a "very dirty and drab" look. Mehta gave assurance that the look of laterite buildings could be improved with the use of surface plaster.[15]

The Orissa government felt that a town planner and a chief engineer should be able to complete the details for the capital, thereby ruling out the idea of consulting with a team of three or four town planners. But the overriding concern of the government was that the Assembly and other government buildings represent Orissan culture and workmanship, while all other buildings—especially residential quarters—be as "simple" as possible in style.[16]

The use of local motifs for government buildings and emphasis on simplicity in housing were dictated as much by the need for austerity as by the simple taste of the people. To stimulate public interest in the capital construction scheme, a capital city committee in the Assembly was created and charged with the responsibility of disseminating information on the capital. Agreeing to deliver the contour plan of Bhubaneswar to Mehta by April 1948, the Orissa government promised full support to the Indian planner in his work. In return, Mehta promised to deliver a master plan which would be "indigenous" in spirit and style.[17]

Clearly, Bhubaneswar was to be an Indian city in shape and spirit, even though the motivation for a modern administrative city was quite different from earlier Indian cities. For that reason, Mehta was selected because he was considered "to be an expert in [the] Indian type of city building" and was thought to have closely studied the "ancient [Indian] science," the *Silpa Sastra.*[18]

Still, the Orissa government did not completely rule out the possibility of calling in "another expert town planner" at some later date.[19] Uncertainty of federal funds demanded flexibility in the master plan, and kept the need for an additional planner open for future development. "It was originally decided to develop an area of 12 sq. miles for the capital," explained the architect Vaz. "It has been recently decided to reduce the area . . . to about 5 to 6 sq. miles with a view to cut down the cost . . . only the essential buildings [are] to be [constructed] immediately and spaces left vacant for future development."[20]

In August 1947, the Orissa government created a planning board to coordinate construction work at Bhubaneswar. The Planning Board had no public representation on it and was made up of mostly government officers. However, the Planning Board was quickly dissolved by the government, ostensibly because it undermined the authority of the Public Works Department, which in the Indian situation typically controlled and directed all government construction work. So it was only natural when the Orissa government authorized the Public Works Department to supervise construction at Bhubaneswar. Such an arrangement was to restrict the role of a town planner to a minimum and certainly to no more than that of a consultant.

In fact, Mehta would not have been invited to Bhubaneswar had the architect Vaz and Superintending Engineer M. L. Bahl, both of the Public Works Department, gone ahead and prepared the master plan for the capital city.[21] But Chief Engineer A. Karim strongly felt the need to consult with a town planner in order "to settle the broad outlines of the plan and to avoid unnecessary delays." Apparently, recognizing their limitations, both Vaz and Bahl agreed with Karim, who suggested the name of Mehta as a town planner. M. Fayazuddin of Hyderabad and Mr. Coets of Lahore were the other two names suggested.[22] Suggested also was the idea of sending a few Public Works officers to study such progressive Indian cities as Hyderabad, Patna, Madras, Mysore, Bangalore, Bombay, and New Delhi, and bring back details which could be adopted in Bhubaneswar.[23]

By the end of 1947 it was manifestly clear that the Orissa government had not found a qualified individual who could draw up the master plan and supervise construction work at Bhubaneswar. The contour survey of Bhubaneswar also remained incomplete, as did any economic survey giving projections of population or industry. No survey of the old town existed either.[24] More than a year had passed since the Orissa government took the decision in September 1946 of placing the capital at Bhubaneswar; but in the absence of a qualified town planner the construction work remained moribund.

It was in such circumstances that the name of Dr. Otto H. Koenigsberger as a possible town planner for Bhubaneswar was first mentioned in Orissa governmental circles. A German Jew by descent, Koenigsberger was raised a Lutheran since his grandfather had converted to ease his way into the predominantly Protestant German society; however, Nazi Germany made no concession for Koenigsberger's religious affiliation, and he fled Germany and arrived in India at the invitation of Diwan (Minister) Mirza Ismail of Mysore in 1939. In India, Koenigsberger had been involved in several developmental projects, including the replanning of the Tata Iron and Steel town of Jamshedpur. He was among a handful of Western town planners in India, along with the Americans Albert Mayer, Frederick Adams, and Roland Greeley, who were in India under President Truman's Point Four agricultural program. Mayer was to eventually prepare the first master plan for Chandigarh.[25]

So late in December 1947, Premier Mahtab wrote to the Mysore government, requesting to borrow the services of Koenigsberger: "We want a good architect and Town Planner to help us [in] preparing a scheme for [Bhubaneswar]." Requesting to borrow the services of Mysore State Architect and Town Planner Otto Koenigsberger for "a few weeks" to draw the master plan for Bhubaneswar, he added, "The remuneration which will be paid to Dr. Konnisberg [*sic*] may be settled by [a] mutual agreement."[26]

That Premier Mahtab believed that the whole new city could be planned in a matter of a few weeks reflects as much the innocence as the inexperience on the part of the Orissa government. Nevertheless, Koenigsberger enthusiastically accepted the assignment, informing Mahtab that the Mysore government had consented to loan his services to the Orissa government, and that "I am looking forward to the opportunity of helping you in this bold and interesting scheme."[27] Promising to visit Bhubaneswar at the end of February or early March 1948, he requested the Orissa government furnish him with statistical data on population and industries in Orissa, and projections of population for the capital city. Topographical sheets and contour maps were among other items requested by Koenigsberger.

However, soon after Koenigsberger accepted the Bhubaneswar project he was offered the directorship of the Department of Housing in the Health Ministry of the government of India, which was to keep his involvement with Bhubaneswar partial and sporadic for the remaining three years of his stay in India. The influx of refugees from Pakistan had created a severe shortage of housing in the north and east, and the government of India was sorely in need of qualified individuals who could deal with the crisis. "We want trained personnel in hundreds of thousands,"[28] Pandit Nehru expressed his concern soon after India's independence.

The induction of Koenigsberger into the government of India was a clear signal to the Orissa government that his principal loyalty would be to the Housing Department of the Health Ministry. In an effort to secure Koenigsberger's services more completely for Orissa, Mahtab wrote Pandit Nehru explaining the needs of the new province. Nehru's response was noncommital, which can be taken as a measure of the central government's involvement with the Bhubaneswar project: "I do not know if they [the Health Ministry] will be able to spare him [Koenigsberger] for any length of time but I suppose he can go to Orissa from time to time. I am sending your letter to Rajkumari Amrit Kaur, our Health Minister."[29]

What made Koenigsberger's employment possible with the government of India was also his newly gained Indian citizenship. Having been stripped of German citizenship two years after he left Germany in 1933, Koenigsberger had been stateless since 1935. Through his work in India, he had come to know Pandit Nehru and Lord Louis Mountbatten, Queen Victoria's great-grandson and the last British governor general. In one of his meetings with Koenigsberger, Mountbatten suggested Indian citizenship for him, which was approved by Mountbatten after Nehru sponsored him and V. P. Menon witnessed in his behalf. Koenigsberger's Indian citizenship automatically made him a citizen of the British Commonwealth, on the basis of which he later emigrated to England in 1951, where he ultimately made his permanent home. He nevertheless was to retain his Indian citizenship until 1991, when he took British citizenship in the wake of the growing hard political rhetoric on immigration policy by the Conservative government. However, it was a difficult decision.

Born on October 13, 1908, to Georg and Katherina Koenigsberger in Berlin, Otto Heinrich Koenigsberger was the second of the five children (two boys and three girls). Family finances precluded private-school education for him, a popular practice of the time among upper-class German professional families, and Otto graduated from the state-supported Korner Schule (High School) in Koepenick near Berlin in 1926. In high school he studied general education, including art, science, French, and Latin; he recalled doing well only in his history class as a boy.[30] Although his father was an architect in the Prussian government, the elder Koenigsberger wanted the younger Koenigsberger to become either a physicist or an engineer, possibly because his own career as an architect had not turned out to be financially successful. In fact, the elder Koenigsberger positively discouraged his son from becoming an architect, fearing that he might not have the single-minded enthusiasm needed by a major architect.[31]

After a short stint as a bricklayer and carpenter soon after high school, Koenigsberger entered the Technical University (Technische Hochschule) of Berlin in 1927, where he studied architecture, civil engineering, and urban planning. It was at the Technical University that he came in contact with Hans Poelzig, Bruno Taut, and Heinrich Tessenow. Discouragement from his father notwithstanding, Koenigsberger selected architecture "because that was the profession I knew most about, and also because my father was a passionate teacher and involved us in everything he did."[32]

To his surprise and encouragement, Koenigsberger won a prize for designing a rowing club building in his first year of college. But concentration in a double major—architecture and civil engineering—proved too much for him, and he eventually dropped civil engineering from his curriculum. Contact with Hans Poelzig (1869–1936) at the Technical University exposed Koenigsberger to free enquiry, which open-mindedness he found liberating and exhilarating. Having ties to the Expressionist tradition of the early twentieth century, Poelzig, who challenged the prevailing orthodoxy of the profession, came to exercise a special influence on the young Koenigsberger.

Koenigsberger completed his education in architecture and urban planning at a time when German architecture, influenced by the changing social and political conditions in Europe, was undergoing evolution. The origins of the new architecture in Germany go back to the last decade of the nineteenth century, to the "Jugendstil." Later, the foundation of the Werkbund in 1907 provided a common forum to architects like Theodor Fischer, Fritz Schumacher, Henry van der Velde, Peter Behrens, and Walter Gropius to work out the problems of modern architecture. But the German optimism in permanent economic stability which had been the main catalyst for the new architecture in Germany suffered a severe blow as a result of the First World War, resulting in a national mood of disillusionment and despair. The mounting mistrust of traditional conventions came to be replaced by a search for new ideas that would lead to new possibilities, especially in architecture.

The center of German architecture was Berlin, where Koenigsberger was a student, and where noted architects like Mies van der Rohe, Erich Mendelsohn, Hugo Haring, Hans Poelzig, Bruno and Max Taut, Heinrich Tessenow, and Walter Gropius were active. The Bauhaus at Weimar, founded through the initiative and zeal of Walter Gropius, became the training school for modern design suited to meet the challenges of the industrial age. In 1927 the Weissenhof housing scheme was carried out at Stuttgart on the occasion of the Werkbund Exhibition—designed to provide innovative answers to the growing problem of housing in Germany.

The new architecture in the 1920s expressed itself in many ways in Germany. Ernst May in Frankfurt, Walter Gropius in Berlin and

Karlsruhe, Bruno and Max Taut, Heinrich Tessenow, and Mies van der Rohe in Berlin undertook large housing projects, especially for the poor. May designed new school buildings, while Poelzig designed the Grosses Schauspielhaus (Great Playhouse) in Berlin. But much of these architectural activities took place after the transition period of 1918–23, since during that period growing inflation did not permit much building. (The German mark, valued at 25 cents in 1914, had fallen to 2 cents by 1922, and a year later it was worthless.) However, the resurgence of construction activity in the late 1920s proved to be short-lived, a span of seven years, because National Socialism, which expressed its ideal of architecture in a monumental pseudo-classicism, smothered any modern inclinations. Prominent architects such as Gropius, Mies, Mendelsohn, along with so many others, finally bowed to the inevitable restrictions and emigrated. Industrial building alone was spared from the restrictive rules of Nazi Germany. Still, straightforward, aesthetically satisfying architecture, as seen in factories and aircraft hangers, survived in the unsympathetic Nazi Germany; and the design of open spans of impressive length broke new ground in the structural field.

The young Koenigsberger's thinking and education was to be shaped in such an environment; but even more important, he was to come under the direct influence of Hans Poelzig, Bruno Taut, and Heinrich Tessenow, and upon graduation in 1931, was to work briefly with Ernst May—all of whom were to have an effect on the young architect. From Hans Poelzig, who held ties to early German Expressionism, Koenigsberger learned the virtue of originality "and not attempting to mimic [his] tutor's designs."[33] Much later in life Koenigsberger remembered with visible relish and affection the unorthodoxy of his teacher, when in a public forum Poelzig challenged the Bauhaus dictum of "form follows function," claiming it to be an overstatement because posterity would only accept the form and not the function that dominated the shape of a building.[34] Poelzig emphasized the significance of a straightforward, practical architecture as seen in his famous water tower (1911) in Posen (Poznan, Poland), although his later involvement with German Expressionism took him toward monumentality, best represented in his administrative building for I. G. Farben in Frankfurt (1928–31).

Poelzig instilled in Koenigsberger the value of traditional architecture. "Poelzig's idea of an architect was that of the nineteenth century, when an architect was a gentleman who designed for gentlemen, and did not concern himself with mass production or housing for labour. He was an elitist who encouraged Expressionist thinking, and, as students, we came to respect his ideas," recalled Koenigsberger.[35]

If Poelzig taught practical architecture to Koenigsberger, Bruno Taut provided lessons in social architecture. "From Bruno Taut," recalled Koenigsberger, "I learned social responsibility."[36] Introspective and solemn, Taut was a political activist, intensely involved with the social and political changes of his time. Driven by the rational process of solving problems of architectural design, and prone to taking a highly subjective delight in abstract color and form, Taut represented duality in his creative character that made him extremely attractive as a teacher.[37] A member of the *Novembergruppe*, a Soviet-style Workers' Council for Art, Taut called for a double revolution in architecture: spiritual and political. The same duality led Taut to combine his own "new crystal architecture" with the new community spirit. The conflict between his earlier Expressionist ties and later concerns with working-class housing and dictates of functionalism was a recurring theme in Taut's prolific career. Also an early member of the Garden City Movement, Taut designed the first garden city suburb of Falkenberg in Germany with Heinrich Tessenow. Before leaving for the Soviet Union at the height of his career in 1930 to engage in large-scale building schemes sponsored under the First Five Year Plan—a plan which stood in marked contrast to economically depressed Europe—Bruno Taut had passed on his teachings to the young Koenigsberger.

Heinrich Tessenow informed his students, among whom sat Koenigsberger, at the Technical University in Berlin that paradise on earth was a small town whose industries were predominantly based on *Handwerk*. A town should be self-sufficient economically, Tessenow, Koenigsberger's third important teacher, reasoned, and it should be able to provide all the food necessary for its survival. Combining the ideology of Heimatkunst with the anarcho-socialism of Kropotkin, Tessenow came to view large cities and the centralized state and its concomitant political system as parasitic and destructive. Large cities were unable to meet their own needs and had to import food from outside, and the centralized state facilitate repressive government which led to war. For Tessenow, industrialization and the development of the modern state and its political and educational systems had been detrimental to the natural development of man. *Geist* had been destroyed in favor of specialization. "We are great specialists, but we are not all great, are not great men, for as specialists we lack harmony and diversity," Tessenow bemoaned in his book *Handwerk und Kleinstadt* (1919).[38]

A member of Der Ring, Tessenow with like-minded architects strove to launch an international architectural movement that would repudiate the restrictions of the past, and provide solutions to contemporary building problems by employing modern technology—a movement which would usher in a new architectural culture better suited to the industrial age. Tessenow regarded contemporary working-class housing as bourgeois in character; instead, he showed a preference for an architectural idiom that was classicist in inspiration, but without elaboration and almost without ornament.

Like Mies van der Rohe, Tessenow believed that designing meant the development and distribution of a small number of constantly recurring elements. Rejecting both avant-garde experimentalism and national nostalgia, Tessenow came to view tradition as neither a link with the past which had to be brutally severed nor an ideal of the past which had to be blindly embraced; he came to view it as a spiritual attitude worthy of adherence and necessary for maintaining consistency. His efforts were centered around functionality rather than around the aesthetic, although he never subscribed to the Functionalist thesis that a house should be built from the inside out. He placed emphasis on simplicity; and while regarding craft-based work as the foundation of design, he grew to appreciate the advantages of industry, since the latter appealed to his intellectual need for an ordered world.

Standardization in industrial production methods provided him with the simple idiom that he searched for in architecture, even though the underlying motives in the two situations were diametrically opposite. His concern for truth, objectivity, and order as being superior to innovation did not contradict in any way his bourgeois and democratic ideals. For Tessenow, it was the architect's responsibility to assess the needs of the individual, while at the same time subordinating those needs to the requirements of the community. Many of Tessenow's ideas were sympathetically close to those of Mahatma Gandhi, and were to prove extremely useful for Koenigsberger in his Bhubaneswar assignment. Tessenow's emphasis on *Handwerk* and small self-sufficient towns was especially suited to the colonial India of the 1930s and 1940s engaged in the Gandhian *Sarvodaya*, the upliftment of all through Gandhian socialism.

Graduating in 1931 from the Technical University, on the basis of a design thesis of a zoological park, Koenigsberger joined the Prussian government as an assistant architect, and worked for the next two years on housing schemes and hospital projects. It was during that time that he came in contact with Ernst May, who had been appointed city architect in Frankfurt. May had been involved in a low-cost housing scheme that mass produced 15,000 apartments which resembled Le Corbusier's freehold maisonettes, with each apartment furnished and equipped with various amenities. The zig-zag blocks enclosed a U-shaped garden court and culminated in the community center. The "Sun, space, and greenery," along with the white planes, flat roofs, and ribbon windows, became recognizable signs of socialist architecture; and the use of precast concrete slab construction in the Frankfurt mass housing scheme came to be popularly known as the "May System" and its aesthetic the "International Style." However, the project was later condemned by Hitler as "*Kulturbolschewismus*" (Cultural Bolshevism).

The improved position of the German mark in 1923, the infusion of foreign capital, and the fiscal policy of the Social Democratic municipal administration formed the financial basis for the mass housing scheme of the Marxist May, who tried to combine as many of the advantages of urban life as possible with those of life in the country—a clear indication that May had been influenced by the satallite town principal of the garden city, although May's housing bloc, unlike the garden city, was not conceived of as detached from the main conurbation. However, in the end the economic savings of the rationalized construction and minimum ground plan failed to put housing within the reach of most workers, for whom the rents remained too high. The Frankfurt housing project failed because "it did not go hand in hand with relevant measures to curb credit and building material costs."[39] Discouraged, May finally left Germany for the Soviet Union, but not before he had announced to the world the benefits of the dwellings of minimal size and cost at the second CIAM (Congrès Internationaux d'Architecture Moderne) Congress called by him to meet in Frankfurt in 1929.

Association with May was to reinforce the principles of social architecture for Koenigsberger. May's ideas on mass low-cost housing were to prove especially useful for Koenigsberger in planning housing in Bhubaneswar, and also in his position as director of housing in the government of India. The experience gained from German housing schemes also proved useful in reworking some of the sketches of his zoological park and integrating them into a new design of facilities for the 1936 Olympic Games in Berlin. The design of facilities for the Olympic

Games won him the first Schinkel Prize in 1933; he thus improved on the accomplishment of his father, who had won the third Schinkel Prize in 1901.[40]

However, that is where the parallels between the careers of father and son ended. Koenigsberger's designs for the Olympic Games were never implemented, and his career in the Prussian government was cut short with the advent of Adolf Hitler as the chancellor of the German Republic in January 1933. The New Order of the Third Reich promised to carry on the process of true German history, and under the new doctrine of "racial science" Otto Koenigsberger, like thousands of other Jews, was summarily dismissed from government service in April 1933. Two years later, he lost his German citizenship under the Nuremberg Laws of 1935.

The next four years proved turbulent for Koenigsberger, but he made the best of his circumstances. The Schinkel Prize helped him secure a job as an archaeologist in 1933 in Egypt, where he was to meet Ludwig Borchardt of the Swiss Institute for the History of Egyptian Architecture in Cairo, and under whom he was to study the funeral temple of Thutmose III in Thebes and the Eighteenth Dynasty remains in the Fayum. If the punishing sun of Egypt was to prepare Koenigsberger for his later stay in tropical India, the arid climate of Egypt also "aggravated a chest condition following tuberculosis at the age of 18 (when the specialist advised him that he had only a few years to live)."[41] Egypt also allowed him the time to complete his doctoral dissertation on the construction of the Ancient Egyptian door, submitted to an examining board under the chairmanship of Professor Herman Jansen at the Technical University in Berlin in 1935.

Koenigsberger's fight with tuberculosis, however, kept taking him back to convalesce in Switzerland from time to time, and it was in Switzerland in 1938 that he was approached by Sir Mirza Ismail, who offered him a position with Mysore State. "I deliberately dragged the negotiations with Sir Mirza because I needed more time to cure myself completely, and at the same time consider another offer from the University of Michigan at Ann Arbor to teach Ancient Egyptian hieroglyphics." Hieroglyphics lost a competent candidate when Koenigsberger decided to accept the offer from the Mysore State "because of the building opportunities."[42]

Colonial India in 1938 appeared far more promising to Koenigsberger than Europe contaminated by anti-Semitism, and certainly preferable to a career in hieroglyphics in the United States. But before moving to India, he had to tie up some important family matters in Germany. After an abortive attempt to move his mother from Berlin to his sister's home in the United States in late 1938, Koenigsberger returned to Switzerland. In February 1939, he flew from Switzerland to London, from whence he took a German ship (he only had German currency with him) to Colombo, and then a ferry across to India. He reached Bangalore by train on April 13,1939, the day of the Tamil New Year. Much later, to his relief he received the good news of his mother's safe passage to the United States in the spring of 1939, albeit after she surrendered all the family assets and property to the German government.

India offered Koenigsberger a fresh start in life. He tenure with the Mysore government was to prepare him for his various Indian assignments, including important lessons in Indian bureaucracy. "Three times a week the Diwan [Minister] met with his government architect, his municipal commissioner, his city engineer, and his garden superintendent at his home, and all of us set out in a very large Buick limousine for town inspection of Bangalore," Koenigsberger recalled. Sir Mirza was very particular about the physical appearance of the city, and Koenigsberger was not only in charge of architecture and city planning but also responsible for industrial designs for the government factories and industrial products. In sum, Koenigsberger became "to the Mysore government what Peter Behrens had been to AEG [Allgemeine Elektrizitats-Gesellschaft], but on a much larger scale."[43]

Planning cities and designing buildings for the next nine years in Mysore, Koenigsberger found the Indian situation very different from what he knew of Europe. In India the government played "a major part in all development projects, even those projects which in other parts of the world are reserved for private enterprise."[44] Consequently, he was mostly involved with public sector-led development projects, although he frequently accepted private projects as well, the most noteworthy being the replanning of the Tata Iron and Steel town of Jamshedpur.

Koenigsberger's years with Mysore State also helped shape his ideas on India's urban future. "The biggest contrast to my European experience was," he later recalled, "the rapid growth of urban population in Indian towns. I also realized that there was no way of stopping this growth and plans had to be made for cities that could grow indefinitely, but at each stage would function efficiently." He added: "For this and many other reasons I came up with the idea of the linear town which had been advocated theoretically by the Spanish planner Soria y Mata and by Frank Lloyd Wright in the U.S.A. Siberia was the only place in the 1930s where these ideas were put into practice in the context of Russia's plans to establish heavy industries at a safe distance from its Western frontier."[45]

Writer and traffic engineer Arturo Soria y Mata had argued in the 1880s that settlements tend to develop along traffic routes, and it was his object to further such trends. But his ideas did not become popular until much later, when in the 1930s such Soviet planners as Nikolayevich Varentsov, Nikolai Alexeyevich Milyutin, and others used them in their works. But it was Ivan Ilyich Leonidov who in 1930 provided a more complete representation of Soria y Mata's thinking in his (Leonidov's) plans for a housing estate near the metallurgical complex Magnitogorsk, which is based on an orthogonal grid of roadways, with large square islands designated as green areas, sports facilities, apartment houses, and single high-rise buildings.

Frank Lloyd Wright, the high priest of Organic architecture and a champion of Functionalism, must have been influenced by the ideas of Soria y Mata as evidenced in Wright's reliance on orthogonal geometry in designing Unity Church (Oak Park, Illinois, 1906). Wright was attracted to using intersecting geometric shapes to provide simple ground plans in architecture. The identification of the building with its natural setting, and development of the house from the inside out without regard for traditional canons of form, are the words of Wright's architectural language, symbolized in the concept of "organic building"—a building made from the use of primary materials like wood and stone, and in consideration of human needs and feelings.

To Koenigsberger, who was working in a completely new environment, the ideas of Soria y Mata and Wright's reliance on nature for solving the intractable problems of function and technique in architecture must have appealed. Moreover, the rural landscape of preindustrial India ruled out the use of glass and steel in buildings. "The need was to find solutions with local resources," Koenigsberger admitted. "Mysore has a beautiful granite, which was cheap and, if used correctly, could be strong and beautiful."[46] Koenigsberger's medium for building in India was going to be different from that of Le Corbusier, who had actually apprenticed with Peter Behrens, and whose search for Machine Art made him antinaturalist.[47] It was therefore not surprising that Le Corbusier's Chandigarh turned out to be much different from Koenigsberger's Bhubaneswar, although both cities were also influenced by local culture, climate, and financial support from the Indian government.

By the time Koenigsberger accepted the planning of Bhubaneswar in

1948, he had acquired extensive experience in India. His ideas are perhaps best detailed in the replanning of Jamshedpur in 1943. Koenigsberger felt that in contrast to London, which suffered from 1) overcrowding and outdated housing, 2) inadequate and poor use of open spaces, 3) jumbling of housing and industries compressed between road and rail communications, and 4) traffic congestion, Jamshedpur and so many other Indian cities suffered from 1) overcrowding and poor housing, and 2) no healthy separation between housing and industry. "Any plan which wants to do away with the two defects of insufficient housing and mixture of houses and industries, and which wants to be guided for the future development of recreation areas and traffic must needs be flexible," he concluded in Jamshedpur.[48] To achieve this flexibility, he recommended linear planning, a popular practice in Europe at the time for planning industrial cities.

Originally planned in 1911 by the American Axel S. Kennedy, Jamshedpur had already undergone two subsequent planning efforts, first in 1919 by F. C. Temple, a British sanitary engineer with the government of Bihar and Orissa, and second in 1936 by P. C. Stokes, a British civil engineer, before Koenigsberger was hired in 1943 by the Tata Iron and Steel Company to replan the city for its burgeoning population. Koenigsberger correctly argued that the Indian urban population was rapidly growing, which was borne out in the 1941 census report which claimed that it "is the fact that city life has begun really to appeal to the ordinary middle class or lower middle class Indians."[49] He reasoned that Jamshedpur was likely to grow, even if the Tata plant itself did not expand any more. He argued that the city was likely to grow because other subsidiary industries were moving to the area to take advantage of the industrial facilities of Jamshedpur, and more people were moving into the city to benefit from urban amenities.

Koenigsberger posited the dilemma for Jamshedpur: "On the one hand, bitter experiences, particularly at ESSEN (Ruhr), have demonstrated the dangers of having a large town depending entirely on one group of economically interrelated industries, on the other, the Steel Workers cannot be expected to continue incurring heavy losses for a town which is becoming less and less 'their own.'" He therefore felt it was "desirable to devise a plan which leaves scope for theoretically unlimited growth, but which, at the same time, is not dependent on the attainment of any given size and provides a suitable town organism at any stage of its development."[50]

The centerpiece of such a plan was to be the neighborhood unit around which Jamshedpur was to be planned on the principles of area planning. Area planning meant separating the four urban functions—1) industry [work], 2) housing, 3) recreation and shopping, and 4) transportation—and ensuring that these areas would not be permitted to change "without very serious reasons," and only in accordance with the safeguarding procedure that protected "the town against short-sighted wishes to change the allotment plan for some purpose or other."[51]

Houses in Jamshedpur were to be grouped into neighborhood units, with the city having a total of twelve units, each to be built around a civic center consisting of a small playground, a shopping center, a police station, a medical dispensary with maternity welfare center and nursery, a postoffice, a cinema, a reading room, and a large recreational hall with provisions for an outdoor stage. Drawing on the plan for Plymouth in Britain, which provided for 6,000 to 10,000 persons per neighborhood unit, Koenigsberger provided for varying sizes of neighborhoods ranging from 10,000 to 18,000 persons to suit local economic conditions.

Joined in linear fashion by a central transportation artery, each neighborhood was to be so designed that the civic center could be reached by a walk of not more than 10 minutes without crossing any of the main traffic arteries, which was considered to be a safeguard feature for children on their way to school, or women on their way to the market. Housing in the city was mostly to be of one-storied settlements, which was thought to favor the Indian way of life and climate that allowed for outdoor living for the greater part of the year. "Their requirements of housing space are therefore small," Koenigsberger concluded, "as long as their houses are one storied and provided with suitable court-yard enclosures."[52] In short, Koenigsberger's ideas were based on the Radburn plan (1929), which called for the use of self-contained neighborhood units and separation of pedestrians and vehicles.

So when Koenigsberger finally reached Cuttack by train at three o'clock in the morning of February 18, 1948,[53] he had already implemented in Jamshedpur the master plan that he was going to redraw with slightest modifications for Bhubaneswar. The purely administrative character of Bhubaneswar made it necessary for him to adapt his ideas for an administrative capital. But he would find it far more difficult adapting to the lackadaisical Orissa administration and the recalcitrant Government Architect Julius Vaz, who might have felt usurped by Koenigsberger's arrival in Bhubaneswar.

A gold medalist graduate of J. J. (Sir Jamsetjee Jeejeebhoy Tata) School of Art in Bombay, one of the few institutions to offer a degree in architecture in India before independence, Julius Lazras Vaz[54] was born to Catholic parents who had moved from Portuguese Goa to British Bombay in search of a better life. Before accepting the position of government architect in the Orissa government in 1945, Vaz had worked with the British architectural firm of Gregson, Batley and King in Bombay—a position which he had secured with the help of Claude Batley, who was also the principal of J. J. School of Art. Batley had gained a measure of national prominence by his outspoken criticism of various government-sponsored development schemes for Bombay, long before it became fashionable to sponsor antigrowth and proenvironmental causes in the financial and film capital of India; he had gained national recognition for his designs for the Braborne Cricket Stadium and Mohammad Ali Jinnah's house on Malabar Hill, both in Bombay; he was known in Orissa for his designs of the Orissa Textile Mill at Chaudwar, near Cuttack; and Principal Batley must have exercised his influence in helping secure the position of government architect for his outstanding pupil Vaz in Orissa.

But predominantly Hindu, rural Orissa had very little to offer socially to the cosmopolitan bachelor Vaz, who continued to spend two months of the year with the British company in Bombay, even after accepting the position with the Orissa government. (Apparently, Vaz's contract with the Orissa government allowed him extended leave in the summer months.) Good-humored but intensely private, Vaz took every opportunity he could find to get away from Orissa to be with his mentor and family in cosmopolitan Bombay. Because Koenigsberger's appointment in the Housing Department of the Health Ministry was to keep him mostly in New Delhi, Vaz never really developed a close working relationship with him. For the same reason, Vaz had little opportunity to consult with Koenigsberger for the majority of the government buildings he designed in Bhubaneswar, principal among them being the Assembly, the Secretariat, the Governor's House, the Assembly Hostel for councillors, B. J. B. College, Agricultural and Veterinary colleges, general hospital, and the Rabindra Mandap Auditorium. Vaz ultimately resigned from the Orissa government and moved to Bombay in 1961.

The poor relationship between Koenigsberger and Vaz, Koenigsberger's long absences from Bhubaneswar, and Vaz's repeated sojourns in Bombay were all to influence the final shape of Bhubaneswar. Before

Koenigsberger arrived in Orissa in February 1948, Vaz had detailed his ideas on the capital city in a note to Governor K. N. Katju, who had assumed office on Independence Day, August 15, 1947. In that note, Vaz had argued for establishing a relationship between old Bhubaneswar and the capital city since the urban facilities—drinking water, sanitation, and electricity—would be shared by both populations, and had also argued for checking the unauthorized growth in old Bhubaneswar resulting from the construction of the capital city next door. Some of his other recommendations included the creation of a municipality, prevention of land speculation, a civic survey for the old town, a network of link roads between the two cities, a railway station, an airport for the capital, development of zoning laws, a green belt between the two cities, and the development of the old town into a tourist resort, which Governor Katju considered important for the financial health of the city and of Orissa. It is possible that Vaz was hoping to implement his ideas with the help of Batley and his Bombay-based British company, when the Orissa government brought planner V. C. Mehta on the scene. But he certainly was hoping to implement his ideas with the help of Mehta. "It would be necessary for V. C. Mehta to visit Cuttack again soon . . . so that we can come to [a] final decision [and] correctly earmark the various zones and plots for the essential buildings to be [constructed] in the first phase of construction and also reserve . . . sites for future expansion," he concluded in his note to the governor.[55]

Vaz's layout plan for Bhubaneswar was to be achieved by combining "the 'Radial' and 'Gridiron' methods of planning," and the architecture of the capitol and the rest of the city was to reflect "the local character" of the area. "The Hindu style of architecture would no doubt be adopted for the [capitol] buildings with of course modifications to [take advantage of] modern methods of construction and [to meet new] social [needs]," Vaz had prophesied as early as May 1947.[56] The Catholic Vaz must have realized that the Hindu leadership of Orissa would require the capital city to look very much like the adjacent temple town. Premier Mahtab and Governor Katju and so many other government officials were enthusiastically calling for recreating temple architecture in the capital city. "Every minister became an architect-planner," recalled M. P. Kini, who served as a draftsman in Bhubaneswar. "We had too much government influence. There was no Le Corbusier like person in Bhubaneswar," Kini lamented much later.[57]

Koenigsberger's task in Bhubaneswar therefore was to devise a master plan which would accommodate all the modern needs of bureaucracy in a city with an essentially medieval character, a master plan which would satisfy the emotional needs of the Oriyas while at the same time meeting the new complex needs of modern government, a master plan which would be a blend between the old Kalinga spirit and the new hope for the young province—a nearly impossible task. In his master plan he was to advise the Orissa government to be concerned about reviving the old ideal, but not the outward shape, in new Bhubaneswar. However, by accepting a position in the government of India, Koenigsberger put himself in the difficult position of balancing good planning principles with narrow administrative requirements, a situation from which Le Corbusier was to be free in Chandigarh.

Visiting Bhubaneswar with Vaz and other government officials, Koenigsberger found the site suitable for building, "well drained and having laterite soil, which is good for building and bad for agriculture." Among other advantages Koenigsberger saw in Bhubaneswar were the presence of a functioning airport in the immediate neighborhood of the capital site, ample land for future expansion, adequate water supply from the local rivers, power supply from the nearly completed Hirakud Dam across the Mahanadi River, the close proximity to commercial Cuttack and religious Puri, the healthy climate of the forest country, the cooling sea breezes coming across the delta, close association with the agricultural riches of the delta area, and the position of Bhubaneswar on the main line of the Bengal-Nagpur railway, linking south India with Bengal, Bihar, and the north; while the proposed north-south national highway was to pass through the neighborhood of the new capital. After a series of discussions with the Orissa government, Koenigsberger returned to Bangalore, promising to deliver the first-draft plan for Bhubaneswar as soon as he had received from the government "a complete contour plan of the site."[58]

No sooner had Koenigsberger returned to Bangalore, than he received a telegram from Chief Engineer R. R. Handa, PWD Orissa, directing him to return to Bhubaneswar for the laying of the foundation stone by Prime Minister Nehru on April 13, 1948. He was also directed to complete his master plan in Bhubaneswar instead of in Bangalore. Koenigsberger declared his reasons for remaining in Bangalore to complete the master plan: " . . . I require specially trained draftsmen and good shorthand typists for my work. Both are more easily available here than in your camp. Therefore I believe that for the progress of the work it is better if I remain here and see to it that you get the necessary plans in good time."[59]

Koenigsberger did attend the foundation stone ceremony, where he was able to make Prime Minister Nehru's acquaintence. The Fabian socialist Nehru must have found the refugee Koenigsberger's ideas on social architecture particularly suited for India, since his embattled government was struggling to rehabilitate millions of refugees in Punjab and Bengal. Soon after his meeting with Nehru, Koenigsberger was offered the directorship of housing in the Ministry of Health, government of India—a position which was to give him the opportunity of planning for refugee towns in India, although his new position would also take him to New Delhi, farther away from Bhubaneswar. Contact with Nehru would also help him gain Indian citizenship, which he would retain until 1991.

However, the move to New Delhi in October 1948 did not solve the problem of finding trained staff for Koenigsberger. "The settling down and fitting in my new place and job has proved more difficult than I had anticipated particularly with regard to staff and office accommodation. I am still without technical staff," he complained to Chief Engineer R. R. Handa in Orissa.[60] He, nevertheless, was to keep his promise of delivering the master plan by December 1948, for which he received Rs. 6,000 in compensation plus his traveling expenses and per diem of Rs. 100.

In spite of Koenigsberger's absence from Bhubaneswar, this arrangement proved to be the most economical solution for the Orissa government in securing the master plan for Bhubaneswar, and certainly much more economical than what the Punjab government was to achieve in securing the master plan for Chandigarh. However, there was a down side to this arrangement. In Chandigarh, Le Corbusier was assisted by his cousin Pierre Jeanneret and the English husband-and-wife team of Maxwell Fry and Jane Drew; in Bhubaneswar, Koenigsberger essentially worked on his own, rarely visiting the city and practically having no say in the construction work. In Bhubaneswar, there was no European team for designing the government buildings or housing, for planning of plots or neighborhood units, and for supervising the general architectural control of the city.

The other important difference in the planning of Bhubaneswar and Chandigarh was that, although neither Koenigsberger nor Le Corbusier had committed to living in their respective cities which they helped build, in Chandigarh Maxwell Fry, Jane Drew, and Pierre Jeanneret made a contract to spend three years; and Le Corbusier, even after his contract with the Punjab government ran out, was to remain active in the development of Chandigarh through his cousin Pierre Jeanneret, who stayed on to become the chief architect of Punjab. In the case of Bhubaneswar, first, Koenigsberger's move to New Delhi in October 1948 was to result in distancing him physically and emotionally from Bhubaneswar; and second, Koenigsberger's move to England in 1951 was to remove him completely from the developments in Bhubaneswar.

Koenigsberger's master plan for Bhubaneswar was a variation of his linear city built of interconnected self-contained neighborhood units that he had been practicing from his office in Bangalore—but with a special concern for the new administrative functions of a capital city as opposed to the industrial requirements of Jamshedpur. He provided the philosophical basis for Bhubaneswar in the introduction to his master plan:

> Most provinces in India had to use one of the existing cities as [the] seat of Government and had to make use of these towns for the functions of a capital as good or bad as circumstances permitted. Orissa is in the fortunate position of being able to build a new town specifically designed for the purposes of a capital. It must be demanded and expected that this town will be so planned as to be equally convenient for the functioning of the Government and the everyday life of its inhabitants. This demand represents in a nutshell the programme and terms of reference for the Master Plan of the New Capital of Orissa.
>
> Had this task been set about 20 years ago, the outcome would have been something fundamentally different from the plan submitted with this report. . . .
>
> Formerly, we would have been concerned mainly with two functions: a) representation and symbolisation of power, and b) day-to-day administration in the sense of maintaining law and order and collecting taxes. New Delhi is a typical example of a town designed to suit this conception of Government with a heavy bias on the side of representations.
>
> The modern conception of Government is a much wider one. The administration is expected not only to play an active part but even to be the major driving force in the economic and cultural development of the country. This change of our ideas about good Government is responsible for the enormous expansion of Government activities and for the rapid increase in the numbers of servants which accompanies the expansion.
>
> Another new feature in our conception of Government is the idea of

the popular Government which implies the active participation of the public or their elected representatives in administrative functions. This has resulted in the extinguishing of the formerly very distinct barriers between officialdom and general public. When New Delhi was planned, an "administrative capital" was a town mainly for Government officers and clerks. In 1948, the term "administrative capital" means much more: It describes the lively nerve centre of provincial activities where workers and their representatives, manufacturers, businessmen, scientists, officials and last but [not] the least, politicians meet and collaborate in the development of all aspects of provincial life.[61]

Elsewhere in the master plan, Koenigsberger continued:

To be successful, the planning of the new Capital of Orissa requires popular collaboration of a similar nature. It is, therefore, suggested that the Master Plan be published with an appeal for constructive criticism and practical collaboration. The principles of the plan are simple and convincing enough to gain the support of all citizens who are genuinely interested in the welfare of Orissa and not prejudiced by vested interests.[62]

In predominantly rural Orissa with a literacy rate of less than 30 per cent, and in a province long accustomed to overcentralized colonial administration, Koenigsberger's democratic principles of planning appeared esoteric. The master plan was never published by the Orissa government for a public debate; and even for its own use, the government did not publish the master plan until 1960. Whatever debate on the master plan that could take place took place within closed government circles by government officials who had no experience in urban planning or aesthetic appreciation for architecture, and public participation in planning remained unrealized.

From the beginning Koenigsberger and the Orissa government had conflicting visions. The government in the colonial bureaucratic tradition wanted Bhubaneswar to become a purely administrative colony, with the difference of architecture borrowed from the temple town rather than from imperial New Delhi; Koenigsberger wanted people of many professions to live in modern, progressive Bhubaneswar, people who would provide the city with economic and cultural diversity. Koenigsberger felt that it was important to mix members of other professions with administrators in Bhubaneswar because "Otherwise we might commit the mistake of thinking of it merely in terms of a segregated settlement for officials and thus set the scene for the growth of yet another caste as harmful to the country as the old castes we are trying to abolish."[63] Aware of the Indian city having distinct levels of segregation based on caste and occupation, familiar with the colonial creations of civil lines and cantonments in cities of British India, and sensitive to the Orissa government's opposition to permitting private construction in Bhubaneswar, he put the idea delicately by suggesting that there was a "need of interspersing the residences for senior [Government] Officers with those of private business men of good standing." He emphasized: "I attach the greatest importance to this matter and would consider it fatal to create new castes and social distinctions separating the residences of Government Officers entirely from those of other people."[64]

Using the caste metaphor proved effective with the Orissa government at a time when India was still under the spell of the Gandhian campaign to rid Hinduism of "the curse of untouchability." Moreover, Koenigsberger's egalitarian housing doctrine appeared compatible with Prime Minister Nehru's commitment to create a secular republic with equal rights for all communities in the Indian family. ". . . I think it is a sensible policy of Gov[ernment] not to do anything which might create a class consciousness of any kind—meaning if we have a particular area inhabitated by only Gov[ernment] servants that means we have segregated them from the rest of the public," Minister Ranjit Singh Bariha, PWD, Orissa, noted in a confidential memorandum to Premier Mahtab. He added:

> Provision in the Capital has been made for education and other public amenities without any class distinction just with a view to encourage mixing of all sections of people inhabiting the area. So if we fall in line with that policy we must also allow non-official citizens to have their residences in between Gov[ernment] officers' residences. There are [*sic*] more than one advantage why it is desirable . . . their designs and maintenance and specification[s] will have to [conform] with Gov[ernment] specifications. Consequently, the general appearance of the town as a whole will not be disturbed in any way. When India was ruled by foreigners, Gov[ernment] in order to magnify their importance . . . had maintaine[d] segregation and preserved distinction between the public and the Gov[ernment] officials. I do not think the National Gov[ernment] should follow that principle.[65]

Recognizing the close proximity of Bhubaneswar to Cuttack and Puri, Koenigsberger suggested developing a traffic system which would serve the tri-city area, but cautioned that in the long run the master plan for Bhubaneswar would have to be supplemented by a regional development plan to include "the whole area from Puri and Khurda to Cuttack and to the north bank of the Mahanadi River."[66] In other words, Koenigsberger's master plan was to be dynamic in character to accommodate future changes and growth, and was to serve as a focal point for developing a regional plan for the area—just as his neighborhood unit was to be the focal point for Bhubaneswar, the capital city being formed through a series of interconnected neighborhood units.

The Orissa government wanted Bhubaneswar to be planned for a population of about 20,000, since they did not expect the city to grow beyond that level. Koenigsberger argued that "it was not possible to determine the rate of growth of a new town merely by considering only the requirements of Government institutions and industrial establishments." Arguing that various public institutions, law courts, the university and other educational institutions, banks, insurance companies, hospitals, businesses, small industries, cultural institutions, and entertainment centers will attract people to Bhubaneswar from the surrounding countryside, Koenigsberger warned the Orissa government that it would be a mistake to plan for a settlement of definitely limited size. "A good Master Plan for a new town," he emphasized, "must provide for unlimited expansion, but at the same time organise the town in such a manner that it forms an organic and healthy structure at each stage of its development."[67]

The neighborhood unit was to be used in achieving flexibility in the master plan, which meant that new self-contained neighborhood units could be added to the master plan as the population of the city grew in size. The concept was compatible with the old Hindu system of planning prescribed in the *Silpa Sastras* wherein the site is divided into a series of units of different geographic shapes. The units fix the approximate zones in a village, as well as help in denoting the exact location of a particular building within the zone. The modern concept of the neighborhood unit was designed to achieve a harmonious unity between the advantages of urban life and the benefits of the country. Koenigsberger defined a neighborhood unit in Bhubaneswar to mean "a group of houses, large enough to afford such major urban [amenities] like schools, dispensaries, shopping centres . . . entertainment, public libraries, etc., but at the same time small enough to keep all these amenities in convenient [walking] distances for the inhabitants and to preserve the main advantage of rural life: the immediate neighbourhood to the open country."[68] Moreover, Koenigsberger thought a villagelike neighborhood was expected to make the Indians "understand their civic responsibilities [much better] than a large amorphous city."[69]

Three-fourths of a mile to a side and shaped like a square, Koenigsberger's neighborhood unit was particularly appealing to the paternalistic instincts of Indian leaders, since the concept concentrated on amenities for women and children. "Children must have as good an education as they can receive in large cities and cultural centres, but they should not grow up in the midst of stones and asphalt miles away from fields and forests," reasoned Koenigsberger. He added, "Women should enjoy benefits of large town shopping, of first class medical attention, of adult education, without losing the intimacy of social life in a small country town and without being compelled to walk for many miles while buying their daily household requirements."[70]

To Pandit Nehru, who celebrated his birthday on November 14 as Children's Day, and who had made a personal commitment for the uplifting of Indian women, Koenigsberger's social ideas appeared naturally suited for transforming traditional India into a modern welfare state. Accordingly, in Bhubaneswar every child was to live within one-quarter or one-third of a mile from school and every housewife was to live within half a mile from the civic center where she could do her shopping and also visit medical facilities. But sensitive to poor Indian wages and ramshackle public transportation, Koenigsberger was equally careful in not putting too much distance between a home and a workplace—a distance that could be conveniently covered by using a bicycle or a city bus. However, the home and the workplace were to be clearly separated since the two functions were different in nature. Residential areas were to be at a distance of two miles from work—a cycling distance—and about the same distance from the railway station so as to allow the residents convenient connection with Cuttack and Puri and other neighboring towns; and all the homes in the city were to be within half a mile of a bus station.

To break down the monotony of uniformity in planning neighborhood units, each unit was to be designed individually, thus providing the residents with a feeling of civic pride and personal attachment to their particular neighborhood. As Koenigsberger put it, the neighborhood unit system was to be "an attempt to transplant into the city one of the healthiest features of country and small town life."[71]

Bhubaneswar was to be a horizontal city, even though the higher density of a vertical city allows for a compact life-style and contributes to economy of costs for roads, services, and sewage lines. For Indians accustomed to living outdoors, a vertical city would require providing expensive balconies and verandahs to higher apartments. "Economic considerations as well as the habits of the people speak . . . in favour of the decision to base the development of [Bhubaneswar] on horizontal expansion," Koenigsberger reasoned. "Wealthy people may have two or three storeyed bungalows, offices and business houses may well have 3 or 4 floors. Quarters for clerks, non-gazetted officers, technicians, peons, artisans, small traders and workers must be in ground floor structures." Even if horizontal Bhubaneswar had to become dependent on a "mechanical transport" system the disadvantages of such a dependence would be much less than the evils of multi-storied development.[72]

Bhubaneswar's horizontal plan demanded decentralization, which was to be achieved through the use of the neighborhood unit—but neighborhood units were not to be considered just as a conglomeration of scattered villages; rather, unity in planning was to be achieved by providing a linear pattern of growth as opposed to a radial pattern. Koenigsberger opposed radial planning because he believed that "[t]hinking in terms of circles, hexagons, squares and axes may produce impressive drawings and interesting patterns but will never result in useful towns which are pleasant to live in." Consequently, Koenigsberger's overall design for Bhubaneswar was "based on the simple device of one main traffic artery to which the neighbourhood units [were] attached like the branch of a tree." He informed his Indian clients that unity in planning was to be achieved by using the main artery to "connect the neighbourhood units with the main centre or centres of business and professional life."[73]

Koenigsberger felt that mass transit had made radial planning obsolete, which was useful when walking was the predominant means of transport, necessitating the shortest distance between home and the center of commercial or professional interest. He felt modern towns were too large for pedestrian traffic, and application of mass transit in radial towns created difficulties. "The converging transport routes overlap, and their entanglement at the centre of the 'spider's web' provides daily headaches to Police Departments and traffic experts."[74]

In Bhubaneswar, Koenigsberger planned to confine the pedestrian traffic to the interior of the neighborhood units, while the mass transit was to run on the main artery to which a few branches were to be added later. Such a traffic system was expected to eliminate the use of complicated circular routes, crossings, and bypasses so visible in older cities of the world; and such a system was easily adaptable to "electrical trains, electric trams, electric trolly buses, petrol, diesel oil or . . . gas driven vehicles."[75]

A shortage of electric power and the expense of gasoline have so far prevented the implementation of a mass transit system in Bhubaneswar. However, the linear design of Bhubaneswar allowed each neighborhood unit quick access to the countryside, which was one of the main considerations in planning the city. This could not be achieved in a radial design for the city "because families housed within the interior of the circle will find themselves further and further away from open country as the town develops." Informing the Indians that a Londoner has "to travel one to two hours" to get to the country, Koenigsberger promised that "the citizens of Bhubaneswar should be able to walk out in the open within 10 to 15 minutes even when the town has reached the size of London."[76]

For the predominantly rural Orissa seeking economic growth and development, access to countryside was not the immediate concern. Still, it was a worthy idea for later urban development. Koenigsberger's plan assumed the introduction of mass transit, and for that reason the unity in design in Bhubaneswar was achieved by attaching the neighborhood units to one main artery of urban life and traffic. The other unifying focus for Bhubaneswar was the central group of public buildings—the capitol complex—not necessarily being placed in the center of the city. "Once we give up as impracticable the idea that it should be in walking distance for everybody, it does not matter at which point of the main artery public buildings are situated, as long as they are at all connected with this artery," reasoned Koenigsberger. "It would even be possible to spread out public buildings evenly along the main road."[77]

However, the government of Orissa had a different idea for the capitol complex. The government wanted the main public buildings—the Secretariat, the Assembly, the Governor's Residence—to be built around a square, and dominating the skyline by their pleasing monumental proportions, just as the Lingaraja temple dominated the view in old Bhubaneswar. Koenigsberger considered the suggestion to be "the old idea of the 'Agora' of the Hellenistic town planners which has its parallel in the temple squares of the medieval Indian towns." Instead, he placed the capitol complex on a ridge west of the railway tracks overlooking the residential neighborhoods on the eastern and southern slopes so as to catch the sea breeze as it comes across the low-lying delta lands. Further, he proposed to intersperse government buildings with a library, a museum, social service centers, and meeting places so that the residents of Bhubaneswar would have "a feeling of belonging together and forming part of one great city, however different they may wish to develop the individual neighborhood units in which they reside." Bhubaneswar was to be saved from what happened in New Delhi, where the Secretariat is "a deserted mass of stone on holidays or in the evenings." In Bhubaneswar, the capitol complex "will be more than merely a 'Central Secretariat' and it will form a lively point for all kinds of public life in the town."[78]

Koenigsberger provided access to the capitol by using a simple *T*-pattern of road system, whereby the cross-bar of the *T* formed the connecting link for two rows of residential neighborhoods, while the stem of the *T* served as a broad avenue lined with trees and park strips, connecting the capitol complex with the business center in front of the railway station. Drawing on the teachings of his German instructors and mentors, Koenigsberger emphasized order, functionality, and simplicity in planning the traffic layout for Bhubaneswar. Familiar with the diversity of traffic on Indian roads—pedestrians, animals, buses, automobiles—he correctly argued that any traffic system "which serves so many different purposes and masters cannot serve any one of them perfectly." To achieve a better road system, "we shall have to analyse the functions which roads serve in particular localities and design them with special regard to such functions. In some instances, we shall have to limit the use of certain roads to restricted groups of users with the object of creating what may be termed as specialized types of roads."[79]

So in Bhubaneswar Koenigsberger came up with seven different types of roads for seven different groups of users and seven different functions. Accordingly, Bhubaneswar was to have: 1) sidewalks, laid out mainly inside the neighborhoods for pedestrian traffic; 2) parkways, laid out informally in recreation areas for strolling and enjoyment of nature; 3) bicycle paths designed to connect residences with work places, but without blind corners and dangerous intersections with fast moving traffic; 4) minor housing streets, designed to interconnect houses in such a manner that vehicular traffic would not get on them (e.g., through the use of cul-de-sacs); 5) major housing streets, intended to collect the local traffic from several minor housing streets and having additional width to accommodate vehicular traffic; 6) main roads, designed for the smooth flow of fast traffic between neighborhoods and workplaces; and 7) main arteries, also intended for fast traffic, but with additional lanes to accommodate slower traffic. Koenigsberger wanted the main artery to have several lanes for pedestrians, bicyclists, bullock carts, slow moving motor traffic, and mass transit, each type of traffic using its own lane.

Over eighty percent of all roads were to be housing streets, and the rest traffic streets and a main artery. With the exception of bicycle paths and sidewalks, all roads in Bhubaneswar were to have avenue trees. Also, there were to be no shopping streets in Bhubaneswar, because the "connection of shopping activities with roads intended primarily for movement of traffic is an unhealthy idea." Instead, Bhubaneswar was provided with shopping squares "accessible from the main roads, but at the same time clearly separated from them, so that fast traffic can [move] undisturbed and people can buy their provisions at leisure without danger of being run over." The shopping squares resembling traditional Indian bazaars "were never meant to be thorough fares [*sic*] for fast moving traffic, but concentrated areas for undisturbed trade."[80]

Clearly it escaped Koenigsberger's notice that Indian bazaars have traditionally thrived on main streets where people make convenient stops for shopping. He nevertheless hoped that his functionally differentiated road system would render the use of roundabouts, traffic lights, and traffic police unnecessary;[81] it is quite another matter that, given the socio-economic and educational levels of the majority of the population, such directive traffic signals are routinely ignored in India. For the Oriya not even accustomed to dirt roads, moreover, distinguishing between a hierarchy of roads proved nothing less than a nightmare. Although Koenigsberger's road system was never fully implemented in Bhubaneswar, his ideas were later adopted by Albert Mayer and Le Corbusier in Chandigarh, not necessarily with any better results.

Success of any town plan in the end depends on how well it is understood by the citizens and how well it is supported by the municipal government. As a result of the predominantly rural character of Orissa, the development of local bodies in that province remained lamentably poor, even after the introduction of Local Self Government by Viceroy Ripon in 1882. There existed only five municipalities in Orissa in 1948—Balasore, Jajpur, Cuttack, Kendrapara, and Puri—all with a limited franchise and a narrow revenue base. The Orissa Municipal Act was not passed until 1950, and soon thereafter Bhubaneswar was upgraded to the status of a municipality. Even so, a municipality remained the weakest local body in India, which was confirmed by the Indian Planning Commission in the *Third Five Year Plan* (1961): "At the local level, municipal administrations alone can undertake satisfactorily the task of providing the services needed for development in urban areas, expansion of housing and improvement in living conditions. Most municipal administrations are not strong enough to carry out these functions."[82]

Although familiar with the poor performance of municipal bodies in India, Koenigsberger was hoping that in Bhubaneswar each neighborhood unit would have "as much administrative autonomy as can be possibly given to so small a unit." Collectively, the neighborhood units were to form a municipal council.[83] But his assurance that the proposed administrative autonomy of the neighborhood units would not result in "splitting up the capital into a number of rival villages"[84] did not persuade the Orissa government, which felt more comfortable with the old colonial practice of centralized control.

Although Koenigsberger's agreement with the Orissa government did not call for detailed architectural schemes and designs for Bhubaneswar, he felt that he had to provide architectural principles which he considered important for the overall urban design of the capital. Familiar with the frequent power shortages so endemic in Indian cities, and also familiar with the poor design of the government buildings in New Delhi, he wanted to use in Bhubaneswar architectural designs which would facilitate both the use of air conditioning and natural ventilation to take advantage of the city's cool southeasterly winds for most of the year. Accordingly, he provided the following design principles:

> All rooms should have through ventilation, inner passages should be avoided. Doors and windows require iron bars or collapsible shutters besides heat resisting shutters and glazing which will make it possible to ventilate rooms during the night and retain the cool air inside them during the day. All outside walls should be protected against direct sun. It is not obligatory to provide deep verandahs on both sides of each room as it was customary in India during the 19th century. Deep verandahs are an expensive remedy and if provided on both sides they affect the privacy and the lighting conditions of an office most unfavourably. New methods of preventing the exposure of outside walls to direct radiation by the provision of protective cushions [to] cool air

have been developed recently in several large buildings in Rio de Janeiro where climatic conditions are similar to those at Bhubaneswar. The methods used recently in Brazil are recommended for careful study and adaptation to Indian conditions.[85]

The abundance of sand and limestone near Bhubaneswar dictated their use in construction of the city's public buildings. But Koenigsberger was opposed to the traditional Indian solid stone masonry because of its ill effects on lighting and ventilation. Instead, he recommended using stone as "facing" or "skin" for steel or concrete frame structures. From the beginning, carports were to be an integral part of the design of the modern public buildings to protect cars from the punishing sun. Also, to avoid endless corridors and large distances between offices so common in government buildings, public buildings were expected to be three or four stories high. This would elevate the group of public buildings over the surrounding areas of one- and two-story residential buildings, thus "providing a pleasant control accent in the overall picture of the town landscape."[86]

Koenigsberger felt that public buildings designed in accordance with his recommendations would have "little need to worry about questions of style. The functions these buildings have to serve and the local conditions which govern their design are particular to Orissa." He was opposed to "the clothing of modern buildings in the fancy dress of decorative features borrowed from the past decades" which had no relevance to the present. Bhubaneswar was to be "a modern city intended to stand proudly by the side of its famous medieval sister." The planning of the capital city was to be separate from the temple town so as to prevent the temple town from getting absorbed by the capital city. The new city was to have its own character, conditioned by the locality and the needs of modern administration. Modern buildings could not be decorated "with the architectural trimmings of past centuries."[87]

The same principles were to govern the design of residential buildings, the major difference being that air conditioning would not be required as much in residential buildings as in public buildings, and that most units in the residential area would not be more than one or two stories. Density was to be achieved by avoiding free-standing, unattached houses so that Bhubaneswar could grow into a modern city and "not remain a village nor even a garden city." Neither the Indian family nor the municipality had the financial strength to afford large gardens, which require water and electricity. High residential density achieved through closely spaced houses and small sites "grouped in rows of 8 or 10," argued Koenigsberger, would not "result in overcrowding and slum formation, because the Master Plan makes ample provision for publicly owned spaces." Terrace housing and closely situated open spaces were to make up for the loss of individual large gardens. "Rows of houses of pleasing proportions lend more dignity to streets and squares than unconnected groups of individual small cottages spaced closely in small compounds," Koenigsberger reasoned. Edinburgh and Jaipur were good examples of terrace housing that added to the beauty of street frontages; and Dadar (Bombay) and Karolbagh (New Delhi) were bad suburban examples of scattered homes and bungalows that created a distorted and uninteresting picture. Where free-standing houses were necessary, continuity in appearance was to be "retained by connecting individual bungalows with the help of collonades [*sic*], pergolas, walls, etc., as it has been done successfully in some streets of New Delhi."[88]

The master plan made no provision for heavy industry or a large labor population because Bhubaneswar's main industry was to be government service. However, the master plan provided for service industries which cater to the daily needs of citizens, for example, laundries, auto-repair shops, tailoring, woodworking, canning, and so on. The service industries were to be located in nonresidential areas, although housing for workers was to be intermixed with those of government employees, traders, and artisans.

For controlling architectural developments in the city, and for preventing land speculation, Koenigsberger recommended leasing plots for 99 years as opposed to selling them outright. Considering the social and economic control which results from leasing land, the Orissa government quickly adopted the policy. Moreover, Koenigsberger felt that the land lease policy would prevent "parasite" settlements from developing in the neighborhood of Bhubaneswar, which normally spring up to take advantage of the urban amenities of a city. In addition, Koenigsberger suggested the acquisition of all surrounding lands by the government.[89] He even submitted a draft for the Orissa Town Planning Act that mandated "ruthless" regulation of any development in Bhubaneswar and its surroundings,[90] but in the end no government effort or urban scheme that ignored economic considerations could prevent the development of unauthorized colonies in the city. In fact, unauthorized developments and land speculation started in Bhubaneswar long before the master plan was ready. Governor Katju expressed his concern:

> Already the news that Bhubaneswar has been chosen as the Capital of Orissa has given rise to enormous speculation in land. . . . Land values have gone up . . . as much as sixteen hundred percent in some cases. I see no reason why the land owners in Bhubaneswar should be allowed to keep in their pocket[s] all these enormous profits and get this unearned income simply because Bhubaneswar has been chosen as the capital site. I think this is a fit case where Government should . . . acquire all land under the Land Acquisition Act . . . at the current pre-capital rates, and then dispose of [*sic*] the same [later] . . . at suitable . . . market prices and apply all the profit . . . for the betterment and improvement of . . . Bhubaneswar. . . .[91]

Koenigsberger strongly believed that town planning legislation alone could create the conditions "under which [his] plan [could] become a reality."[92] But the old colonial practice of controlling socioeconomic problems through legislation has not succeeded in postindependence India. Governor Katju possibly understood that when he proposed to expand the economic base of the city by encouraging tourism and other economic activities which would result in rising standards of living. He wrote after his first trip to Bhubaneswar:

> There should be an industrial survey of the old town with a view to finding out the best methods for providing employment to the residents. The sole occupation at present seems to be that of squeezing and living on the pilgrims. . . . I am struck by the possibility of establishing numerous health resorts in Orissa. . . . Everybody knows that Switzerland practically lives upon two industries: the tourist industry and . . . watches. . . . We can, with the beautiful climate of Puri, of Gopalpur, of Bhubaneswar, of Jajpur and other places of great reknown, make them all into wonderful health resorts attracting a large number of well-to-do people who would visit us and bring us money.[93]

Orissa did not experience an economic renaissance. In fact, wages were so low that government employees could not be expected to afford housing in Bhubaneswar. Fearing that his master plan for Bhubaneswar might suffer the same fate that Ernst May's mass housing scheme had suffered in Frankfurt because of unaffordable rents resulting from high construction costs, Koenigsberger suggested calculating rents for housing in Bhubaneswar based on 10 percent of salaries rather than on the actual construction costs.

He suggested two ways of making up the deficit. In the first instance, all residential quarters in Bhubaneswar were to be treated as a single, undivided estate, and rents from the higher wage earners and the earnings from the lease of commercial and residential properties to private parties were expected to make up the deficit in the collection of rents from the lower income groups. In the other instance, housing for lower income groups was to be fully subsidized by the government; and housing for higher income groups was to be combined with housing for businessmen and commercial properties, thereby attracting private capital for construction in Bhubaneswar. But Koenigsberger's suggestion for managing private capital through a government controlled joint stock company appeared confusing,[94] and there was no realistic provision made for the recovery of construction costs in Bhubaneswar.

The last provision in the Bhubaneswar master plan called for a memorial for Mahatma Gandhi, who had been assasinated by a Hindu militant in New Delhi just before sundown on January 30, 1948. The Gandhi Memorial Pillar was to "form the spiritual centre of the new town." Similar in purpose to the pillars erected all over northern India by the Mauryan ruler Ashoka to spread the teachings of Buddhism, the Gandhi Pillar was intended "to remind [the] citizens of Bhubaneswar of the teachings of Gandhiji [on] which the town was founded."[95]

Made from reinforced concrete, the Gandhi Pillar was to be a hundred feet tall, standing as a landmark and greeting people from afar. It was to be flood-lit at night and crowned by a special torch or light, reminiscent of the pillars in front of ancient Hindu temples. The concrete core of the pillar was to be covered with local stone, and "decorated by the best sculptures of India." The stem of the pillar was to be engraved with scenes from Gandhi's life and his teachings.[96]

But to extol the Gandhian teaching of religious and communal tolerance, the Orissa government wanted to place the pillar next to a cluster of religious shrines belonging to the Hindus and Muslims; Koenigsberger objected to the location, arguing that "the new India [was] intended to be a secular state." The proper place for the Gandhi Memorial "obviously" belonged next "to the Representative Assembly of Orissa and to other public buildings of this type rather than [next] to mosques and temples."[97]

The conflict between Koenigsberger's modernism and the Orissa government's traditionalism is possibly best reflected in Koenigsberger insisting that the Gandhi Pillar should "not be an exact replica of an Ashoka Column" and the Orissa government's wanting to duplicate the Ashoka Pillar. The Orissa government had vetoed Koenigsberger's drawing for the Gandhi Memorial on the grounds that it was "un-Indian" in character. Koenigsberger responded to his Indian clients in the Bhubaneswar master plan by declaring: "It is the ideal which we want to revive, [and] *not* the outward shape."[98] But the conflict between the "ideal" and the "shape" was to remain the enduring theme for Bhubaneswar.

·5·

THE CAPITAL CITY

Bhubaneswar as the capital city of Orissa was to be a secular city. But the modern mission of creating a capital was shaped by a rural vision, whose origins go back to the days of antiquity when city building was considered a religious act. Traditionally, villages and cities were laid out in India to reflect the pattern of *Devnagari*, the city of gods. These villages and towns were generally walled, with two wide main streets dominating the otherwise irregular and narrow street system, while the palace, fort, or temple formed the core area. Residential areas were divided along class and caste lines, and the internal layout of the houses was determined by building regulations specified in the *Silpa Sastras*. Kautilya's *Arthasastra* provided the details of urban administration. As the home of gods, the city represented eternal values and revealed divine possibilities, which were purportedly present in the old temple town of Bhubaneswar, and which the Oriya leaders wanted to recreate in the new capital.

The desire to recreate the city of the old in Bhubaneswar was further reinforced by the discovery of the ruins of an ancient city near the capital site. "It is now definite that there was another Capital underneath the site where the new Capital is being built," Premier Harekrushna Mahtab enthusiastically reported to Prime Minister Jawaharlal Nehru. He added that the Orissa government had "decided to preserve these remains as monuments . . . for the public to know and feel that there was a capital underneath the present site."[1]

Driven by the sacred desire to duplicate the buried ancient city as a *tirtha* (a religious crossing or place), the Oriyas hoped to preserve the old memory in the new city—a desire sanctioned by the Hindu polytheistic view, which calls for important events and places to be seen from many perspectives and to be widely shared and duplicated. For planner Otto Koenigsberger, this view stood in marked contrast to his Western monotheistic insistence that important events represent a singular, more linear view of history.

The hold of Hindu tradition was so strong on the Indian that, while laying the foundation stone for the capital a year earlier on April 13, 1948, even Cambridge-educated Nehru could not resist admitting that the creation of a city was a "godlike" act, and that he was most happy "to be associated . . . with the construction of the city. . . ." Declaring New Delhi to be a city of big buildings "meant to impress people," and designed to preserve imperial rule by separating the British from the Indians, Nehru emphasized that Bhubaneswar "would not be a city of big buildings for officers and rich men without relation to common masses. It would accord with our idea of reducing differences between the rich and the poor." Further, the new capital would embody the beautiful art of Orissa, and it would "be a place of beauty . . . so that life might become an adjunct to beauty."[2]

Even though the objectives in New Bhubaneswar had changed, the realities behind them remained the same. The mixture of divinity, power, and personality still made for a powerful potion in fueling the passions of the Indians: a potion which had fueled the passions for the creation of the old temple town but which had to be weighed anew in terms of ideology and culture to create the new capital city, and poured into fresh civic, national, and environmental concerns. Religion, with its many symbols, was yet to play an important role in shaping New Bhubaneswar.

Whatever the attitude towards Bhubaneswar, the dichotomy between the old and the new became almost a category in the Kantian sense in terms of which the city came to be viewed. Both the temple town and the capital city exerted influence on each other to establish their dominance. If in time the capital city was to replace the old *jajmani* (the patronage system of barter prevalent in most traditional Indian village economies) relationships with commercialized ones in the temple town, the temple town was to attract numerous educated professionals from the capital city as the new patrons of monasteries and temples. It is not uncommon to find a popular ascetic or a religious teacher providing political forecasts to some government official who is his patron, or to find a government official receiving privileged information from a religious person about the political climate in the old town. Premier Mahtab himself provided financial support to several religious organizations in old Bhubaneswar, and refused to remove his residence from the temple town to the capital city, even while serving in the government.[3]

It was precisely this encounter and reciprocal interaction between the two social entities—the town and the temple—that intellectually and emotionally separated the planner Koenigsberger from his Indian clients in Bhubaneswar. Reared in the tradition of the German Reformation, which, in the words of A. G. Dickens, "was an urban event,"[4] Koenigsberger viewed the city as an autonomous body, having its own law and jurisdiction, political independence, right of self-determination, and an organized sense of communal relationships along secular lines. Having experienced no Hindu Reformation, the Indian town retained its close relationship with religion, and continued to grow more or less organically with the people living together more or less without a sense of community obligation, the principle of city-residence never transcending primordial ties to clan, caste, or village.

The rise of urban civilization and the fall of traditional religion are two enduring modern themes. Urbanization constitutes a massive change in the way people live together, which became possible in its contemporary form only with scientific and technological advances. Secularization, another equally important movement, marked a change in the way people grasp and understand their life together; and it occurred only when cosmopolitan confrontations and conflicts of city life forced people to question the validity of prevailing myths.

Steeped in the ideology of the Reformation and armed with scientific inventions, Western planners and architects experimented in social and urban engineering to design the secular city, no longer concerned with patterning their concepts after the Heavenly City. But the movement for secularization did not necessarily aim at persecuting religion; rather, it aimed at privatizing religion, thereby creating the conditions that eventually led to the rejection of the sacred city and acceptance of the secular city.[5] These intellectual and social movements have been slow in making their impact felt in India, and therefore the symbiotic relationship between the town and the temple has survived much longer.

It has been suggested that two chief characteristics of a modern metropolis are electronic communications and rapid mass transportation—made possible by scientific inventions—which have produced *anonymity* and *mobility*. Both *anonymity* and *mobility* are essential in shaping the character of the secular city, while at the same time both are under attack by religious and nonreligious critics for making city life vacuous.[6] Whereas each group has its own separate reasons for attacking city life, practically everyone agrees that urbanization leads to depersonalization.

Similarly, it has been suggested that *pragmatism* and *profanity* constitute the two main components of style of the secular city.[7] *Pragmatism* suggests that an individual in a modern city is concerned with efficiency. The test of shape and style of a modern city is whether it will yield desired results in practice. *Profanity*, on the other hand, literally puts an individual outside the temple, forcing him to engage in "this world." *Profanity* provides an earthly perspective on life, forcing an individual to take a nonreligious, not necessarily a sacrilegious, view of his daily life. Anonymity, mobility, pragmatism, and profanity therefore become the four pillars of the secular city, and are viewed not as obstacles but "avenues of access to modern man."[8]

Paradoxically, these four pillars of the secular city are the modern equivalents of the old gods of destruction, and they must be reconciled to modern man's need to maintain balance between nature and city life. "Otherwise," as urbanist Lewis Mumford has warned us, "the sterile gods of power, unrestrained by organic limits or human goals, will remake man in their own faceless image and bring human history to an end."[9]

So while the secular city removes religion from its calculus, it is nevertheless bounded by a religious perspective which continues to renew the human spirit for interpreting new scientific discoveries on a human scale. After all, "Man grows in the image of his gods, and up to the measure they have set."[10] It is, therefore, not surprising that Bhubaneswar has grown in the image of its gods, and up to the measure they set. The development of the capital represents that struggle, on the one hand, between man and his gods, and on the other, between man and technology. The final shape and style of Bhubaneswar bears as much the imprint of local religion as that of rational, scientific knowledge imported from the West.

The planner Otto Koenigsberger hoped to reconcile in Bhubaneswar the conflict between scientific rationalism and religious symbolism—between the town and the temple—by using the neighborhood unit as the basic building block. On the principle that, if one looks after the pennies, the pounds will look after themselves, it seemed obvious to him that if the neighborhood unit were healthy, harmonious, and autonomous, then the life of the city as a whole would also become healthy, harmonious, and autonomous. Such a neighborhood unit was to be self-contained and close to the countryside: the presence of industry was a disturbance.

But for the Oriyas, the secular city, with its distinct modern structure, cultural milieu, urban refinement, and rational human behavior was largely a new phenomenon, in which the traditional parochial structure was strained to the breaking point. The ruling priest class of old Bhubaneswar had opposed urban growth of the temple town to preserve its power and the religiously inspired traditional social structure. The response of the priest class in old Bhubaneswar was consistent with the traditional brahman opposition to towns, since urbanism was equated with secularism—no doubt a threat to brahman power. Later when brahmans were forced into compromising with urbanization and the secular power of the kshatriyas, they did so only after making certain that the highest ritualistic rank belonged to the brahmans in the *varna* (Hindu class) system. Clearly, the construction of the capital city next door was not good news for the priest class of old Bhubaneswar.

But the "brown sahibs" of the new state were quick to take a lesson from the history of old Bhubaneswar, and restricted the population of new Bhubaneswar to no more than 20,000 so as to secure their own power and the administrative character of the capital city. In large cities it is difficult to develop human relationships when so many inhabitants are newcomers; and in large cities it is difficult to maintain class cohesiveness and caste solidarity; and in large cities men are forced to live in different parts of the city where their position is threatened. Social amenities, such as schools, temples, parks, and so on, come under pressure of a large population. Consequently, there developed among the administrative elite at Bhubaneswar a fear of the urban mob, angry, sullen, and impure. How could a city like that become "a little commonwealth?"

Koenigsberger's answer in Bhubaneswar was to divide the city into small manageable neighborhood units, sufficiently compact to preserve a sense of community. The concept of the neighborhood unit was thus, paradoxically, based on the ideal of a rural vision. The rural community was the norm, and the town was thought of as an unnatural growth on the face of the gods' countryside and all that was sacred in the area. As Koenigsberger himself admitted, a village-like neighborhood was likely to make the Indians feel much more comfortable with their civic responsibilities than a large "amorphous" city. "There is . . . a live tradition of rural self-government (the so-called 'village panchayats') and people are used to thinking in terms of village communities." He added, "For them neighborhood units of the new towns [in India] form the best possible link with the type of community life they know from their villages."[11]

However, Koenigsberger was aware from his European experience that the neighborhood unit was not without its faults. Just as ethnic and racial considerations in the West had turned the neighborhood unit into a "ghetto formation," so, too, the Indian caste system served as a sanction for segregated communities. Moreover, urban settlers in India "are [no] more than one generation removed from the land, and most of them still have rural family ties." The solution that he offered in Bhubaneswar was to provide in "each neighbourhood a cross-section of the population, taking good care to have each social and professional group represented in it roughly in [proportion to] its relative strength in the whole community"[12]—a solution reminiscent of Western man's effort to perform social surgery in his segregated neighborhoods with the cutting knife of scientific knowledge.

Koenigsberger had provided the Orissa government with the master plan for Bhubaneswar. What remained to be done was the design of important buildings in the capitol complex, the planning of residential plots, the detailing of neighborhood units, and the general architectural treatment of various blocks, squares, parks, and so on. In Bhubaneswar, Koenigsberger's contract did not call for architectural planning, nor did he have an architectural team to implement his plan. The Orissa government had committed the same mistake which the Punjab government would commit later in Chandigarh: that of not employing planners and architects as one. Nevertheless, Koenigsberger in the remaining three years of his stay in India made various efforts to put together a team of architects and train them in modern design principles.

Concerns for the architectural style of the capital city had occupied many in the Orissa government. As early as August 1948, the Governor's Office sent a telegram to Secretary R. R. Handa, Orissa Public Works Department (PWD), inquiring about the decisions relating to "the general [architecture] of the principal buildings in the new Capital."[13] Soon after submitting the master plan, Koenigsberger himself wrote from Delhi, where he had taken up a position in the central government, to PWD Minister Ranjit Singh Bariha, expressing his concern for the architectural treatment of his master plan: "The town planning for the new capital is of course not completed with the submission of my detailed report. A good deal of site planning remains to be done. Further neighbourhood units must be developed, the station square and the area of the public buildings laid out and so on." He added, "I am anxious to continue with this work as speedily as possible. . . ."[14] In the same letter he informed the minister of the prefabricated 'small houses' which had been developed by the government of India's Department of Housing for low-income government employees, and which he hoped to use in Bhubaneswar to cut construction costs.

Adding to Koenigsberger's anxiety was the announcement by the Punjab government that it had hired Le Corbusier, his cousin Pierre Jeannearet, and the English husband-and-wife team of Maxwell Fry and Jane Drew for the planning and architectural design of Chandigarh. That decision of the Punjab government would inevitably place Chandigarh in competition with Bhubaneswar—a circumstance which made the lack of qualified architects in Orissa all the more noticeable. Koenigsberger immediately wrote to Chief Engineer C. M. Bennett, Capital Project, that "I do not propose that Orissa should go to the same lengths [as Punjab], but it is undoubtedly necessary that . . . [Government] Architect [Julius Vaz] be given adequate staff to cope with [the architectural] tasks [in Bhubaneswar]."[15] Later, he suggested that the Orissa government should develop a proper architectural office, sufficiently staffed to manage efficiently architectural work in the capital, "have it trained in Delhi [under himself], and then transferred [back] to Bhubaneswar."[16]

In making such a recommendation Koenigsberger was clearly concerned about retaining some measure of control over architectural developments in Bhubaneswar. His concerns focused on two issues: one was the planning of the area that lay between old Bhubaneswar and the capital city; and the other was the design of public buildings in the capitol complex. Planning of the area between the two sister cities was important because that would "prevent the development of two entirely different standards of living and housing in the old and new town[s]." As for developing an architectural design for the capitol complex and other public buildings in the city, he felt that Vaz could not possibly handle the job single-handedly. Besides, Koenigsberger felt that it was necessary for Vaz to visit him in Delhi and "work with proper staff which I can recruit for him if the Government of Orissa accords the necessary sanction."[17] This was yet another example of the popular Indian belief that all wisdom must be found in the center, ironically provided this time by an outsider.

Julius Vaz did spend some time in Delhi with Koenigsberger, however. But the two men remained separate in their vision of new Bhubaneswar. Vaz felt that Bhubaneswar planned as a linear city would give the impression of "a very elo[n]gated town" when it expanded with population. He also called for more space for government offices in the master plan, and felt that the shopping center needed to be expanded by reducing the number of residential plots. As for the neighborhood concept, he felt that it promoted monotony in the capital city. But above everything else, he disagreed with Koenigsberger on the architectural design of Bhubaneswar. The Lingaraja temple in the old town and the nearby Dhauli hills and caves at Khandagiri-Udayagiri hills, he felt, should be treated as "vantage points" in the master plan.[18]

The record on the prevailing thinking in Orissa government circles strongly suggests that the demand for making the capital city conform to the temple town was widespread, and Architect Vaz must have been influenced by that thinking. Moreover, Governor Asaf Ali had clearly instructed Vaz and Minister Ranjit Singh Bariha, PWD, "that the architecture of the new capital should conform to the . . . ancient art of Orissa." The governor had also called Koenigsberger's modern design of the Gandhi Memorial unsuitable for Bhubaneswar. In fact, to ensure that the architectural design of the capital city conform to the temple town, the governor had his office send the two volumes of R. L. Mitra's *Antiquities of Orissa* (1880) to Vaz. The governor demanded that "Dr. Koenisberger [*sic*] may now be asked to give his definite suggestions on this point."[19]

Koenigsberger's response was that since "the new India is intended to be a secular state, I do not think that there is a strong case for associating . . . religious institutions in some way or [another] with the Gandhi Memorial, to say nothing of the fact that a proposal of this kind would meet with almost unsurmountable practical difficulties."[20] For the same reason, he was opposed to associating the rest of the architecture of the capital city with the temple town, although he was prepared to include important religious monuments of the old town in his master plan to "form interesting view-points at the end of our main road."[21]

In opposing making the capital city a twin of the temple town, Koenigsberger was not against the practical proposal of planning for old Bhubaneswar. But his training in practical architecture and respect for order moved him in the direction of keeping the functions of the two towns separate. Moreover, he feared that modern urban amenities of the capital city would encourage the growth of parasitic communities in the area; and although he had moved to Delhi in his new position, he was not inclined to surrender the implementation of his master plan to the ill-trained, government-run Public Works Department. On the other hand, he found it increasingly difficult to control architectural design of Bhubaneswar from Delhi.

Visiting Bhubaneswar for the sixth time in June 1950, Koenigsberger noted that the long intervals between his visits to the capital provided "a good opportunity of observing and gauging the progress of the work." He added:

> In the two years since the site clearing and construction work was started at Bhubaneswar about 1800 houses have been constructed or are nearing completion. About 30 miles of roads have been laid, 7 1/2 miles of which are main roads of 34' width with tarred surface. Avenue trees have been planted, street lighting provided and a temporary water supply is functioning. . . . the total expenditure incurred so far is [Rs.] 1.1 crores. [1 crore = 10 million.]
>
> On the whole, this picture compares favourably with other towns started in India during [the] last two or three years, particularly with Faridabad [Haryana], Rajpura [West Bengal], Kalyan[i] [West Bengal], Gandhidham [Gujrat] and Chandigarh [Punjab].[22]

However, Koenigsberger was less sanguine about old Bhubaneswar and about the architectural design of the buildings in the capitol complex. "The most urgent problem which has to be dealt with . . . is the integration of [the] old and new towns and the control over . . . the old town and the area between the two settlements . . ." he noted in his report. To maintain the integrity of the master plan, he urged the Orissa government "to exercise the necessary [architectural] controls with the help of the existing legislation," and called for an "early enactment of a Town Planning Bill," which he hoped would "solve a multitude of problems and provide . . . means to guide urban developments (in Orissa)."[23]

The same legislation was also expected to discourage the growth of parasitic communities near the capital city—communities which would take "advantage of the civic amenities of Bhubaneswar without contributing to their costs." He warned the Orissa government that if it did not take charge of the land surrounding the capital city, all improvements made in Bhubaneswar "will soon be completely obliterated by slum developments in the immediate neighborhood." Emphasizing that planning of new Bhubaneswar must include old Bhubaneswar, he recommended that old Bhubaneswar must become a self-contained town with standards of living comparable to those in the capital, and that "construction [should] take place only where it is desirable in the interest of the planned development of the capital as a whole."[24]

Requesting the Orissa government to furnish him with a survey of old Bhubaneswar and of the area that existed between Bindu Lake and the Railway Station so that he could "prepare a plan for the integration of the existing town into the development of the whole capital area," he warned the government to avoid the mistakes of New Delhi, where "the spacious luxuries of [the capital city existed] side by side with the slums of Old Delhi."[25] In Bhubaneswar, both towns must achieve the same standards of living, diversity of occupations, and provision of amenities.

Koenigsberger felt that legislative controls were imperative for achieving such a noble urban objective. The Punjab government was already contemplating such legislation for their "city beautiful" at Chandigarh, patterned after the British Town and Country Planning Act of 1947.[26] Municipal acts introduced by the British government in India in the late nineteenth century had not proved effective in regulating urban development, largely because municipalities lacked both trained personnel and financial resources to enforce legislation. The Indians viewed the British act of 1947 as a legal tool for modernizing and rehabilitating slums and blighted areas of their cities.[27] It is another matter that in Indian cities, where a very mixed pattern of land use is the rule rather than the exception, it is increasingly difficult to secure public understanding and support for a zoning ordinance, whose purpose is, in the main, to discourage additional mixing of activities.

Recognizing the special Indian situation, one urban planner has concluded "that the [Indian] condition of public administration renders the enforcement of elaborate controls on private development too difficult to be worth the effort." Instead, he has argued that, "[g]iven the severe shortages of money, administrative capabilities, and political support available for plan implementation, planning and development organizations [in India] must forego the delusion that private development can be effectively controlled and concentrate their efforts and resources on direct public investment."[28]

The Orissa government finally did pass the Town Planning and Improvement Trust Act in 1956, but it was not until 1964 that it became operational when the first qualified town planner was hired. The reason given was scarcity of funds. Even so, the department became tied up in political knots, since politicians interfered and prevented the authorities from upsetting their constituents who had illegally occupied government land.

However, writing his report in June 1950, when India still moved under the old colonial momentum that called for legislation as a remedy for all ills, Koenigsberger was unaware of the later crystalized thinking on Indian cities; and his own experience was too deeply rooted in the Western tradition to penetrate the reality of Indian cities. Nevertheless, he felt that something had to be done to streamline the conflicting functions of three authorities—the PWD, the Notified Capital Area Committee, and the Collector—all having powers to grant licenses for building in Bhubaneswar. Consequently, he proposed:

1. That applications for building should be accompanied by a certificate of approval from the Chief Engineer, PWD, stating that the proposed building fits into the development plan of the capital area.
2. That construction on leased land must be completed within 18 months of obtaining the lease; failure to complete construction was to result in cancelling of lease and the land was to be repossessed by the government.
3. That land values in the capital were to be frozen at the existing market rates so as to prevent land speculation later when the government was ready to acquire additional lands for building.[29]

To buttress his proposal, he cited the familiar British Ordinance of 1939 that froze land values in London at the levels of 1939, and the British Town and Country Planning Act of 1947, which replaced the 1939 Ordinance with the same objective of transferring all development rights of nonurban land to the state.

As for designing the capitol complex—which was to contain the Gandhi Memorial, the Assembly, the Secretariat, the State Public Library, the Museum, and the Accountant General's Office—Koenigsberger felt that the choice lay between hiring a reputable architectural firm or "strengthening" the architectural unit of the Orissa PWD. He explained: "The second alternative will be less expensive but it will be successful only if the term 'strengthening' is interpreted in the right way. It should mean not merely the employment of some additional staff but also the training of the existing Architect [Julius Vaz] and his staff to cope with the very important task of the design of the Capitol buildings."[30]

Driven both by personal pride to see his master plan for Bhubaneswar translated into an architecturally attractive city, and the altruistic instinct to educate the Indians in the vocabulary of modern architecture,

Koenigsberger requested the Orissa government to release Vaz for six months to train under him in Delhi. He hoped that such an arrangement would allow Vaz to profit from his (Koenigsberger's) "senior experience in designing . . . large public buildings"—an experience which would also give the Orissa government the "permanent benefit" of training its architectural staff, and building modern public buildings at a substantially low cost.

For Koenigsberger, the public buildings in the capitol complex had even greater "sentimental value . . . than their practical importance." They were intended to form the heart of Orissa and "designed with a view to this position." They were to serve as monuments "to the pioneer spirit and patriotism of the leaders of the New Orissa—to the group of workers who were converting a neglected province and conglomeration of backward princely states into one of the leading states of the Indian Union."[31]

Forever looking to the future—and *not* to the past—of Orissa, Koenigsberger forcefully argued: "Luxuries must be avoided, but austerity does . . . not preclude monumentality and architectural dignity. Our Capitol [Complex] should, under no circumstances be a testimony of narrow-mindedness and stinginess." He exhorted: "Let us design something really good and build it in stages in accordance with the funds which we can make available each year. . . . the planning work must be done now, even if the execution is to be staggered in accordance with the availability of funds."[32]

But the lack of qualified architects in Orissa and the debate over architectural controls and designs delayed construction work, which forced Koenigsberger to end his inspection report of 1950 by calling for "An Order of Urgency."[33] He hoped that such an order issued by the government would galvanize the indolent administration and lackadaisical planning staff into stepping up the actual building work in Bhubaneswar.

Actual building work remained dormant in Bhubaneswar until Chief Minister Nabakrishna Choudhury (May 12, 1950–Oct. 19, 1956) transferred his residence to the capital city in 1951, however. By the end of that year, nine important government departments—the PWD, the Secretariat, the Directorate of Health, the Inspector General of Prisons, the Registrar of Cooperative Societies, the Public Relations, the Agriculture, the Forestry, and the Tribal and Rural Welfare—had moved from Cuttack to Bhubaneswar into temporary buildings. It would be yet another decade before the Capitol Complex, Governor's House, and Utkal University would be completed in Bhubaneswar.

All early architectural designs in Bhubaneswar were done by Government Architect Julius Vaz and his skeleton staff. It was a cheerless assignment, since about the same time Le Corbusier and his international team of architects were planning and designing Chandigarh in Punjab, which must have put pressure on Vaz and his team to measure up to international standards. After Koenigsberger left for Great Britain in 1951, Vaz lost an enthusiastic ally in Bhubaneswar, even though Vaz himself had been a reluctant partner. Worse, with the arrival of Le Corbusier in Chandigarh and the departure of Koenigsberger from India, world attention came to be focused on Chandigarh, removing Bhubaneswar once again from any public discussion, and certainly from the minds of national leaders. Nevertheless, Vaz discussed the thinking that shaped the architectural designs in Bhubaneswar in a radio talk delivered from Cuttack on April 13, 1954:

> With the advent of Independence, amongst other revivals, architecture has a great part to play in [India]. . . .
>
> . . . The tendency . . . in the contemporary [Indian] architecture is to accept the glamorous experiments in architectural innovation of "novelty" and "stunts" borrowed from . . . European and American [cities] . . . without discriminating their use and relevancy in our case. The result is what we generally see today in some of our larger cities[,] "a mongrel style" . . . correctly termed by the Prime Minister of India.
>
> . . . [W]hat is the architectural character to which we in India should aspire for our . . . buildings? Some of us are in favour of the strict revival of the Indian Traditional [*sic*] forms [in] architecture; others feel that an international style would automatically be the outcome due to the tremendous impact of [the] world civilization in India; and . . . still [others] pray for an evolution of a new character by accepting all the ideas the world has to offer us and [assimilating] the new forms [into] our aesthetic traditions. I belong to the last school of thought.[34]

Evidently, Vaz saw no contradiction between what he advocated as "a new character" in architecture and what he denounced as "a mongrel style." The architectural style that finally evolved in Bhubaneswar was a mixture of colonial and traditional forms, with some modern ideas borrowed from Chandigarh. The fundamental difference between Chandigarh and Bhubaneswar was that in Chandigarh all "architectural work was subjected to the rigorous test of functional analysis as codified in the Charter of Athens by CIAM (1933)."[35] In Bhubaneswar, no such guidelines existed. In general, the Orissa PWD supervised the construction of all government buildings, government housing, and neighborhood shops, while private housing developed haphazardly under minimal supervision—although looking at the government housing it is difficult to determine how private housing could have been improved under greater supervision.

The architecture of Bhubaneswar is inspired by the architecture of India: It is an architecture of indoor and outdoor spaces merging into each other, the use of which is influenced by the climate and the seasons, and not by the activity within them. It is an architecture of horizontal planes: of roofs and platforms, open colonnades, verandahs and courtyards, gardens and fountains, statues and temples commemorating local leaders and gods. It is an architecture which has risen from the native soil, sacred and pure.

The City Center is located near the Railway Station and occupies parts of Neighborhood Units 1 and 2. It contains the civic and commercial buildings, shops, restaurants, banks, and so on. A slow-traffic road encircles the City Center, with areas set aside for parking. However, because of its location, it is not easily accessible to residents living in distant neighborhoods. The poor accessibility of the City Center has caused several government reports to conclude that shopping facilities are inadequate in the capital city—reports which have called for additional shopping centers.[36] Consequently, new shopping centers have been developed in Madhusudan Nagar (Neighborhood Unit 4), Shaheed Nagar, the Central Reserve Police Complex, Birasurendera Sai Nagar (behind Vani Vihar) to cater to the needs of the residents. In addition, plans for developing new shopping centers in other parts of the city are in various stages of implementation.

Architecturally, the main City Center near the Railway Station has been influenced by New Delhi's commercial district of Connaught Place, with some ideas borrowed from Old Delhi's Chandni Chowk. For lack of elevators, it contains low-rise buildings which are embellished with temple-inspired turrets, spires, pillars, perforated patterns (*jali*) and so on. PWD engineers discouraged any structures over three stories throughout the city for fear of "earthquakes"—even though Bhubaneswar is not situated in a seismic zone and is therefore not prone to earthquakes. However, the Public Works Department has recently started permitting multistoried commercial and office buildings to develop, although resistance to multistoried apartment complexes remains strong among the Oriyas. In accordance with Koenigsberger's instructions, there is no provision for housing in the City Center. However, local socioeconomic conditions have contributed to the development of unauthorized housing near the City Center—as in fact unauthorized housing has also developed near the new shopping centers.

In 1960, in the Capitol Complex, located in Neighborhood Unit 5, the Secretariat was the first building to be completed. Originally, the Secretariat was placed in a two-story bungalow, popularly called the "Red Building" after its red-colored bricks. But when that building failed to accommodate the government offices, a new three-story structure was erected in front of the Red Building. The New Secretariat, as the latter structure is called, was clearly inspired by Le Corbusier's design of the Secretariat in Chandigarh, and was completed at a cost of Rs. 5,000,000.[37] The Red Building represents temple architecture, while the New Secretariat pretends to represent modern architecture, even as it retains some features of temple design.

Placed on a plateau, the New Secretariat is a part of the cluster of administrative buildings. The parking for dignitaries was originally provided in the basement of the building, which also contained storage facilities. But with the proliferating bureaucracy the parking in the basement proved inadequate and had to be moved outside—although the general parking problem for the employees remains unresolved. The upper three levels of the building are provided with seven staircases, six elevators, and three service staircases.

The main consideration in designing the New Secretariat was to catch the cool breeze from the south in order to eleminate the use of expensive air conditioning,[38] although Koenigsberger had strongly argued for designs that would allow the use of air conditioning on the grounds that it improved productivity of workers which would offset the expense. Senior government officers have had independent units installed in their offices, but this is not efficient. Still, Vaz placed the building facing the east to catch the southern breeze, and provided perforated concrete screens for ventilation.

Aligned on a slight slant and stretching 880 feet in length, the New Secretariat is the longest building in the city. The facade of the New Secretariat building is broken by evenly distributed entrances and embellished with projections, recesses, stair towers, changes in pattern, and so on. Each floor has a running balcony, while the main entrance is approached by a lofty marble-paved palm court. The court contains no reception office and waiting hall, which facilities are located in a separate building adjacent to the main structure. Across from the main entrance are sprawling gardens bearing the Mughal touch. Also provided in the back of the New Secretariat Complex are carports and bicycle stands for the employees. The parade grounds in front of the Secretariat have now been converted into Indira Gandhi Park.

Inside, the New Secretariat contains meandering corridors with offices on both sides. There are two large conference rooms and one cabinet committee room. The conference room on the third floor is the largest and is flanked by terrace gardens on both sides. In the original plan, the governor was assigned an office on the third floor, while the chief minister was given an office in the second floor, both in the Central Wing. After the New Secretariat was completed, the chief minister occupied the third floor, the cabinet ministers took over the second floor, and the governor moved his office to his residence at the Raj Bhavan. Still, the space in the building proved insufficient for the proliferating bureaucracy, which has resulted in plans for adding new blocks to the New Secretariat Complex. A multistory building behind the New Secretariat also had to be erected to house several administrative heads of departments, who had been functioning in scattered offices in Cuttack and Bhubaneswar.

The two-story Assembly of the unicameral Orissa legislature is built of baked bricks, bearing the firm imprint of Vaz's English civic training. There are three entrances—east, north, and south—to the building. The Assembly administrative staff uses the entrance to the south, the ministers and the public use the entrance to the north, while the entrance to the east is reserved for ceremonial occasions. The building itself is a monolithic pile, with reception rooms located to the north. Perforated screens made out of concrete ventilate the building. The front of the building has a cluster of concrete columns set in a deliberately curved pattern, to which the rest of the structure hangs in the background as an appendage.

The Assembly Hall has a dome roof, while the remaining wings of the building have flat roofs. The facade of building has been provided with columns, arches, and other Indian motifs for ornamentation. A projecting canopy hangs in front of the building to provide shade to visitors and also serves as a portico at the entrance. The Gandhi Memorial, which was intended for the Assembly Complex, has remained unconstructed. Instead, the gardens in front of the Assembly contain the statutes of

Mahatma Gandhi, and the Oriya nationalists Gapabandhu Das and Madhusudan Das.

Not as long as the Secretariat but with the same layout, the Accountant General's Office is the third important building in the Capitol Complex. The three-story structure is broken in several places with projections, recesses, stairways, and changes in pattern to create an interesting facade. Inside, offices are arranged on both sides of the corridors, and there are conference halls, committee rooms, and so on. Except for scale and size, the building has no other architecturally attractive features. The other buildings in the Capitol Complex include the State Guest House, the PWD building (Nirman Sauda), the Office of Chief Engineer of Irrigation and Electricity, the Directorate of Public Relations, and some other government offices, along with a few houses for senior government officers. The poor planning of the Capitol Complex not only failed to produce unity in architectural design but also resulted in several government offices' having to locate along the Sachivalya Marg (Secretariat Road) in Neighborhood Units 4, 3, and 2.

Vaz also designed the Rabindra Mandap (auditorium) in Unit 4 and the Governor's House in Unit 8. The Rabindra Mandap is a circular, domelike structure which is broken in design in several places to provide varying geometric configurations. The structure is embellished with superficial Indian detailing and protruding perforated screens, the use of *jali* so common to the Indo-Islamic style. The entrance is protected by a portico, which succeeds in blocking the sun but also blocks natural lighting. Clearly Vaz in designing the Rabindra Mandap must have been inspired by the traditional Buddhist *stupa*, a beehive-shaped funerary mound to the Buddha's memory found in so many places in India. (A modern *stupa* was built much later with Japanese money in nearby Dhauli.) The top of the dome of the auditorium is shaped like a *chattri* (umbrella) so often seen in the Indian style.

The Governor's House, situated on a plateau at the end of the Raj Path (Royal Road), was also conceived by Vaz as an oversize government bungalow, but without the overlay of Gothic details that characterized the mid-nineteenth century Indian bungalow. (The term "bungalow" is derived from the seventeenth-century Hindustani word "bangala," commonly used in Bengal to refer to local village huts. It was later corrupted by the British to describe any single-story building with a verandah.) Set in a large landscaped compound, and approached from the Raj Path lined will tall palm trees, the Governor's House has a rectangular plan and raised floor. The two-story house is entered through a colonnaded portico which functions as a porte cochere. This leads to a wide colonnaded verandah, which leads to an entrance lobby. On the west side of the lobby is the ADC's office, on the south is the governor's office and the office of the secretary to the governor. To the north of the lobby are located a lounge, a dining room, a kitchen, and guest rooms. The family quarters of the governor are on the first floor of the southern wing of the building. There are also guest rooms on the first floor of the northern wing, separated from the governor's private quarters by a terrace garden. Guest rooms for dignitaries are reserved in the ground floor of the southern wing. Room ceilings are 14 feet high to allow air circulation, since the building is not centrally air conditioned—although special rooms have individual air conditioners. The large front verandah is designed to provide shade from the harsh Indian sun and protection during the monsoon rains, just as the gardens in the back of the house are designed for relaxation.

The architect Vaz hoped that the Capitol Complex in new Bhubaneswar would radiate the same architectural harmony that can be seen in the temple complexes of old Bhubaneswar. He believed that "reinforced cement concrete . . . will naturally bring about its own structural forms, symmetry and characteristics." The reinforced concrete was to give the buildings ancient patina as if they had been standing there for centuries. He declared: "We, in Bhubaneswar, are striving to create a new capital for . . . Orissa on the lines dictated and prompted by the immense amount of culture that surrounds us here, both in humanity and stone. Bhubaneswar and its surroundings excel in some of India's most prized monuments of architecture—the temples of Lingaraj, Lord Jaganath, and Konarak, the Khandagiri caves and the Ashoka Pillar [at] Dhauli. . . ."[39]

It is not clear whether Vaz in Bhubaneswar intended self-parody or was simply trying to comply with the wishes of his political masters. It is, however, clear that his dilemma in Bhubaneswar resulted from the old debate over the question of "What is Indian style?"—a debate which has occupied many practitioners of architecture since the second half of the nineteenth century, and a debate which surrounded the construction of both New Delhi at the beginning of the twentieth century and contemporary Chandigarh in the middle of the century.

Not having the stature of the imperialist Edwin Lutyens, who had bluntly declared in New Delhi that "I do not believe there is *any* real Indian architecture or any great tradition,"[40] or the reputation of the modernist Le Corbusier, who would later remark in Chandigarh that "What is the significance of Indian style in the world today if you accept machines, trousers and democracy,"[41] Vaz could not reject in Bhubaneswar the politicians' demand for adopting the Indian style or inserting Indian features. "Vaz confessed to me," recalled A. K. Biswal, who eventually succeeded him as the chief architect of Orissa in the 1960s, "that the politicians will not allow him to bring in modern ideas. They wanted a 'glorified village.'"[42]

That might be a harsh judgement by Vaz, possibly prompted by his marginal position in relation to the more powerful administrators of Orissa. But like the rest of some two hundred architects practicing in India at the time of independence, Vaz himself was caught between India's romantic past and potential future—a conflict which could only be resolved through a historical process, but which some might argue remains unresolved even today. But Vaz was trained under the eclectic influence of the liberal Claude Batley, who worried so much about the virus of the modern movement which had already infected "India's youngest generation of architects . . . with an inferiority complex [so that they] take their cue from the hastily developed, inadequately tested but ready to hand ideas of the West." And Vaz could not completely disregard the solemn message of his venerable mentor to his generation to build a new Indian architecture "on the solid base of their own tradition as eminently suited by long usage and experiment to the India of the future."[43] For the liberal Claude Batley the imperialist Edwin Lutyen's dismissal of India's architecture, like the utilitarian Thomas Macaulay's of her literature, was based on ignorance and arrogance.

It is therefore not surprising that Vaz instinctively combined colonial and traditional Indian styles in his architectural designs in Bhubaneswar—the same hybridization that Lutyens was forced into using against his wishes in New Delhi, and which has continued to be used in varying degrees by Indian architects since. Sensitive to matters of architectural integrity, Koenigsberger, like his predecessor Lutyens and his contemporary Le Corbusier, was opposed to hybridization. But for Indian politicians, who felt bound to have an Indian-style city, this style appealed because it was seen by them to make a politically correct statement. As for Vaz, an attempt at the fusion of Eastern and Western traditions was simply a matter of adapting the Western architectural vocabulary to the conditions in Bhubaneswar. After all, the modern international style was all-encompassing. He explained:

Being in the hot and humid region, our problems must have a definite approach climatically. We cannot just imitate what others are doing in other regions [a clear reference to Chandigarh] . . . we find that the traditional Indian house lends itself [to] adjustment to fit in the modern concept of living and the use of new and local material.

The Indian way of [living], especially in the dwelling place, we cannot and do not propose to . . . alter basically.

The privacy of [the] rear shaded courtyard, the copious verandahs [facing] the prevalent breeze and the sanctity of the kitchen and dining space, etc., are all maintained, because, in this transitional rush for absorbing new ideas in the art of living it is imperative that we retain the healthy characteristics of Indian culture. . . .

Another aspect that brings about its own architectural effect in Bhubaneswar is the absence of the multi-storeyed buildings. Vast open and healthy areas are available for expansion, and the need for developing vertically, [e]specially for residences, is not called for. Except for the public [buildings] and other places of common activities, most of the dwellings, especially those intended for the middle class and lower middle class groups, are single-storeyed, each with a rear courtyard and front garden space. This [open space], besides serving as additional living area over and above the limited number of rooms that [these] group[s] must necessarily have, also facilitates vegetable gardens and poultry breeding.[44]

Considering the socioeconomic conditions and living habits of the Indians, Koenigsberger himself had ruled out vertical planning, instead recommending a horizontal plan on the pattern of a postwar garden town in the West. But to protect the town from the urban congestion that he saw in older Indian cities, he had also recommended separating the functions of automobile traffic from other modes of transportation and the promotion of greater pedestrian movement. But while implementing the Koenigsberger plan, Vaz redefined the purpose in Bhubaneswar:

We have again tried to maintain the typical Indian [r]oad [p]icture. The layout of . . . Bhubaneswar, [e]specially the new areas under development, accepts and absorbs the universal principle of [the] self-contained Community Unit, but we have tried to keep the local character of small informal domestic group of houses. Market centers [in residential neighborhoods] are developed on the lines of [Delhi's] Chandni-Chowk and the village life is grafted by [the] provision of

> [daily] bazaars in [enclosed areas]. Even pan-biri kiosks are . . . neatly hidden away in convenient corners [away from the dangers of fast moving traffic].
>
> The twin watchwords of modern architecture are said to be "function" and "structural form." The vertical sunbreakers, the air-fins . . . the "fenestration" treatment [of buildings]. . . [are] a few devices . . . used to solve the problem[s] of sun, wind and rain.[45]

However, Vaz must have recognized the contradiction between Western functionalism and Indian traditionalism, for he admitted that "no Indian is happy with any form of severe or rigid laws of function [for] use of space." The average Indian, he felt, was temperamental and easy-going. Even a disciplined, freedom-loving Indian, "loves to loiter and use space for varied purposes according to the dictates of his moods," Vaz reflected, inquiring ironically into the mind of the Indian.[46]

Understanding the Indian mind was essential in planning for India, and Vaz used his psychological profile of the Indian in defense of his architectural style in Bhubaneswar. Traditional architectural treatment of the Indian house seems "to fit in well with the mental and physical make up of the individual, who is happy to see decorative patterns of jallies [literally, a net; a lattice or perforated pattern] . . . which, besides breaking the sun's rays, play patterns of shadows on the floor—[and] who likes to see rambling [*chujja* (an over-hanging cornice; eave)] protecting him from the direct sun and rain, who even likes spouts of rain water falling from the terrace [in front of] him, who flourishes in his deep set breezy verandah, where he lounges, chats and often sleeps."[47]

Forced by his beliefs and influenced by Claude Batley's *The Design Development of Indian Architecture* (1934), a volume of scale drawings of details of smaller domestic traditional Indian architecture, Vaz attempted to recapture in Bhubaneswar India's lost magnificent spiritual and building traditions but without lapsing into a spurious orientalism or pastiche. He rhetorically asked in Bhubaneswar: " . . . where is the waste in providing oriental turrets or chattries [umbrellas] on . . . roof tops of . . . our buildings if [they] can provide [shade for] squatting . . . wherefrom to watch the city life? . . . Are [they not] features [of] topographical landmarks and sky-lines [found in Indian cities]?" He answered himself: "I am not trying to say that we must be static and revert back to our traditions. After all, architecture is not merely an art or a profession, but it is [a] unifying philosophy of life . . . the climatic conditions and local characteristics [govern the modes of life] of a people [and shape] the . . . external environment and [the] internal use of space."[48]

Modern critics of Bhubaneswar might argue that the use of a material (sand and limestone) so unsuited to the local climate that it appears shabby within forty years of construction displays not so much respect for tradition as unconcern for reality. They might also argue that experiments in architectural styling in India since independence are based on the doubtful lesson of history that greatness of a civilization reveals itself in its architecture. But for the newly independent India engaged in the exercise of city building, rediscovering its lost past through the visual medium of architecture was an attractive way of affirming its identity. "Whatever view we [might] take of architecture, of its shortcomings and vagaries, the fact [still] remains that our native instincts and sensibilities remain alive," Vaz perceptively noted.[49]

So the basic religious instincts of the Oriyas were not destroyed by the secular master plan of Bhubaneswar. The Oriya administrators ensured that the capital city contained ample provision for religious shrines. Most of these new temples have been constructed since the capital city came into existence, and are built in the Orissan style in stone or burnt brick covered with cement plaster. Devoid of "architectural skills," "designs," and decorations, these temples are meant to meet the social and religious needs of the people, such as daily worship, marriage ceremonies, sacred thread ceremonies, Janmashtami, and so on.[50] The simplicity of these temples can be measured from their construction costs: the Radha-Krushna temple in Unit 9 was completed in 1975 by the Kalpataru Seba Sangha of Kendrapara (popularly known as the Baya Baba Matha) at a cost of Rs. 300,000. The same religious organization also built a *matha* (monastery) in the capital city in 1973.[51] In the early 1980s, the Rama temple was built on Janpath (People's Avenue) in Unit 3, and within a short span it has become a popular place of worship for residents of both old and new Bhubaneswar.

In addition to Hindu temples, the capital city is dotted with other religious shrines, mostly constructed under sacred banyan (*ficus indica*) or pipal (*ficus religiosa*) trees and commemorating Lords Vishnu or Shiva or Shiva's consort Shakti. The local popular worship of Trinath or the Holy Hindu Trinity—Brahma, Vishnu, and Shiva—had to be accommodated in the master plan by providing a row of single-roomed shops selling religious offerings in Asoka Nagar,[52] even though the original plan carried no such provision.

The other religious institutions in the capital city include one Muslim mosque, two Christian churches, one Sikh temple, one Buddhist temple, and one Jain temple. Located to the west of the Secretariat, the mosque was completed in 1959 and contains a small *madrasa* (Muslim religious school). Located in Bhauma Nagar, near the mosque, the Protestant church was completed in 1960; while the Roman Catholic church in Satya Nagar was finished in 1968. The Sikh temple located in Kharavela Nagar was completed in 1960; while the Buddhist temple is located in Unit 9, and the Jain temple in Asoka Nagar.

Anticipating a proliferation of religious shrines in the capital city, the planner Koenigsberger had provided guidelines for their development in Bhubaneswar. Differentiating between religiously supported teaching institutions and places of worship, he had recommended that the former be accommodated together with other educational institutions, while a few large religious buildings might form suitable vistas at the ends of the roads leading east and west. Smaller religious institutions were to be assigned smaller spaces reserved specifically for religious purposes. However, this mixing of interests in Bhubaneswar resulted in achieving mixed results.

It was to be expected that a plan and style so much associated with fantasy and illusion would eventually find its critics. Curiously, the severest criticism came from within the ranks of the Orissa officialdom. Equating the conversion of lush forest land into poorly planned neighborhoods that looked like "glorified slum[s]," N. Senapati of the Indian Civil Service complained that the entrance to his Indian-style home was so narrow that not even a car could get through it. He thought that the absence of public latrines in the city created a "feeling as if [one was] inside a latrine." He chided the planners for neglecting the sanitary needs of "thousands of people . . . permanently living in huts," who were forced into using public lands for their sanitary needs. He also felt that the planners, knowing the Indian affection for cows, should have provided a cow pasture outside the city or made proper cow patches near homes to prevent the city from becoming "a breeding ground for flies."[53] In fact, he was so strongly provoked by the urban environment of Bhubaneswar that he provided a rather humorous account:

> To meet the demand [of restaurants and other eating houses] we find ugly tin shacks called "cabins" all over the town. All these cabins are without authority and . . . encroach . . . on the Government land. Yet

[the] Government is [unwilling to] do [anything]. . . . [The] Government [has] surrender[ed] to anarchical condition.

It is no use calling . . . Lewis Road . . . a State High Way [*sic*], if you have a College on [the] one side and the Law Courts on the other. . . . At certain times [each] day there is such congestion on that road that it becomes a slum and not a High Way [*sic*]. . . .

At Bhubaneswar the cinema . . . which was meant to be a temporary cinema, is for all purposes permanent.

. . . The road to Cuttack has already become a ribbon [growth]—an ugly, dirty, moth-eaten ribbon. . . .

I can look at a plain, featureless building or a straw-thatch [hut] day after day and not get tired. But arches on top of Raj [Bhavan] or the Museum or the new bus station bore me. . . . The Rabindra Mandap . . . What a waste. What lack of utility. The Secretariat . . . looks [like] a house of cards: The Office of the Accountant General . . . [is] borrowed from Venice. . . . The Assembly—no comments . . . Krushi Mahabidyalya [High School] . . . might have been a palace of a Maharaja. . . . The Police Station—haunch back [*sic*]—an object of ridicule. The [M]arket [P]lace—stables. When will the horses come out? The shopping centre [has] a temple-[like] entrance. But no temple. You [can] go in and come [out] with a vacant mind and empty pocket[s], if you can wade your way through bicycle[s] and packing cases . . . [and] lumps of cowdung. . . . The Public Library . . . What film is on tonight? The [Govenment] Guest House—o.k.—thanks to [politicians] who rejected it. The Courts [are] as crooked as the cro[o]ks who loiter about [in] its corridors. When will "Your Honour" hold [the Durbar] on the covered terrace? [The] Vani-Bihar [*sic*]—reaching to [the] heaven: But theology is not taught. Or is it pointing to space travel?

The builder was a child playing [with] building bricks. He took ideas from the Ganges, from Lutyens' [New Delhi], from Michael Angelo, from ancient Greece and indeed from [the] latest Delhi. But [he] stopped short. The temples—the eye[s] cannot stop looking—the mind cannot stop thinking. How childish—the wrangles [of modern architecture] in the presence of eternity.[54]

One has to admire the wit as much as the perception in such criticism. But the irony was that to most of India's ruling elite, trained in the idiom of Western education, modernism meant Westernism; and in their determination to build a new future, they frequently found themselves suspended between two separate worlds. It was as logical for them to turn to the West for forms of modern urban architecture as it was for them to dress those forms in traditional Indian motifs to reaffirm their identity. This contradiction was in keeping with the dualistic instinct so basic to the Indian tradition.

Still, the contradiction created its own tension. As one observer of Indian architecture has noted, the Indian practitioners of architecture "did not wish to return to historicism of the last century, nor to any kind of craft revivalism, and they did not wish to jettison everything that had been learned from the West; yet still they wanted their own, independent voice."[55] Only recently as a result of political self-consciousness gained through a historical process have Indian architects started to find their own position in the modern international style. As one of them explained: Before "Independence, to many people the question of style was the question of how much Indianization to allow without appearing to make political concessions to the subject people. But after Independence, the question changed to: 'How much indigenisation could a newly independent nation afford without appearing backward and weak both in its own eyes and in the image it presented to the rest of the world?'"[56]

Such a refinement of thought processes was as yet absent in Bhubaneswar, which was reflected in its architecture. Neither the Westerner Koenigsberger nor his Indian clients had discovered a language in which to communicate the subtleties of architecture, which might explain why the modern, socialist, and secular architecture of Koenigsberger was not understood by the Indians accustomed to imperial architecture and religious monuments. Perhaps this is best reflected in the housing in Bhubaneswar.

In his egalitarian efforts, Koenigsberger had called for mixed neighborhoods of private citizens and government employees that were expected to eradicate the "bureaucratic caste" from Bhubaneswar. Instead, the Indians graded housing in Bhubaneswar according to eight types for three social groups—upper, middle, and lower—distinctions between types often depending on the amount of land, the grouping of units in two- or four-family structures, and so on. All houses were provided with certain basic features—even the lowest paid employee was provided with two rooms, sanitary facilities, a kitchen, front and rear verandahs, and a courtyard. Efforts were also made to distribute space more equitably amongst various income groups, and excess rooms and luxuries in residences for senior officials were discouraged.[57] But when senior officials protested, their homes were built in the bungalow style with four to six rooms and separate servants' quarters and garages.

To attract private housing in Bhubaneswar, the Orissa government, using the practice followed in New Delhi, initially leased 8,000 plots for 99 years. Measuring about three-fourths of an acre, each plot cost Rs. 5,000 in down payment and Rs. 100 in monthly rent.[58] Sixty percent of these plots were reserved for housing, the remaining were meant for small consumer businesses.[59]

Covering roughly an area of 150 acres, each neighborhood unit was to have a different approach road plan and informal layout in order to make the grouping of houses "more interesting" and discourage "the same rigid grid-iron pattern" that led to monotony. For the same reason, each neighborhood was to have several small open spaces evenly distributed throughout and houses grouped around them to form courts, instead of "only one open space in the centre of a unit."[60] All neighborhood units were named after historical figures and royal dynasties of Orissa.

Disaggregating architectural form into a series of separate but interdependent volumes is a common practice in India. Born of the culture of a warm climate, where during the day minimum protection against the sun is achieved by using a *chattri* (umbrella) and in the early morning and at night the best place to be is outdoors—under the open sky—Vaz understood the significance of open spaces. By arranging individual plots in clusters around a hierarchy of open spaces Vaz hoped to give the citizen his separate space and yet keep him as a part of the community. The Indian mode of living allows for rapid movements from the inside of a house to open spaces outside: one step out of the house and into a verandah outside, and from there into a courtyard—the centerpiece of the temple—and then under a tree—which may well have some religious significance—and beyond onto a terrace covered by a bamboo trellis, and then perhaps back into a room and out onto a balcony, and so on.[61]

Koenigsberger was still in India when Vaz revised the plan for neighborhood units, which he (Koenigsberger) found "objectionable" on the grounds of town planning principles and instead gave his own revised plan. Koenigsberger explained: "You will notice that the [new] drawing provides a more informal layout and spacing of houses than Neighbourhood Nos. 1 and 2 [drawn by Vaz]. This will improve the appearance of the whole colony." The other important change that Koenigsberger made was to arrange houses in such a manner [so] as to allow the cool southern breeze to pass through the maximum number of houses unobstructed. He, however, kept the total number of houses in a neighborhood the same "as in Vaz's proposal."[62]

As for industry, Koenigsberger had argued that "administration" was to be the main industry in Bhubaneswar, although his plan provided for service industries. His reasons for opposing industry in Bhubaneswar were essentially the same for which Le Corbusier opposed industry in Chandigarh. Both planners shared the European theoretical wisdom of the "Three Human Establishments" that divided cities into three separate categories, each with its unique plan and design according to function: agriculture, industry, and administration. The last was meant to be a city of cultural exchanges, commercial transactions, and administrative "authority."[63]

The concept of linear planning that Koenigsberger used in Bhubaneswar was actually meant for an industrial city, but he had used it in Bhubaneswar with modification to allow for administrative functions and rapid Indian urbanization. But in Bhubaneswar he made it "a principle that even small consumer industries must be separated from residential districts and that mixing of two must be avoided under all circumstances." However, he was careful in putting industrial plots "within convenient walking distance from the corresponding residential areas."[64]

Accordingly, Koenigsberger in his plan designated the area east of Neighborhood Unit 3 for service industries, although he never completed the layout for the industrial estate.[65] But when purely administrative character failed economically to sustain the population, the Orissa government reconsidered its original position on industry. D. R. K. Patnaik, who became the first town planner of Orissa in 1964, lamented in a report that Bhubaneswar will always remain "under the shadow" of industrial Cuttack, and proposed "incentives like cheap land and [electrical] power" as inducements to attract small and medium industries to Bhubaneswar. It was with that wisdom that he replanned the industrial area north of Bhubaneswar near the Mancheswar Railway Station. The 532 acres of industrial estate was considered to be at a safe distance from the residential districts of Bhubaneswar because the flow of prevailing winds was expected to blow the dust, fumes, and foul odors of industry away from the capital city. Another 110 acres were allocated to industry in Bomikhal.[66] More recently, the Chandika Industrial Complex has been developed in the northern part of the city. But the result has been unauthorized ribbon growth, with its attendent problems of congestion and sanitary pollution, along highways leading out of Bhubaneswar.

Disagreements also surrounded the planning of cemeteries, slaughterhouses, and fish markets in the capital city. Koenigsberger had reasoned that "cemeteries should not be too far out [of the city], but at the same time [they] should be in a place where they will not [become an obstruction] in the way of future development [of Bhubaneswar]." As for the slaughterhouses, he considered them "troublesome." But he reasoned: "Theoretically, it would be best to intercept herds of [animals] before they enter the town. Meat vans cause less traffic difficulties and less dirt than herds of goat and sheep which will be driven right through the main streets of the capital if slaughter houses [*sic*] are wrongly located." For that reason it would be better to "locate slaughter houses [*sic*] on the main in[coming] roads where the herds can be intercepted before entering the Capital."[67] But the slaughterhouse initially placed at Bargarh became a source of "nuisance" to the residents of the Kalpana Cinema area, and the cemetery and the cremation grounds in Satya Nagar became a source of "annoyance" to the local residents. Consequently, the slaughterhouses, the cemetery, and the cremation grounds were shifted to seven different areas on the outskirts of the city in the revised plan of 1968,[68] although the sanitary problems of the city remain unresolved.

The area between Neighborhood Units 3 and 4 that Koenigsberger had designated for the educational and cultural complex proved inadequate after the government revised plans. Consequently, Utkal University, which had been functioning with its departments scattered in different places, partly moved to Vani Vihar in July 1962. Located east of the proposed central business district and north of Unit 9, and covering an area of over 2000 acres, Vani Vihar was destined to become the regional cultural center. The master plan for the complex was prepared by the Calcutta-based architectural firm of Chatterjee and Polk. Disagreement over whether to make the complex completely self-sufficient or to integrate it with the capital city delayed construction, and what was eventually constructed was a result of several changes introduced by different planners, including a revision done by the Chief Architect's Office. Embellished with architectural motifs drawn from the Indian tradition, the new campus was to be a fully self-contained community: classrooms, departments, dormitories, laboratories, shopping facilities, restaurants, and so on. The housing for faculty and the staff was allocated on the basis of rank and income grouping, the same principles which were applied in the capital city.

It was only natural that many of the ideas and designs in the planning of Utkal University were borrowed from the Capital Project—but the university complex lacked integration with the capital city. Clearly, frequent changes in the master plan by different planners have contributed to the lack of unity in design and purpose. M. P. Kini, who served as an architect in Bhubaneswar, complained that there was too much interference from the government. "What we did then was o.k. for the time, but now we think that modern architecture is missing," he reflected, adding, "I am not too pleased with the results."[69]

Also not pleased with the results in Bhubaneswar were many others, both within and outside officialdom. "The urban scene[s] in Bhubaneswar and other towns of Orissa are chaotic and ugly, when compared to beautiful cities like Chandigarh, Ahmedabad, Bangalore, New Delhi . . ." declares the opening surly sentence of the *Report on Architectural Control Commission Rules* prepared by the Chief Architect's Office. "The main reason [for the haphazard] urban scene is that [not] all . . . buildings are . . . designed by [a]rchitects. . . . there is no [code] that [requires] private buildings [to] be designed by [a]rchitects."[70] The report calls for the creation of a panel of architects selected by the Chief Architect's Office which alone would have the authority to design buildings throughout the state.[71]

Although well intentioned, the idea aims at disenfranchising qualified private architects from building in Orissa. Apparently, the idea has its origin in the old rivalry between the Chief Architect's Office and the Chief Engineer's Office, both part of the Public Works Department. Historically, the Chief Engineer's Office has dominated all decisions relating to construction, which has resulted in resentment by the Chief Architect's Office. It was the same relationship between the two offices that led architect Maxwell Fry to challenge engineer P. L. Varma in Chandigarh. Although the chief architect is responsible for designing all public buildings, they must be approved by the Chief Engineer's Office, which also approves private construction. In Bhubaneswar, the proliferation of several competing authorities—the Bhubaneswar Development Authority (BDA), the Bhubaneswar Municipality, the Capital Project Office, the Town Planning Office, and so on—has further resulted in the erosion of the chief architect's powers. "There is no clear line of administrative authority in Bhubaneswar, and all architectural decisions are influenced by political forces," lamented Chief Architect A. K. Biswal.[72]

Recognizing the labyrinthine Indian bureaucracy, John Hansman of the Ford Foundation Group who studied urbanization in India in the late 1950s argued against administrative controls in the management of Indian cities.[73] The group was also the first outside agency to provide an assessment of Bhubaneswar when it was invited to study the capital in 1958. The group found low-rise, low-density planning uneconomical, and Vaz's architectural designs not conducive to natural lighting and the free flow of breezes. "To obtain a more efficient use of the land by building at higher densities would at the same time yield great savings in costs of land, services, utilities and other site improvements," concluded the Ford Foundation Group. Arguing that climate, not topography, should influence the shape and style of neighborhoods, houses, and streets, the group recommended that "houses should be oriented with the long axis or living area to the south; a 20 degree variation east or west would be permissible to obtain a minimum of sun radiation and maximum wind benefits."[74]

The Ford Foundation Group was also critical of the purely administrative character of the capital city. For higher density and a wider economic base, the group called for more industries in Bhubaneswar. "Even a purely administrative center needs service industries . . . which could be located in a service-cum-industrial center." As for the government's idea of joining Bhubaneswar with Cuttack with a linear development of 18 miles, the group felt that that would be "most impracticable" and would quickly make the highway between the two cities "choked with all sorts of encroachments on the right-of-way. This has already occured [*sic*] at the entrance to both the towns."[75] Many of the group's recommendations were implemented by D. R. K. Patnaik in the 1960s, but with the results that the Ford Foundation Group and other well-wishers of the city wanted to avoid most.

A Harvard University team led by the sociologist Cora Du Bois visited Bhubaneswar for an interdisciplinary study at the beginning of the 1960s. The Harvard-Bhubaneswar Project stretched over ten years, and in the end concluded that the development of the city had widely strayed from its original plan. Poor planning of the capital was attributed to piecemeal construction, the absence of proper authority, the lack of commercial developments, the shortage of well-trained administrators, planners, and funds, the uneconomical distribution of land, and so on.[76] The team expressed its concern for the shortage of shopping facilities, water supply, and recreational facilities in the capital, and lamented the absence of a mass-transit system to provide mobility to people, especially to women.

"The government has finally realized that land was used rather extravagantly [and] the outlying areas are rows of monotonous two- and three-storey flats," a member of the Harvard team in Bhubaneswar wrote to the planner Koenigsberger in London.[77] Still, the popular "aversion to apartment living" remained unabated in Bhubaneswar;[78] and so did the popular passion for religion, which shaped the attitudes of the residents. Vaz had correctly concluded: "We can fully accept all that the world has to offer us and . . . we can adopt and absorb all the influences into . . . [the] Indian Renaissance"—but "the fact will remain that our native instincts and sensibilities remain alive. . . . The hereditary character of a people is not easily destroyed by any foreign influence."[79]

.6.
CONCLUSIONS

As in Chandigarh, so also in Bhubaneswar the decision to build the capital was fraught with controversy, the major difference being that the Orissa government's decision to build a new capital was taken before India achieved its independence. Surely other differences—funding from the central government, Nehru's lack of personal involvement in Bhubaneswar, relative cultural and financial differences between Orissa and Punjab, Punjab's close proximity to Pakistan, the absence of European architects in Bhubaneswar, and so on—all played a role in shaping the outcome of the two capital cities. But the Oriyas engaged in a much longer and protracted debate that lasted more than a decade before agreeing to place the capital at Bhubaneswar. Even then, doubts about Bhubaneswar lingered much longer in the minds of many leaders, who preferred to view the whole exercise of capital construction more from personal perspectives than from the larger needs of the new province eager to administer its affairs efficiently.

The political reasons for building a new capital for Orissa are to be found in the Constitution of Orissa Order that transformed that province into the eleventh district of British India on April 1, 1936. The psychological reasons for building are to be found in the romantic passions of the Oriyas for rediscovering their identity that had been lost, politically, to the overbearing British. But nationalism that fueled the passions of the Oriyas was not so much directed against the British, who were still needed to broker differences with neighboring provinces, rather, it was directed against the neighboring Bengalis, Biharis, and Tamils who occupied Oriya jobs and exploited the province for their personal gain—ironically, as a result of British policies.

The British takeover of the province in 1804 had resulted in a series of administrative experiments and social engineering, all of which were implemented in the higher interest of administrative convenience and efficiency but which resulted in dismembering and scattering the Oriya-speaking territories to neighboring administrative units of Bengal, Bihar, Madras, and the Central Provinces. Having thus lost its political unity, Orissa languished in official neglect until Oriya nationalism, buoyed by local linguistic passions,in successive stages achieved unification for Orissa in 1936.

Although created as "the most homogenous province in the whole of British India, both racially and linguistically,"[1] the Oriyas could not agree on where to locate their capital city for the administration of the new province. The O'Donnell Commission (1931), which had brokered the boundary disputes between Orissa and its neighbors, recommended Cuttack as the capital of Orissa. The commission did not consider the spatial needs of the new administration and gave its recommendation purely on the basis of Cuttack's historical claim to that position. Competing with Cuttack for designation as the capital initially were Berhampur, Puri, and Angul. But neither Berhampur nor Angul possessed any historically unifying force, which led the Orissa government to conclude that popular sentiment would "not view their claim with favour."[2]

By the time the protracted debate had come to focus on Cuttack and Puri as the two most viable alternatives for the capital city, a decade had lapsed and India's independence loomed large on the horizon. But independence also meant maintaining commitment to secularism, experienced in a limited measure under British rule, as a necessary prerequisite for maintaining the political unity of India, which had already been tarnished by the partition of India. The British experiment in India had clearly demonstrated that, despite all its faults, a secular government was the only force capable of keeping the country politically united. For that reason, the Hindu city of Puri was ruled out because the government felt that there were inherent disadvantages in "making an all-India centre of [Hindu] pilgrimage the seat of a provincial Government."[3]

Commercial Cuttack, on the other hand, proved too crowded to accommodate the proliferating functions of a new administration. Later frivolous attempts to locate the capital at Rangailunda, Khurda, Barang, and Chowdwar (near Cuttack) also proved abortive. Finally, the government decided to build the capital at Bhubaneswar, a site discovered by the Maharastrian brahman B. K. Gokhale, special advisor to Governor Hawthorne Lewis, who, visiting it on April 13, 1945, strongly endorsed it. But the Oriyas remained undecided until Gokhale was able to persuade the rising young Oriya Congressman Harekrushna Mahtab of the advantages of placing the capital at Bhubaneswar, next to the temple town of Bhubaneswar. The charismatic Mahtab succeeded in winning the approval of the Orissa Assembly in September 1946.

Bhubaneswar was a romantic city steeped in pious Hindu sentiment, and was viewed as a powerful force in unifying sectarian sentiments. Gokhale was originally attracted to Bhubaneswar because of the presence of the airport, which had been carved out of scrub jungle west of the temple town by the Allies during the war. Certainly if the Allies could succeed in taming the jungle, the Orissa government could take the rest of the land which belonged to itself and build a new city. Moreover, Bhubaneswar had a mild climate throughout the year, and the main railway line connecting Calcutta and Madras ran past the site.

The urban vision that formed in the mind of Gokhale looked to Bhubaneswar becoming an educational and cultural center of the region, with Cuttack retaining the commercial functions, and Chowdwar (a Cuttack suburb) growing into an industrial center. "I would like to establish a school of arts and other educational institutions on the beautiful healthy upland near Bhubaneswar," Gokhale declared. He added, "The place is ideally suited for the location of educational institutions where a truly educational atmosphere could be created." In his vision Gokhale saw "factories spring up on both banks of the Mahanadi and the Kathjuri with Cuttack itself as a big centre of commerce." He reassured the supporters of Cuttack that that city would remain the principal commercial city of Orissa, retaining cultural and legal functions as well; but Bhubaneswar would become Orissa's administrative capital as well as its educational center, and suburban Chowdwar, just across the Mahanadi, would develop as the major industrial center of the new province.[4]

But the selection of Bhubaneswar did not put the capital site controversy to rest. Instead, the old controversy quickly changed into a new one over the question of architectural design of the capital. Worsening the situation was the fact that Orissa's inspired impulse to build a new capital was not matched by its resources and building skills. After yet another long and protracted debate, the government hired Otto Koenigsberger, a German Jew who had fled Nazi Germany and arrived in Mysore to work as a town planner. Koenigsberger had gained extensive experience in India by the time he was offered the position of town planner of Bhubaneswar in 1948. Soon after accepting the Bhubaneswar project, he was offered the position of director of housing in the Housing Department of the government of India, which took him to Delhi. Consequently, the capital at Bhubaneswar was built under the supervision of the Public Works Department (PWD)—that venerable but monolithic institution created by the British in the aftermath of the Great Rebellion of 1857 to ease the expansion in civil engineering work, but whose productions Rudyard Kipling described as "bungaloathsome"[5]—a cynical term for government bungalows built by PWD.

Although attracted to egalitarian principles and eager to build a secular city as their new capital, the Oriyas in the very nature of things were caught in their own tradition. From the very beginning, Koenigsberger and the Orissa government disagreed in their vision of the capital city. The Orissa government searched for shapes and styles for new Bhubaneswar in its past, in the temples of old Bhubaneswar, and in the religious caves of the Khandagiri-Udayagiri hills. Koenigsberger, driven by his Western instincts, looked to modern secular architecture as a solution to India's future—an egalitarian, secular India which, while acknowledging its past, would be moving forward on the new road to prosperity. Almost in the tenor of a tutor he informed his clients in Bhubaneswar: "It is the ideal which we want to revive, [and] *not* the outward shape."[6] It was a hard lesson to teach to the government which was determined to build a purely administrative colony with architecture borrowed from the temple town.

Perhaps Koenigsberger's strongest opponent in Bhubaneswar was Government Architect Julius Vaz. Vaz never really developed a close working relationship with Koenigsberger, and instead looked to his mentor Claude Batley for solutions to Indian architecture. A strong critic of the imperialist Edwin Lutyens and the modernist Le Corbusier, Batley felt that the Indians should search for solutions to their building needs in their own tradition, and not in the international style. For that reason, Vaz must have used his flexible contract with the Orissa government to spend as much time in Bombay as he could possibly manage, since that gave him the opportunity to continue working in Batley's private architectural firm and also remain in contact with his family and friends; and after resigning in 1961, Vaz permanently moved to Bombay.

The poor relationship between Koenigsberger and Vaz, Koenigsberger's long absences from Bhubaneswar, and Vaz's repeated sojourns in Bombay all influenced the final shape of Bhubaneswar. That would not have been so bad for Bhubaneswar had the Public Works Department functioned harmoniously and implemented the plan quickly. Feelings between architects and engineers of the Public Works Department remained strained for the duration of the construction, and have not improved significantly since. The adversarial relationship between the chief architect and the chief engineer goes back to the days of the British Raj, when their unresolved professional relationship was often exacerbated by social condescension on the part of the chief engineer.

But perhaps the most important factor influencing Bhubaneswar was the absence of Prime Minister Jawaharlal Nehru. In postindependence India, Nehru emerged as the successor of Mahatma Gandhi, which gave him a special status. In the very nature of things, and by his sheer stature and standing, Nehru became the architect of Modern India; and he played a far greater role in the development of Chandigarh than he allowed himself in Bhubaneswar. His special attention to Chandigarh might have been influenced as much by Le Corbusier as by Punjab's border state status. Orissa, on the other hand, was located at a politically safe distance, and had no refugee problem. In Chandigarh Nehru declared: "Let this be a new town symbolic of freedom of India, unfettered by the traditions of the past . . . an expression of the nation's faith in the future."[7] But in Bhubaneswar he informed his audience that the new capital would not "be a city of big buildings . . . and it would accord with our idea of reducing differences between the rich and the poor." Bhubaneswar would represent the art of Orissa, Nehru emphasized, so that it would "be a place of beauty [where] life might become an adjunct to beauty."[8]

Nehru's two different visions shaped the outcome of Bhubaneswar and Chandigarh differently. But the two cities were also influenced by the visions of their own leaders, drawing from their own cultural traditions. A Punjabi leader could proclaim, making no reference to the past: "As a Punjabi I want the new capital of the Punjab to be the last word in beauty, in simplicity and in standards of such comfort as it is our duty to provide to every human-being."[9] But an Oriya leader could only ask for the capital city to represent Orissan culture and workmanship, and the buildings to be as "simple" as possible.[10] Even when the expression of an Oriya bordered on hyperbole, the greatest excessiveness that he allowed himself was to declare: "Let us in developing [the capital city] and fashioning it be inspired by art and architecture and show to the world that the new capital of Orissa is not merely a copy of a Western town but a town which has grown out of the culture of the Orissan people and that it is an artistic and architectural symbol of Orissan culture."[11]

Even allowing for the limited vision, the shortage of economic resources, the absence of European architects, the ties to tradition, and the conflict between architects and engineers of the PWD, Bhubaneswar might have been a different city were it not for the mixing of purposes by so many different planners involved with the designing of the capital city. The long intervals in the development of the city assured that Bhubaneswar could not be planned by a single planner, and the capital city is a proverbial example of the dictum that too many cooks spoil the broth.

Since work on Bhubaneswar started in the early 1950s, the master plan for the capital has undergone three revisions—in the mid-1960s, the mid-1970s, and the mid-1980s—practically all inspired by the Ford Foundation Report on Bhubaneswar in the late 1950s. Specifically, the Ford Foundation Report recommended: 1) Bhubaneswar should expand northward in accordance with Koenigsberger's linear plan; 2) a physical separation should be maintained between commercial Cuttack and administrative Bhubaneswar, and between the old and new Bhubaneswar; 3) Bhubaneswar should be allowed to develop a more diversified economic base along the lines suggested by Koenigsberger; 4) Bhubaneswar should have higher density, perhaps even higher than suggested by Koenigsberger; 5) multi-storied buildings should be encouraged; and 6) developments on the periphery of the capital should be discouraged.[12]

The two-part, voluminous *Comprehensive Development Plan for Bhubaneswar (1988–2001)* prepared by the Bhubaneswar Development Authority (BDA) repeats many of the findings of the Ford Foundation by admitting that economy was not adopted in allotting land for different activities, and that the earlier planning of Bhubaneswar followed "horizontal growth." The BDA report admits that both these factors have "contributed" to the spread of urban sprawl in the capital and to the lack of controls, and calls for higher density, vertical development, and diversification of the economic base.[13]

Similarly, the equally voluminous *Interim Development Plan for Bhubaneswar (Final)*, 1985, prepared by the Town Planning Unit of the Directorate of Town Planning, Orissa, correctly places emphasis on regional planning for the improvement of the urban environment in Bhubaneswar. Admitting that Bhubaneswar has become the "central city" in a system of urban centers of the region, the report laments that the amenities of Bhubaneswar have served to encourage unauthorized urban developments in the region,[14] just as Koenigsberger had predicted might happen if the whole region were not brought into the planning process.

More important, the report correctly recognizes that planning should aim at coordinating the agricultural (rural) and industrial (urban) developments in the region. Specifically, the report calls for:

1. All State Government Offices to move from Cuttack to Bhubaneswar, which will complete the administrative character of Bhubaneswar and free space in Cuttack for commercial developments.
2. All State and Regional institutions in Orissa to locate in Bhubaneswar.
3. Development of Bhubaneswar as a tourist center.
4. Dispersion of Industries to cities other than Cuttack, such as Chowdwar, Jagatpura, and Pradeep—all of which form a regional urban unit.
5. Development of Jatni and Khurdas, near Bhubaneswar, as centers of transportation and trade, respectively.[15]

Although well intentioned, most of these reports neglect to address the basic problem plaguing Indian cities: weak local government. Independent India inherited a highly centralized government from the British, and nothing was done to decentralize power in postindependence India. Consequently, the central government continued to administer in a paternalistic style, reminiscent of the British government; and the local bodies became increasingly dependent on the central government for their existence. This unhealthy overinvolvement with the center also served as an excuse by the local bodies to escape responsibility to the public. The distinguished A. N. Khosla, governor of Orissa (Sep. 9, 1962–Jan. 30, 1968), eloquently summarized the condition of the local bodies in his address to representatives of the local urban bodies meeting in Bhubaneswar in 1966:

> The basic problem of local bodies is the [lack of] provision of adequate funds to meet the increasing cost of services and amenities, and their use in the best interest of improving civic amenities and undertaking development schemes, which [should] . . . not only [be] self-financing, but leave sufficient margin of profit for . . . plough[ing] back into other

> essential welfare activities. The tendency on the part of local bodies to depend mainly on [Central] Government grants and loans has acted as an opiate and a disincentive to self-help. That explains the growing trends towards [*sic*] shirking responsibilities in raising [local funds] through prescribed taxation and levies. To make local bodies consciously alive to their developmental responsibilities, it is necessary that they should be fully associated with the planning process and programmes not only of the local bodies, but of the country as a whole, so as to become aware of the necessity of economic self-reliant [*sic*] and self-sufficient [*sic*] in the context of all-India resources and plans of development.[16]

In Orissa there was a wide gap between the needs and resources of urban local bodies, estimated at Rs. 91 crores (one crore equals ten million). The governor diagnosed the problem as one of "unwillingness" and "corruption" widespread among urban local bodies, and for remedy he prescribed "selfless" dedication to work and eschewing "groupism or the craze for personal gain."[17]

More important, the strengthening of urban local bodies was deemed necessary for encouraging public participation, which in turn depended on education. People could only be persuaded through education into taking an active interest in civic matters; and education was also important for persuading people into questioning old beliefs and searching for new solutions. It was with that intention that Koenigsberger had pointedly noted in his master plan that to be successful "the planning of the new Capital of Orissa requires popular collaboration. . . . It is, therefore, suggested that [the] Master Plan be published with an appeal for constructive criticism and practical collaboration."[18] Nearly two decades later, the governor of Orissa admitted that "No substantial improvement can be possible unless mass public opinion is roused in favour of responsive clean civil administration and civic consciousness among all the people. . . ."[19]

Tagged in parts until 1936 to the tails of Bengal, Madras, and Bihar, and having no political identity, Orissa inevitably had a late start in developing local government. The Orissa Municipality Act was not passed until 1950, and the Orissa Town Planning Act was passed six years later in 1956, making it possible for the creation of Improvement Trusts to implement master plans for urban areas; and that in turn necessitated creation of the Town Planning Section under the Local Self Government

Department, Orissa. The minister for local self government admitted:

> The Municipal Administration requires special training and aptitude of its officers in view of the ever-increasing problems of Urban Local Bodies. . . . We intend to make arrangement to introduce facilities of such training in the Administrative Officers' Training School, Hirakud. We would also like to move . . . Utkal University to introduce . . . subject[s] like Local Administration and Town Planning in their curricula.[20]

The measure of any good government is to create the conditions under which people can realize their full potential. But the efforts of the government notwithstanding, Orissa continues to lag behind many other states of the union in literacy, and has not succeeded in achieving its full potential, even though the state possesses roughly half the mineral wealth of India, a rich forest land, and 250 miles of coastline.

Poor socioeconomic conditions in rural areas continue to push migration to cities, which in turn creates haphazard urban growth. Minister Banamali Babu hopelessly admitted that because of the lack of basic amenities in rural areas—drinking water, health care, sanitation, education, economic opportunities, and so on—increasing numbers of people were moving into towns and cities. "Unfortunately in our state," he added, "there is an absence of awareness among all sections of the urban population about the importance and desirability of reorganizing . . . towns."[21]

But in a country like India, where population continues to grow unabated, where paucity of resources frequently forces people to act out of self-interest at the expense of community interest, and where traditions persist in the face of modernization, "awareness" is not always sufficient to bring about social change. A leading Indian architect admitted recently that architects in India are not able to influence social change—although that does not stop them from trying.[22]

Bhubaneswar represents that effort—an effort characterized as much by the natural tastes of the people as by their acquired habits. After all, the city as a civic entity remains a dramatic example of man's effort to fashion his physical and social world—a world made up of man's basic nature and acquired practices. Small wonder then that even recent critics of Bhubaneswar have faulted the city, not for what it is not but for what it is: an administrative capital. The administrator-turned-activist M. N. Buch, driven by his natural impulses, remarked: "Bhubaneswar has been planned as if the Lingaraja temple does not exist. . . . No city can lay claim to greatness whose focal point is an office building housing government clerks. This is the real tragedy of Bhubaneswar."[23]

How that "tragedy" could have been averted by making the Lingaraja temple the focal point of the city the critic of Bhubaneswar does not explain. But he clearly laments the planners' neglect of Orissa's ancient past in designing the modern capital city of Bhubaneswar. Consequently, Bhubaneswar turned out to be "a typical PWD township. . . . "[24] The sentiment is reminiscent of Kipling's invented term "bungaloathsome"

Oriya Biju Patnaik, who played a prominent role in the early development of Orissa and who reemerged from political oblivion to become chief minister of the state in 1991, was nearer the point perhaps when he admitted that "Bhubaneswar is a poor man's town. Keeping the poverty of Orissa in mind, it was not to be a grandiose town like Chandigarh. Its potential was limited by the poverty of the people and the imagination of the planners."[25]

Still, the story of Bhubaneswar is one in which a people attempted a break with the past in hope of a new future, accompanied by urban transformation that was conditioned by the collective unconscious. Somewhere in the experiment, it would seem, the local familiar gods, close to the hearth fire, overpowered and replaced, and certainly outranked, the distant gods of modernism identified with secularism.

NOTES

SELECTED BIBLIOGRAPHY

INDEX

NOTES

CHAPTER 1. THE TEMPLE TOWN

1. Cited by Krishna Chandra Panigrahi in his *Archaeological Remains at Bhubaneswar* (Bombay: Orient Longmans, 1961), p. 2.
2. Ibid., p. 17.
3. Kanwar Lal, *Temples and Sculptures of Bhubaneswar* (Delhi: Arts & Letters, 1970), p. 4.
4. Some local sources say that it took four Kesari kings to complete the Lingaraja.
5. Panigrahi, *Archaeological Remains*, pp. 164–66. The date of the completion of the temple remains controversial, differently described from c. A.D. 600 to 1000. Also see, R. K. Das, *Bhubaneswar and its Environs* (Puri: Sri Printers, 1982), p. 35; Kanwar Lal, *Temples and Sculptures*, p. 68; W. W. Hunter, *A History of Orissa*, vol. 1, edited by N. K. Sahu (Calcutta: Susil Gupta [India] Ltd., 1956), p. 90.
6. Krishna Deva, *The Temples of North India* (New Delhi: n.p., n.d.), cited by Kanwar Lal in his *Temples and Sculptures*, p. 68.
7. Panigrahi, *Archaeological Remains*, pp. 99–100.
8. Cited by Kanwar Lal in his *Temples and Sculptures*, p. 8.
9. Ibid., p. 4.
10. Panigrahi, *Archaeological Remains*, pp. 177–79.
11. Ibid., p. 179.
12. Ibid., pp. 181–82. Dhauligiri has assumed new importance after the erection of a Chaitya (sacred Buddhist Shrine) called Santi Stupa (Mound of Peace) in 1972 by the Kalinga-Nippon Buddha Sangha (an Indo-Japanese joint venture), providing a striking landmark in the skyline of Bhubaneswar. There is also a Buddha Vihara (resthouse) set up by the Japanese Baudda Vikshus. A ruined Shiva temple at Dhauligiri has also been renovated by the Rural Development Department, Government of Orissa, in an effort to preserve the historical monuments in the area.

13. Rock Edict No. 13. Trans., by Romila Thapar in her *Asoka and the Decline of the Mauryas* (Oxford: Oxford Univ. Press, 1961), pp. 255–57.
14. There is some speculation that Buddhism may have existed in Orissa before Ashoka's conquest of Kalinga in c. 261 B.C. See Kanwar Lal, *Temples and Sculptures*, p. 12.
15. Rock Edict No. 12. Trans. by Romila Thapar, *Asoka*, p. 255.
16. First Separate Edict (Dhauli & Jaugada). Trans. by Romila Thapar, *Asoka*, pp. 257–58.
17. Second Separate Edict (Dhauli & Jaugada). Trans. by Romila Thapar, *Asoka, pp.* 258–59.
18. Debala Mitra, *Bhubaneswar* (New Delhi: The Director General, Archaeological Survey of India, 1978), pp. 4–5; also see K. C. Panigrahi, *Archaeological Remains*, p. 193.
19. Panigrahi, *Archaeological Remains*, pp. 183–86.
20. Ibid., pp. 187–88. Also see, Harekrushna Mahtab, *The History of Orissa*, vol. 1 (Cuttuck: Cuttuck Student's Store, 1981), pp. 48–49.
21. Panigrahi, *Archaeological Remains*, p. 192 ff.
22. Mahtab, *The History of Orissa*, vol. 1, pp. 35–36.
23. W. W. Hunter, *A History of Orissa*, vol. 1, pp. 58–59.
24. Ibid., p. 59.
25. Panigrahi, *Archaeological Remains*, p. 296.
26. S. A. Wolpert, *A New History of India* (New York: Oxford Univ. Press, 1989), p. 76.
27. Ibid.
28. Panigrahi, *Archaeological Remains*, p. 208.
29. Ibid., p. 209.
30. Ibid., p. 210.
31. R. D. Banerji, *History of Orissa, vol.* 1 (Calcutta: R. Chatterjee, 1930), p. 117.
32. Panigrahi, *Archaeological Remains*, p. 213.
33. Ibid., p. 220.
34. For a detailed description of the rise of the Pasupata sect in Bhubaneswar, see Panigrahi, *Archaeological Remains*, pp. 224–29.
35. Wolpert, *A New History*, p. 82.
36. Charles Louis Fabri, *History of the Art of Orissa* (Bombay: Orient Longmans Ltd., 1974), p. 104.
37. Ibid., p. 107.
38. Ibid., p. 105.
39. K. C. Panigrahi, *History of Orissa* (Cuttuck: Kitab Mahal, 1981), p. 61.
40. Mahtab, *The History of Orissa*, vol. 1, p. 210.
41. Fabri, *History of the Art*, p. 105.
42. Panigrahi, *Archaeological Remains*, p. 233.
43. Hunter, *A History of Orissa*, vol. 1, pp. 90, 118.

44. Ibid., pp. 121–22.
45. Ibid., p. 123.
46. For a detailed discussion of the influence of the Jagannatha cult on the Lingaraja temple, see Panigrahi, *Archaeological Remains*, pp. 257 ff.
47. *Ekarma Purana*, chap. 5, p. 29, cited by Panigrahi in his *Archaeological Remains*, p. 259.

CHAPTER 2. THE NEW PROVINCE

1. *Hansard's Parliamentary Debates* (Cornelius Buck: London, 1867), vol. 189, p. 816.
2. Andrew Stirling, "Religion, Antiquities, Temples and Civil Architecture," reprinted in *A History of Orissa*, ed. N. K. Sahu (Delhi: Bharatiya Publishing House, 1980), vol. 2, pp. 267, 270. Stirling's *The History of Orissa* was originally printed in 1822.
3. R. L. Mitra, *Antiquities of Orissa* (Calcutta, 1880); cited in "Bhubaneswar Notified Area Council, Custodian of important Ancient Monuments of Orissa," in the *Orissa Historical Research Journal* (hereafter referred to as *OHRJ*), ed. H. K. Mahtab (Bhubaneswar, 1982), special vol., sec. 2, p. 28.
4. Nivedita Mohanty, *Oriya Nationalism: Quest for a United Orissa, 1866–1936* (New Delhi: Manohar, 1982), p. 6.
5. For the Maratha administration of Orissa, see Bhabani Charan Ray, "Maratha Administration of Orissa," in *Sidelights on History and Culture of Orissa*, ed. M. N. Das (Cuttack: Pitamber Misra, 1977), p. 153. For the Mughal administration of Orissa, see M. A. Hague, "Muslim Rule in Orissa," in *History and Culture of Orissa*.
6. For a detailed discussion of the impact of British rule on the regional ruling elites in India, see John Broomfield's "The Regional Elites: A Theory of Modern Indian History" in his *Mostly About Bengal* (New Delhi: Manohar, 1982).
7. *Memoirs of Sir John A. Hubback* (Governor of Orissa, 1936–41), document ref. no. Photo Eur. 152, India Office Library and Records (hereafter referred to as IOLR), London, p. 238.
8. King Edward VIII's message cited by Sunit Gosh in *Orissa in Turmoil: A Study in Political Development* (Calcutta: Sankha Prakashan, 1978), p. 9.
9. W. W. Hunter, "Orissa or the vicissitudes of an Indian Province under Native and British Rule," reprinted in *A History of Orissa*, ed. N. K. Sahu, vol. 1, p. 178.
10. T. Fortesque, letter to Charles Grome, Nov. 2, 1804, cited by Asha Mitra in "Cuttack, Immediately After British Occupation (1803–1805)," *OHRJ*, vol. 9, Nov. 4 (Bhubaneswar, 1963), p. 238.
11. Nivedita Mohanty, *Oriya Nationalism*, p. 10.

12. "The Lessons of the Famine," *Calcutta Review*, no. 8, Oct. 1866; also see *Hansard's Parliamentary Debates*, vol. 189, pp. 770 ff.
13. G. N. Barlow, letter to R. B. Chapman, member Board of Revenue, Nov. 26, 1865. Also, see "Orissa Famine of 1866," P. Mukherjee in *OHRJ*, vol. 6, part 1, Apr. 1957.
14. Reprinted in "The Lessons of the Famine," *Calcutta Review*, no. 8, Oct. 1866.
15. G. N. Barlow, letter to T. E. Ravenshaw, Dec. 29, 1865.
16. For a full text of the debate, see *Hansard's Parliamentary Debates*, vol. 189, pp. 770–818; the cited quote is from Sir James Fergusson's speech in the House.
17. *Calcutta Review*, no. 8, Oct. 1866.
18. *Utkal Dipika*, Mar. 6, 1886.
19. *British Parliamentary Papers*, pub. no. 99, vol. 51, 1867.
20. Major Chesney, *Indian Polity*, 1868, pp. 120–21; reprinted in "Rebirth of Orissa," *OHRJ*, special vol., sec. 2 (Bhubaneswar, 1982).
21. *British Parliamentary Papers*, pub. no. 99, vol. 52, 1867.
22. *Utkal Dipika*, Jan. 1, 1868.
23. Ibid., May 16, 1868.
24. Ibid., Jan. 4, 1868.
25. Ibid., Feb. 1, 1868.
26. Ibid., Apr. 4, 1868
27. Ibid., Apr. 18, 1868.
28. Ibid., Feb. 8, 1868.
29. Ibid., Sept. 5, 1868.
30. Ibid., Mar. 3, 1869.
31. Cited in "Rebirth of Orissa," *OHRJ*, special vol., sec. 2 (Bhubaneswar, 1982), p. 11.
32. Ibid., pp. 11–12.
33. Ibid., p. 13.
34. *Utkal Dipika*, July 8, 1882.
35. Ibid., May 26, 1883.
36. Ibid., Dec., 25, 1886.
37. Two Bachelors of Arts, *The Oriya Movement* (Ganjam: n.p., 1919), p. 22.
38. *Utkal Dipika*, Nov. 24, 1886.
39. P. Mukherjee, *History of Orissa in the 19th Century*, vol. 6 (Utkal University History of Orissa [series]; Cuttack: Utkal Univ. Pub., 1964), p. 423.
40. *Annual General Administration Report of the Orissa Division* (Cuttack, 1894–95), p. 26.
41. Two Bachelors of Arts, *The Oriya Movement*, p. 35.
42. Ibid., p. 24.
43. *Utkal Dipika*, Feb. 21, 1903.

44. H. H. Risley, secretary to the government of India, letter to the chief secretary, Bengal, Dec. 3, 1903, no. 3678 *Records on Journals and Papers, 1903*, London.
45. *Utkal Dipika*, Jan. 1, 1904; Mar. 3, 1904.
46. Ibid., Apr. 13, 1912.
47. Two Bachelors of Arts, *The Oriya Movement*, p. 42; also see K. M. Patra, *Orissa State Legislature and Freedom Struggle 1912–47* (New Delhi: Indian Council of Historical Research, 1979), pp. 16–17.
48. Soilabala Das, *Life of Madhusudan as Seen by Many Eyes* (Cuttack: n. p., n. d.), p. 15. That Congress in an effort to maintain its preeminent corporate position in national politics frequently worked to depoliticize regional and local movements has been the subject of several recent scholarly studies. N. Gerald Barrier, Ranjit Guha, David Hardiman, Ravinder Kumar, D. A. Lowe, Gyanendra Pandey, Richard L. Park, Sumit Sarkar, and Paul Wallace are only some of the scholars who have examined Congress' elitist position and its relationship to regional and communal movements. These studies confirm that Congress' single-minded goal of representing a national Indian political community led its leaders to support only those movements which they felt involved struggle against the British Raj, and not those which involved "conflict *within* Indian society and *between* classes or castes." It is in this context that Soilabala Das' comment on the meeting between Madhusudan Das and Surendra Nath Banerjee has to be examined. It is on the basis of this point that it might be explained why the Congress party in the postindependence period has continued to dominate the center, while in states it has been frequently voted out of office. For an eloquent review of the literature on the relationship between Congress and regional and communal movements, see Richard Sisson's "Congress and Indian nationalism: Political Ambiguity and Problems of Social Conflict and Party Control," in *Congress and Indian Nationalism: The Pre-Independence Phase*, Richard Sisson and Stanley Wolpert, eds. (Berkeley: Univ. of Calif. Press, 1988).
49. *Utkal Dipika*, Mar. 30, 1912.
50. Utkal Union Conference, "Presidential Address," Cuttack, 1918.
51. Edwin Montagu, *An Indian Diary*, ed. Venetia Montagu (London: William Heinemann Ltd., 1930).
52. Two Bachelors of Arts, *The Oriya Movement*, pp. 298–301.
53. "The Utkal Union Conference Resolutions," Cuttack, Sept. 22, 1918: reprinted in Two Bachelors of Arts, *The Oriya Movement*, pp. 50–51.
54. Proceedings, Home-Pub., May 1920, File no. 203–203A; National Archives of India, New Delhi.
55. Government of India, *Proceedings of the Indian Legislative Council*, Apr. 1919–Mar. 1920, vol. 57, National Archives of India, New Delhi, pp. 831 ff.

56. Government of Bihar and Orissa, *Proceedings of the Legislative Council*, Nov. 1921, IOLR, London, v/9/1433. p. 164.
57. Ibid., pp. 163–64.
58. Ibid., pp. 164–65.
59. Ibid., p. 165.
60. Ibid., p. 166.
61. Ibid., p. 165.
62. Ibid., p. 170.
63. Ibid., pp. 171, 180–81.
64. For a detailed discussion of the position taken by the four concerned governments on the question of amalgamating the Oriya-speaking tracts, see P. K. Mishra, *The Political History of Orissa: 1900–1936* (New Delhi: Oriental Pub. & Dist., 1979), pp. 140 ff.
65. *India Gazette*, no. 4, Oct. 4, 1924.
66. *The Philip-Duff Inquiry Report* (1925), cited by P. K. Mishra in his *The Political History of Orissa*, p. 159.
67. Reprinted in P. K. Mishra's *The Political History of Orissa*, p. 175.
68. Ibid.
69. *The Report of the Indian Statutory Commission (1930)*, vol. 12, p. 172, v/26/261/28 IOLR, London.
70. Ibid., p. 408.
71. *The Report of the Indian Statutory Commission*, vol. 4, p. 554.
72. *The Report of the Indian Statutory Commission*, vol. 1, p. 68.
73. *The Report of the Indian Statutory Commission*, vol. 2, pp. 24–25.
74. Ibid, p. 24. The recommendation was made in the cases of Orissa and Sind.
75. Lord Edward Wood Irwin, letter to Wedgewood Benn, Sept. 20, 1930.
76. He was the ruler of Delang estate in the Puri district. The governor of Bihar and Orissa was not enthusiastic about the Raja of Parlakimedi representing Orissa to the Round Table but later approved his appointment.
77. *Amrita Bazar Patrika*, Sep. 19, 1931.
78. Ibid.
79. *Orissa Boundary Commission Report* (Calcutta, 1932), p. 34.
80. Ibid., p. 74.
81. *Utkal Dipika*, Sept. 24, 1932.
82. Ibid., June 6, 1932.
83. *Proceedings of the Legislative Council of Bihar and Orissa*, vol. 27, 1993, p. 1529.
84. Reforms Office, File no. 47/3/33-R, National Archives of India, New Delhi.
85. Ibid.
86. Reforms Office, File no. 47/1/34-R & K. W., National Archives of India, New Delhi.
87. *Report of the Joint Parliamentary Committee on Indian Constitutional Reform*, vol. 1 (London, 1934), p. 36.

88. Sind was the other province to be separated from Bombay under the Government of India Act of 1935.
89. *Report of the Joint Parliamentary Committee*, p. 35.

CHAPTER 3. THE CAPITAL SITE

1. Proceedings, Home-Pub., 214/1933, National Archives of India, New Delhi.
2. "Memoirs of Sir John Austin Hubback, Governor of Orissa, 1936–41," Photo-Eur 152, IOLR, p. 238.
3. Ibid., pp. 238–39.
4. *Report of the Orissa Administration Committee* (New Delhi: Govt. of India Press, 1933), V/26/242/8, IOLR, p. 2.
5. Ibid., p. 2.
6. Ibid., p. 4.
7. Ibid.
8. Ibid.
9. Ibid., p. 5.
10. G. S. Das, "History of Cuttack," *OHRJ*, vol. 3, no. 4, Mar. 1955, p. 197.
11. Ibid., p. 198.
12. Ibid., p. 204.
13. *Report of the Orissa Administration Committee*, p. 5; also see G. S. Das, "History of Cuttack," p. 205.
14. *Report of the Orissa Administration Committee*, p. 5
15. Das, "History of Cuttack," p. 212.
16. *Report of the Orissa Administration Committee*, p. 5.
17. Ibid.
18. Ibid.
19. Ibid., p. 6.
20. Ibid.
21. Ibid.
22. "Minute of Dissent," in *Report of the Orissa Administration Committee*, pp. 35–36.
23. *Report of the Orissa Administration Committee*, p. 8.
24. Ibid.
25. "Preliminary Examination of Site of a new Capital at Cuttack," cited in *Report of the Orissa Administration Committee* as Appendix 1, p. 37.
26. *Report of the Orissa Administration Committee*, p. 12.
27. Ibid., p. 13.
28. Ibid., p. 19.
29. Ibid., pp. 18–19.
30. Ibid., p. 22–23.
31. Ibid., p. 21.

32. J. A. Hubback, "Financial Aspects of the Alternative Schemes for the Higher Judiciary on [*sic*] Orissa," Appendix 3 in *Report of the Orissa Administration Committee*, pp. 42–45.
33. *Report of the Orissa Administration Committee*, p. 23.
34. Ibid., pp. 23–24.
35. Ibid., p. 35.
36. Ibid., pp. 27–28.
37. Ibid.
38. Ibid., pp. 30–31.
39. Ibid., p. 33.
40. *Orissa Legislative Assembly Proceedings, Sept. 24, 1937* (Cuttack: Orissa Govt. Press, 1937), p. 1083.
41. Ibid., p.1084.
42. Ibid., pp. 1103–8.
43. Ibid., p. 1103; also see Governor C. M. Trivedi, letters to Finance Minister Sir Eric Coates, Aug. 17, 1946.
44. *Orissa Legislative Assembly Proceedings, Sep. 24, 1937*, p. 1106.
45. Ibid., p. 1117.
46. Ravi Kalia, *Chandigarh: In Search of an Identity* (Carbonadale: Southern Illinois Univ. Press, 1987), p. 8.
47. *Orissa Legislative Assembly Proceedings, Sep. 24, 1937*, p. 1138.
48. Ibid., p. 1192.
49. Ibid., p. 1122–23.
50. Babu Atala Behari Acharya in *Orissa Legislative Assembly Proceedings, Sep. 24, 1937*, p. 1129; also see Babu Jadumoni Mangaraj, idem, p. 1136.
51. *Orissa Legislative Assembly Proceedings, Sep. 24, 1937*, p. 1156.
52. Ibid., p. 1136.
53. Ibid., p. 1129.
54. Ibid., p. 1163.
55. Ibid., p. 1164.
56. A. H. Kemp, "Extracts of Notes Taken from Reconstruction Dept. File," Jan. 16, 1945.
57. Ibid.
58. Ibid.
59. Ibid.
60. Harekrushna Mahtab, *While Serving My Nation* (Cuttack: Sri Pitambe Misra, 1986), p. 57.
61. Governor C. M. Trivedi, letter to Premier Mahtab, Sept. 9, 1946.
62. *Orissa Legislative Assembly Proceedings, 1949*, p. 24.
63. Secretary, PWD, Orissa, letter to Secretary, Finance, Govt. of India, Oct. 17, 1946.

64. Secretary, PWD, Orissa, letter to Secretary, Finance, Govt. of India, Dec. 20, 1946.
65. Ibid.
66. Ibid.
67. For a recent study of the "Imperial Vision," see Thomas R. Metcalf's *An Imperial Vision: Indian Architecture and Britain's Raj* (Berkeley: Univ. of Calif. Press, 1989).
68. Secretary, PWD, Orissa, letter to Secretary, Finance, Govt. of India, Dec. 20, 1946.
69. Ibid.
70. "Minutes of the Meeting on Town Planning for the Proposed New Capital at Bhubaneswar," Cuttack, June 21, 1947.
71. Ibid.
72. Ibid.
73. Trivedi, letter to Sir Eric Coates, Aug. 17, 1946.
74. Ibid.
75. Trivedi, letter to Mahtab, Sep. 7, 1946.
76. Mahtab, letter to Sardar Vallabhbhai Patel, Sept. 6, 1946.
77. Mahtab, letter to Patel, May 22, 1947.
78. Patel, letter to Mahtab, May 28, 1947.
79. Mahtab, letter to Patel, Sept. 19, 1947.
80. Trivedi, letter to Mahtab, Mar. 2, 1947.
81. Trivedi, letter to Liaquat Ali Khan, Mar. 12, 1947.
82. Trivedi, letter to Mahtab, Mar. 18, 1947.
83. Liaquat Ali Khan, letter to Trivedi, Mar. 18, 1947.
84. Trivedi, letter to Liaquat Ali Khan, Apr. 1, 1947.
85. Trivedi, letter to Mahtab, Apr. 18, 1947.
86. Trivedi, letter to Liaquat Ali Khan, May 21, 1947.
87. Liaquat Ali Khan, letter to Trivedi, May 15, 1947.
88. "Minutes of the Meeting on New Capital of Bhubaneswar," May 28, 1947.
89. Mahtab, *While Serving My Nation*, p. 59.

CHAPTER 4. THE ARCHITECT

1. *Orissa Legislative Assembly Proceedings, Sep. 24, 1937* (Cuttack: Orissa Govt. Press, 1937) p. 1115. Assemblyman Raju was hoping Rangailunda would become the capital.
2. Ibid., p. 1097.
3. Ibid., p. 1110.
4. A. Karim, letter to Premier Harekrushna Mahtab, Aug. 8, 1946.
5. Governor C. M. Trivedi, letter to Brig. Sir Millis Jefferies, Mar. 31, 1947.

6. Mahtab, letter to Prime Minister Jawaharlal Nehru, May 26, 1948.
7. *Times of India* (Bombay), Dec. 28, 1946.
8. Trivedi, letter to Minister R. K. Biswasroy, PWD, Orissa, Apr. 24, 1947. The letter provides a detailed discussion of the incident relating to Governor Trivedi's speech.
9. Ravi Kalia, *Chandigarh: In Search of an Identity* (Carbondale: Southern Illinois Univ. Press, 1987), p. 23.
10. Nehru, letter to Mahtab, Jun. 7, 1949.
11. Nehru cited the relevant part of his finance minister's letter in his letter to Mahtab. Nehru, letter to Mahtab, July 14, 1948.
12. "Minutes of the Meeting on Town Planning for the proposed New Capital at Bhubaneswar," Cuttack, June 21, 1947.
13. Ibid.
14. Ibid.
15. Ibid.
16. Ibid.
17. Ibid.
18. Ibid.
19. Julius Vaz, "Notes giving the Present Position of Work done for the Capital Construction at Bhubaneswar," Cuttack, undated.
20. Ibid.
21. "Jungle Clearance [of] the Proposed Site of the New Capital at Bhubaneswar and Planning the New Capital," Minutes of the Meeting held on May 28, 1947, at the Honourable Premier's Residence, Cuttack.
22. Ibid.
23. Julius Vaz, "Questions by Architect: For Clarification by Town Planning Expert," Cuttack, undated.
24. Governor K. N. Katju, "A Note on the New Capital," Oct. 23, 1947.
25. See Kalia, *Chandigarh.*
26. Mahtab, letter to Sir Ramaswamy Mudaliar, Dec. 31, 1947.
27. Otto H. Koenigsberger, letter to Mahtab, Jan. 27, 1948.
28. Govt. of India, Planning Commission. Nehru's address to the "Third Meeting of the National Development Council." Nov. 9, 1954.
29. Nehru, letter to Mahtab, Sep. 1, 1948.
30. Koenigsberger, interview with the author, London, July 4, 1987.
31. Ibid.
32. Ibid.
33. "Biographical Notes on O. H. Koenigsberger," eds., *Habitat International*, vol. 7, no. 5/6. Oxford, 1983, pp. 7–16.
34. Koenigsberger, interview with the author, July 4, 1987.
35. Ibid.

36. Ibid.
37. For a good biography of Burno Taut, see Iain Boyd Whyte, *Bruno Taut and the Architecture of Activism* (Cambridge: Cambridge Univ. Press, 1982).
38. Heinrich Tessenow, *Handwerk und Kleinstadt* (Berlin, 1919), p. 4.
39. Vittorio Magnago Lampugnani, *Architecture and City Planning in the Twentieth Century* (New York: Van Nostrand Reinhold Co., 1980) p. 132.
40. "Biographical Notes on O. H. Koenigsberger," p. 7.
41. Ibid.
42. Koenigsberger, interview with the author, London, July 4, 1987.
43. Ibid.
44. Ibid.
45. Ibid.
46. Ibid.
47. Kalia, *Chandigarh*, p. 82.
48. Koenigsberger, *Jamshedpur Development Plan* (Bombay: Tata Iron and Steel Co., 1944[?]), p. 1.
49. Govt. of India, *Census of India*, 1941, vol. 1, p. 26. Also see Kalia's *Chandigarh*, p. 2.
50. Koenigsberger, *Jamshedpur*, p. 1.
51. Ibid., p. 1–2.
52. Ibid., p. 2. Also see, Koenigsberger, "Town Planning in India," *Eastern World* (London: Aug. 1953).
53. Undersecretary, Orissa, letter to Collector, Cuttack, Feb. 2, 1948. There was no direct rail route to Cuttack from Bangalore; consequently, Koenigsberger flew to Vizagpatnam from Bangalore, and then took the Calcutta mail to Cuttack from Waltair.
54. Unfortunately, Julius Vaz died in the early 1980s, leaving behind no papers or family. He was one of six siblings, of whom only two married. Vaz himself never married. To construct information on Vaz, I have had to rely on his scanty letters, and on an interview with M. P. Kini, who served as assistant to Vaz in Bhubaneswar.
55. Vaz, "Governmnt Architect's views on His Excellency's visit to Old Town of Bhubaneswar and the Capital Site," Bhubaneswar, undated.
56. Vaz, "Architect's Notes: Town Plan for Capital at Bhubaneswar," May 13, 1947.
57. M. P. Kini, interview with the author, Bhubaneswar, July 15, 1989.
58. Koenigsberger, interview with the author, London, July 4, 1987. Also see Koenigsberger's *Master Plan for the New Capital of Orissa at Bhubaneswar* (Cuttack: Orissa Govt. Press, 1960), p. 3.
59. Koenigsberger, letter to H. S. Kahai, superintending engineer, Central Circle, Bhubaneswar, Mar. 29, 1948.

60. Koenigsberger, letter to Chief Engineer R. R. Handa, PWD Orissa, Nov. 15, 1948.
61. Koenigsberger, *Master Plan for the New Capital*, p. 1.
62. Ibid., p. ii.
63. Ibid., p. 2.
64. Koenigsberger, letter to M. N. Bhuyan, PWD Orissa, Feb. 5, 1949.
65. Ranjit Singh Bariha, memorandum to Premier Mahtab, Apr. 7, 1949.
66. Koenigsberger, *Master Plan for the New Capital*, p. 3.
67. Ibid., p. 4.
68. Ibid., p. 5.
69. Koenigsberger, "New Towns in India," *Town Planning Review*, vol. 23, no. 2, July 1952, p. 105.
70. Koenigsberger, *Master Plan for the New Capital*, p. 5.
71. Ibid., p. 6.
72. Ibid., p. 7–8.
73. Ibid.
74. Ibid., p. 9.
75. Ibid., p. 10.
76. Ibid.
77. Ibid.
78. Ibid. p. 11.
79. Ibid. p. 12.
80. Ibid. p. 15.
81. Ibid. p. 14.
82. Govt. of India, Planning Commission, *The Third Five Year Plan* (New Delh: Govt. of India Press, 1961) p. 693.
83. Koenigsberger, *Master Plan for the New Capital*, p. 16.
84. Ibid.
85. Ibid. p. 18.
86. Ibid. p. 19.
87. Ibid.
88. Ibid. p. 20.
89. Koenigsberger, letter to M. N. Bhuyan, Feb. 25, 1949.
90. Koenigsberger, *Master Plan for the New Capital*, p. 24, and Appendix C on p. 35.
91. Governor K. N. Katju, cited by Koenigsberger in his *Master Plan for the New Capital*, pp. 25–26.
92. Koenigsberger, *Master Plan for the New Capital*, p. 26.
93. K. N. Katju, "A Note on Bhubaneswar," Oct. 23, 1947.
94. Koenigsberger, *Master Plan for the New Capital*, pp. 22–23.
95. Ibid. p. 27.
96. Ibid.

97. Koenigsberger, letter to Chief Engineer C. M. Bennett, Orissa, Jan. 3, 1950.
98. Koenigsberger, *Master Plan for the New Capital*, p. 27.

CHAPTER 5. THE CAPITAL CITY

1. Premier Harekrushna Mahtab, letter to Prime Minister Jawaharlal Nehru, July, 15, 1949.
2. From Nehru's speech, reported in *Hindustan Standard*, Calcutta, Apr. 14, 1948; also see *Statesman*, Calcutta, Apr. 14, 1948.
3. David Miller, "Religious Institutions and Political Elites in Bhubaneswar," in *The Transformation of a Scared Town: Bhubaneswar, India*, ed. Susan Seymour (Boulder: Westview Press, 1980) pp. 86–87.
4. A. G. Dickens, *The German Nation and Martin Luther* (New York: Harper & Row, 1974).
5. For some of these ideas, I am indebted to Harvey Cox's *The Secular City* (New York: The Macmillian Co., 1966).
6. Ibid., p. 33.
7. Ibid., p. 52.
8. Ibid., p. 54.
9. Lewis Mumford, *The City in History* (Harmondsworth, Middlesex: Penguin Books, 1966) p. 655.
10. Ibid.
11. Otto Koenigsberger, "New Towns in India," *Town Planning Review*, vol. 23, no. 2, July 1952, p. 105.
12. Ibid. p. 107.
13. B. Mishra, Secretary to the Governor, telegram, to Secretary R. R. Handa, PWD, Aug. 18, 1948.
14. Koenigsberger, letter to PWD Minister Ranjit Singh Bariha, Jan. 13, 1949.
15. Koenigsberger, letter to C. M. Bennett, Dec. 20, 1950.
16. Koenigsberger, letter to Bennett, Feb. 19, 1951. Also see Koenigsberger, letter to Bennett, Dec. 20, 1950.
17. Koenigsberger, letter to Bennett, Dec. 20, 1950.
18. Julius Vaz, "A note on Bhubaneswar to Chief Engineer," Apr. 2, 1949.
19. Secretary to the Governor, Orissa, letter to Chief Secretary, Orissa, May 30, 1949.
20. Koenigsberger, letter to Bennett, Jan 3, 1950.
21. Ibid.
22. Koenigsberger, "Bhubaneswar Inspection Report, June 1–5, 1950," New Delhi, Sept. 12, 1950, p. 2.
23. Ibid., p. 3.
24. Ibid., p. 4.
25. Ibid.

26. For details, see Ravi Kalia's *Chandigarh.*
27. K. Baldeva Mehta, "Planning Legislation in India," paper presented at the Ninth Annual Town and Country Planning Seminar, Bangalore, India, Sept. 1960.
28. John A. Hansman, "Planning Yes, Zoning No," *Journal of the Institute of Town Planners, India*, nos. 49–50, Dec. 1966–Mar. 1967, pp. 89–94.
29. Koenigsberger, "Bhubaneswar Inspection Report, 1950." p. 6.
30. Ibid., p. 8.
31. Ibid.
32. Ibid.
33. Ibid., p. 13.
34. Julius Vaz's radio talk on All India Radio, Cuttack, Apr. 13, 1954, published as "Archictecture of Bhubaneswar, New Capital, Orissa," *Journal of the Indian Institute of Architects*, vol. 20, no. 2, Apr.–June 1954, pp. 3–4.
35. Kalia, *Chandigarh*, p. 111.
36. *Greater Bhubaneswar Master Plan Report*, part 1 (Bhubaneswar: Directorate of Town Planning, 1969), p. 117.
37. S. Mumtaz Ali, "Secretariat Building," *Souvenir of Indian Science Congress: Orissa Past and Present*, eds. P. Parija and S. Mukherjee (Cuttack, 1960), pp. 225–26.
38. Ibid.
39. Vaz, "Architecture of Bhubaneswar."
40. Cited in G. H. R. Tillotson, *The Tradition of Indian Architecture: Continuity, Controversy and Change Since 1850* (New Haven: Yale Univ., Press, 1989), p. 107.
41. Cited in Kalia's *Chandigarh*, p. 105.
42. A. K. Biswal, interview with the author, Bhubaneswar, July 14, 1989.
43. Cited in Tillotson, *The Tradition of Indian Architecture*, p. 134.
44. Vaz, "Architecture of Bhubaneswar."
45. Ibid.
46. Ibid.
47. Ibid.
48. Ibid.
49. Ibid.
50. Govt. of Orissa, *Orissa District Gazetteers, Puri*, Bhubaneswar, Aug. 15, 1977, p. 721.
51. Ibid., p. 722.
52. Ibid.
53. N. Senapati, "Rumblings on New Towns of Orissa," *Journal of the Institute of Town Planners, India*, nos. 49–50, Dec. 1966–Mar. 1967, pp. 52–54.
54. Ibid.
55. Tillotson, *The Tradition of Indian Architecture*, p. 136.

56. Malay Chatterjee, cited in Tillotson's *The Tradition of Indian Architecture*, p. 137.
57. R. R. Handa & J. Vaz, New Capital at Bhubaneswar," *Marg* (Bombay), vol. 8, no. 4, Sept. 1955, pp. 82–88.
58. Vaz, a note to Chief Secretary, Orissa, Apr. 1949.
59. Bennett, letter to Koenigsberger, Feb. 16, 1949.
60. Vaz, a note to Chief Engineer, Aug. 20, 1948.
61. Charles Correa, "Transfers and Transformations," in *Charles Correa*, ed. Hasan-Uddin Khan (New York: Concept Media Pvt. Ltd., 1987), p. 167.
62. Koenigsberger, letter to Bennett, Aug. 4, 1950.
63. Kalia, *Chandigarh*, p. 119.
64. Koenigsberger, letter to M. N. Bhuyan, PWD, Orissa, Feb. 25, 1949.
65. Koenigsberger, letter to Bhuyan, PWD, Orissa, Feb. 5, 1949.
66. "A Short Note on Draft Master Plan for Greater Bhubaneswar," Town and Country Planning Organization, Orissa, Bhubaneswar, undated, p. 7.
67. Koenigsberger, letter to Bennett, Jan. 3, 1950.
68. *Greater Bhubaneswar Master Plan, 1968* (Bhubaneswar: Town and Country Planning Office, 1968).
69. M. P. Kini, interview with the author, Bhubaneswar, July 15, 1989.
70. "The Report on Architectural Control Commission Rules," prepared by the Chief Architect's Office, Bhubaneswar, undated, p. 1.
71. Ibid., pp. 3–5.
72. A. K. Biswal, interview with the author, Bhubaneswar, July 21, 1987.
73. John A. Hansman, "Planning Yes, Zoning No."
74. Edward Echeverria, memorandum to Minister of Public Works, Govt. of Orissa, Apr. 2, 1958.
75. Ibid.
76. Peter Grenell, letter to Koenigsberger, Nov. 23, 1965.
77. Ibid.
78. Ibid.
79. Vaz, "Architecture of Bhubaneswar."

CHAPTER 6. CONCLUSIONS

1. *Report of the Joint Parliamentary Committee on Indian Constitutional Reform, vol.* 1 (London, 1934), p. 35.
2. *Report of the Orissa Administration Committee* (New Delhi: Govt. of India Press, 1933), p. 4.
3. Ibid. p. 5.
4. B. K. Gokhale, cited by D. R. K. Patnaik in "Site Selection of Bhubaneswar as the New Capital of Orissa," *Jr. of the Institute of Town Planners, India*, nos. 49–50, Dec. 1966–Mar. 1967, pp. 55–60.

5. Rudyard Kipling, cited in G. H. R. Tillotson's *The Tradition of Indian Architecture,* pp. 72–73.
6. Otto Koenigsberger, *Master Plan for the new Capital of Orissa at Bhubaneswar* (Cuttack: Orissa Govt. Press, 1960) p. 27.
7. *Hindustan Times* (New Delhi), July 8, 1950. Also see Ravi Kalia's *Chandigarh,* p. 21.
8. *Hindustan Standard* (Calcutta), Apr. 14, 1948.
9. Rajkumari Amrit Kaur, letter to Sardar Gurbachan Singh, Apr. 27, 1954, cited by Kalia in *Chandigarh,* p. 21.
10. "Minutes of the Meeting on Town Planning for the Proposed New Capital at Bhubaneswar," Cuttack, June 21, 1947.
11. Assemblyman Vysyaraju Kasiviswanadham Raju's statement recorded in *Orissa Legislative Assembly Proceedings,* Sept. 24, 1937 (Cuttack: Orissa Govt. Press, 1937), p. 1115.
12. Cited in Peter Grenell, "Planning the New Capital of Bhubaneswar," in *The Transformation of a Sacred Town: Bhubaneswar, India,* ed. Susan Seymour (Boulder: Westview Press, 1930), p. 48.
13. Bhubaneswar development Authority, *Comprehensive Development Plan for Bhubaneswar (Draft),* Part 1 (Bhubaneswar, March 1989), pp. 55–70. Part 2 was published simultaneously, and provides projections up to the year 2001.
14. Town Planning Unit, Bhubaneswar, *Interim Development Plan for Bhubaneswar (Final)* Bhubaneswar: Directorate of Town Planning, Orissa, 1985), pp. 40–65.
15. Ibid., pp. 57–58.
16. A. N. Khosla, "Address of Dr. A. N. Khosla, Governor of Orissa," reprinted in *Proceedings of the Second Conference of Chairman* [*sic*] *and Executive Officer* [*sic*] *of Urban Local Bodies of Bhubaneswar,* Cuttack: Govt. of Orissa, Feb. 5 and 6, 1966, pp. 1–6.
17. Ibid.
18. Otto Koenigsberger, *Master Plan for the New Capital of Orissa at Bhubaneswar* (Cuttack: Orissa Govt. Press, 1960) p. ii.
19. A. N. Khosala, "Address by Dr. A. N. Khosla."
20. Banamali Babu, "Welcome Speech by Shri Banamali Babu, Minister local Self-Government, Orissa," reprinted in *Proceedings of the Second Conference of Chairman* [*sic*] *and Executive Officer* [*sic*] *of Urban Local Bodies of Bhubaneswar,* pp. 7–13.
21. Banamali Babu, "The Need for Town Planning," *State Level Conference of Urban Local Bodies,* Govt. of Orissa, Feb. 1966, pp. 49–56.
22. Charles Correa cited by Sherban Cantacuzino in his "Ideas and Buildings" in *Charles Correa,* ed. Hasan-Uddin Khan (New York: Concept Media Pvt. Ltd., 1987) p. 10.

23. M. N. Buch, "Bhubaneswar: The Lost Opportunity," *Design* (New Delhi), Jan.–Mar. 1982, pp. 25–27.
24. Ibid.
25. Biju Patnaik, interview with the author, Aug. 5, 1987.

SELECTED BIBLIOGRAPHY

The unpublished sources, government records, and correspondence between officials, which are cited in notes only, include the personal papers of Sir John A. Hubback at the India Office Library and Records, London, the Harekrushna Mahtab papers at the Nehru Memorial Museum and Library, New Delhi, and the Cora Du Bois papers at the Southern Asia Reference Center, University of Chicago. In Bhubaneswar, I consulted the Capital City Project papers at the General Administration Department and other relevant documents at the Orissa State Archives, the Town Planning Office, and the Chief Architect's Office, where the original Koenigsberger drawings are also located; in New Delhi, I consulted legislative debates and other relevant planning documents at the Central Secretariat Library, the Town and Country Planning Office Library, and the National Archives; and in London, I received the use of the personal papers of Otto Koenigsberger directly from himself. In addition to these sources, I also interviewed several individuals, who either had worked in Bhubaneswar in the early stages or who have been connected with the city's later developments. These include, in India, Abdul Ali, A. K. Biswal, C. S. Chandrashekhra, P. K. Hota, M. P. Kini, P. K. Mohanty, R. S. Padhi, Biju Patnaik, D. R. K. Patnaik, J. B. Patnaik, E. F. N. Ribeiro, and S. S. Shafi, and in England, Otto Koenigsberger. For data and statistical information, I have relied on the Government of India Census, 1941, 1951, 1961, 1971, 1981, and 1991 (*Provisional Population Totals: Papers 1 and 2*), the yearly statistical abstracts of the Orissa government, and the *Orissa Gazetteer*; for legislative debates, on *Hansard's Parliamentary Debates*, London, *British Parliamentary Papers*, and the *Proceedings of Legislative Council*, Orissa; and for news reports, on the *Amrita Bazaar Patrika*, the *Calcutta Review*, the *Hindustan Standard*, the *Statesman*, and the *Utkal Dipika*. I also consulted the *Journal of Orissa Historical Research* (Bhubaneswar), the *Quarterly Review of Historical Studies*

(Calcutta), and the *Journal of the Institute of Town Planners, India* for historical discussions relating to urban developments in Orissa. These sources, along with other journal references, are also generally cited in notes only. Soon after the publication of this work, the author hopes to deposit all the original sources collected in India and the United Kingdom on Bhubaneswar with the Special Collections, University Research Library, University of California, Los Angeles, where the original sources collected by him on Chandigarh are also housed.

ABELL, AARON IGNATIUS. *The Urban Impact on American Protestantism, 1865–1900.* Hamden, CT: Archo, 1962. Originally published in 1943 by Harvard Univ. Press in the series Harvard Historical Studies.

ACHARYA, PARAMANANDA. *Studies in Orissan History, Archaeology and Archives.* Cuttack: Cuttack Students' Store, 1969.

AHMAD, QUAZI. *Indian Cities: Characteristics and Correlates.* Chicago: Dept. of Geography, Univ. of Chicago, 1965.

AHMED, SHARIF UDDIN. *Dacca: A Study in Urban History and Development.* London: Curzon Press, 1986.

AHMED ALI, M. *Historical Aspects of Town Planning in Pakistan and India.* Karachi: al-Ata Foundation, 1972.

ALLESWORTH, DON T. *The Political Realities of Urban Planning.* New York: Praeger, 1975.

ANANTHALWAR, M. A, et al., eds. *Indian Architecture.* 3 vols. Delhi: Indian Book Gallery, 1980.

L'Association Française d'Action Artistique. *Architectures en Inde.* Paris: Electa Moniteur, 1985.

BACKLAND, CHARLES E. *Bengal Under the Lieutenant Governors.* 2 vols. Calcutta: K. Bose, 1902.

BADCOCK, BLAIR. *Unfairly Structured Cities.* Oxford: Basil Blackwell, 1984.

BAILEY, FREDERICK GEORGE. *Caste and the Economic Frontier: A Village in Highland Orissa.* Manchester: Manchester Univ. Press, 1960.

———. *Politics and Social Change: Orissa in 1959.* Berkeley: Univ. of Calif. Press, 1970.

BAKER, DEREK. *The Church in Town and Countryside.* Oxford: Basil Blackwell, 1979.

BALLHATCHET, KENNETH, and JOHN HARRISON. *The City in South Asia.* London: Curzon Press, 1980.

BANERJEE, TRIDIB, and WILLIAM C. BAER. *Beyond the Neighborhood Unit.* New York: Plenum Press, 1984.

BANERJI, R. D. *History of Orissa.* 2 vols. Calcutta: R. Chatterjee, 1930–31.

BANGA, INDU, ed. *The City in Indian History.* Columbia, MO: South Asia Publications, 1991.

BARRIER, N. GERALD. *Banned: Controversial Literature and Political Control in British India. 1907–1947*. Columbia: Univ. of Missouri Press, 1974.

———. *The Census in British India*. New Delhi: Manohar, 1981.

BASHAM, A. L. ed. *A Cultural History of India*. Oxford: Oxford Univ. Press, 1975.

BATLEY, CLAUDE. *The Design Development of Indian Architecture*. 3rd ed. New York: St. Martin's, 1973. Originally published in London in 1934.

BAYLY, C. A. *Indian Society and the Making of the British Empire*. The New Cambridge History of India, vol. 2. Cambridge: Cambridge Univ. Press, 1988.

BOSE, ASHISH. *India's Urbanization, 1901–2001*. 2nd ed. New Delhi: Tata McGraw–Hill Pub. Co., 1966.

BRANCH, MELVILLE CAMBELL. *Continuous City Planning: Intergrating Municipal Management and City Planning*. New York: Wiley, 1981.

———. *Comprehensive City Planning*. Chicago: Planners Press, American Planning Assoc., 1985.

BROOMFIELD, J. H. *Elite Conflict in a Plural Society*. Berkeley: Univ. of Calif. Press, 1968.

———. *Mostly About Bengal: Essays in Modern South Asian History*. New Delhi: Manohar, 1982.

BROWN, HILTON. *The Sahibs*. London: W. Hodge [1948].

BRYCE, HERRINGTON *Planning Smaller Cities*. Lexington, MA: D.C. Heath, Lexington Books, 1979.

BUCH, M. N. "Bhubaneswar: The Lost Opportunity." *Design*, New Delhi, Jan.–Mar. 1982.

BUCKLAND, CHARLES. E. *Bengal Under the Lieutanant Governors*. 2 vols. 2nd ed. Calcutta: K. Bose, 1902.

BURCHELL, ROBERT W., GEORGE STERNLIEB, eds. *Planning Theory in the 1980s: A Search for Future Directions*. New Brunswick, NJ: Center for Urban Policy Research, Rutgers Univ., 1978.

BURROWS, LAWRENCE B. *Growth Management: Issues. Techniques and Policy Implications*. New Brunswick, NJ: Center for Urban Policy Research, Rutgers Univ., 1978.

CASTELLS, MANUEL. *The Urban Question: A Marxist Approach*. Trans. Alan Sheridan. Cambridge, MA: MIT press, 1977.

———. *City, Class and Power*. Trans. Elizabeth Lebas. New York: St. Martin's Press, 1978.

CATANESE; ANTHONY JAMES, and W. PAUL FARMER, eds. *Personality, Politics and Planning*. Beverly Hills: Sage Publications, 1978.

CHAPIN, FRANCIS STUART, Jr., and EDWARD J. KAISER. *Urban Land Use Planning*. Urbana: Univ. of Illinois Press, 1979.

CHATTERJI, SUNITI KUMAR. *The People, Language, and Culture of Orissa*. Bhubaneswar: Orissa Sahitya Akademi, 1966.

CHAUDHARY, VIJAY CHANDRA PRASAD. *The Creation of Modern Bihar.* [*Patna ?*]: *Yugeshwar Prakashan,* 1964.

City and Nation in the Developing World: Selected Case Studies of Social Change in Asia, Africa, and Latin America. Compiled by American Univ. Field Staff. New York: American Univ. Field Staff, 1968.

CLAVEL, PIERRE, JOHN FORESTER, and WILLIAM W. GOLDSMITH, eds. *Urban and Regional Planning in an Age of Austerity.* New York: Pergamon Press, 1980.

COBDEN-RAMSAY, L. E. B. *Feudatory States of Orissa.* 1910. Rpt. Calcutta: Firma KLM Pvt. Ltd., 1982.

COPPA, FRANK J., and PHILIP C. DOLCE, eds. *Cities in Transition: From the Ancient World to Urban America.* Chicago: Nelson Hall, 1974.

COX, HARVEY G. *The Secular City.* Rev. ed. New York: Macmillan Co., 1966.

CROSS, ROBERT D., ed. *The Church and the City, 1865–1910.* Indianapolis: Bobbs-Merrill Co., 1967.

CURTIS, WILLIAM J. R. *Balkrishna Doshi: An Architecture for India.* New York: Rizzoli, 1988.

DALLAPICCOLA, ANNA LIBERA, and STEPHANIE ZINGEL-ALE LALLEMANT, eds. *The Stupa: Its Religious, Historical and Architectural Significance.* Wiesbaden: Franz Steiner Verlag, 1980.

DAS, DHARMANARAYAN *The Early History of Kalinga.* Calcutta: Punthi Pustak, 1977.

DAS, DIPAKRANJAN. *Temples of Orissa: The Study of a Sub-Style.* Delhi: Agam Kala Prakashan, 1982.

DAS, GOPABANDHU. *Gopabandhu: The Legislator.* Introduction by Sadasiv Misra. Cuttack: Gopabandhu [Das] Centenary Celeberation Committee, 1977.

DAS, H. C. *Resources and Responses in Two Orissa Villages: The Influence of the New State Capital 1950–1970.* Orissa Studies Project No. 6. Calcutta: Punthi Pustak, 1979.

DAS, MANMATHA NATH. *Glimpses of Kalinga History.* Calcutta: Century Publishers, 1949.

———. ed. *Sidelights on History and Culture of Orissa.* Cuttack: Pitamber Misra, 1977.

DAS, N. K. *Madhusudan's Immortal Words.* Cuttack: N.p., 1958.

DAS, R. K. *Bhubaneswar and its Environs.* Puri, Orissa: Sri Printers, 1982.

DAS, SOILABALA. *Life of Madhusudan as Seen by Many Eyes.* Cuttack: N.p., n.d.

DAVIES, PHILIP. *Splendors of the Raj.* New York: Penguin, 1987.

DEUTSCHKRON, INGE. *Bonn and Jerusalem: The Strange Coalition.* Philadelphia: Chilton Book Co., 1970.

DICKENS, A. G. *The German Nation and Martin Luther.* New York: Harper and Row, 1974.

DONALDSON, THOMAS E. *Hindu Temple Art of Orissa.* 3 vols. Leiden: E. J. Brill, 1985–87.

Dwyer, Denis John, ed. *The City in the Third World.* New York: Barnes and Noble Books, 1974.

Fabri, Charles Louis. *History of the Art of Orissa.* Bombay: Orient Longmans Ltd., 1974.

Feuerstein, Gunther *New Directions in German Architecture.* New York: George Braziller, 1968.

Gangooly, O. C. *Orissan Sculpture and Architecture. Calcutta: Oxford Book and Stationery Co.*, 1956.

Germani, Gino, ed. *Modernization, Urbanization and the Urban Crisis.* Boston: Little, Brown, 1973.

Ghosh, Pradip K., ed. *Urban Development in the Third World.* Westport, CT: Greenwood Press, 1984.

Ghosh, Sunit. *Orissa in Turmoil: A Study in Political Development.* Calcutta: Sankha Prakashan, 1978.

Girouard, Mark. *Cities and People: A Social and Architectural History.* New Haven: Yale Univ. Press, 1985.

Green, Leslie, and Vincent Milone. *Urbanization in Nigeria: A Planning Commentary.* New York: International Urbanization Survey, 1972–73. An International Urbanization Survey Report to the Ford Foundation, no. 273.

Greenway, Roger S., ed. *Discipling the City: Theological Reflections on Urban Mission.* Grand Rapids: Baker Book House, 1979.

Grewal, J. S., and Indu Banga, *Studies in Urban History.* Amritsar: Guru Nanak Dev Univ., [1981].

Grover, Satish. *The Architecture of India: Buddhist and Hindu.* New Delhi: Vikas, 1980.

———. *The Architecture of India: Islamic, 727–1707 A.D.* New Delhi: Vikas, 1981.

———. *Know India: Architecture.* Bombay: Welcomgroup, n.d.

Gupta, Narayani. *Delhi Between Two Empires, 1803–1931.* New Delhi: Oxford Univ. Press, 1981.

Handa, R. R., and J. L. Vaz. "New Capital at Bhubaneswar." *Marg*, Bombay, vol. 3, no. 4, Sept. 1955.

Hansen, Niles M., ed. *Human Settlement Systems: International Perspectives on Structure, Change and Public Policy.* Cambridge, MA: Ballinger Pub. Co., 1978.

Harloe, Michael, and Elizabeth Lebas, eds. *City, Class and Capital: New Developments in the Political Economy of Cities and Regions.* London: E. Arnold, 1981.

Hausur, Phillip M. *Handbook for Social Research in Urban Areas.* Paris: UNESCO, 1965.

Head, Raymond. *The Indian Style.* Chicago: Univ. of Chicago Press, 1986.

Hibbert, Christopher. *Cities and Civilizations.* New York: Weidenfeld and Nicolson, 1986.

———. *Rome: The Biography of a city*. Harmondsworth, Middlesex: Penguin Books Ltd., 1987.

HOBERMAN, LOUISA SCHELL, and SUSAN MIGDEN SOCOLOW, eds. *Cities and Society in Colonial Latin America*. Albuquerque: Univ. of New Mexico Press, 1986.

HOLLAND, CECELIA. *City of God: A Novel of the Borgias*. New York: Knopf, 1979.

HUNTER, W. W. *A History of Orissa*. See N. K. Sahu's (ed.) *A History of Orissa*.

Indian National Trust for Art and Cultural Heritage. *Ekamra Kshetra Heritage Project: Bhubaneswar*. New Delhi: INTACH, Apr. 1989.

Jena, B. B. *Orissa: People, Culture and Polity*. New Delhi: Kalyani Publishers, 1980.

JENCKS, CHARLES. *Modern Movements in Architecture*. Garden City, New York: Doubleday Anchor, 1973.

JHA, MAKHAN. *Readings in Tribal Culture: A Study of the Ollar of Orissa*. New Delhi: Inter-India Publications, 1983.

JOEDICKE, JURGEN. *A History of Modern Architecure*. Trans. James C. Palmes. London: The Architectural Press, 1959.

JONES, ARNOLD HUGH MARTIN. *The Cities of the Eastern Roman Provinces*. Revised by Michael Avi-Yonah et al. 2nd ed. Oxford: Clarendon Press, 1971.

KAGAL, CARMEN, ed. *The Architecture of India*. Bombay: The Festival of India Pub., Oct. 1986.

KALIA, RAVI. *Chandigarh: In Search of an Identity*. Carbondale: Southern Illinois Univ. Press, 1987.

KHAN, HASAN-UDDIN. *Charles Correa*. New York: Concept Media, 1987.

KING, ANTHONY. *Colonial Urban Development*. London and Boston: Routledge and Kegan Paul, 1976.

KOENIGSBERGER, OTTO H, *Jamshedpur Development Plan*. Bombay: Tata Iron and Steel Co., 1944 (?). Published for private circulation by the Tata Iron and Steel Co.

———. *Master Plan for the New Capital of Orissa at Bhubaneswar*. Cuttack: Orissa Govt. Press, 1960.

———. "Design for an Olympic City." *Deutsche Bauzeitung*, vol. 68, Mar. 1933.

———. 'Schinkel Competition 1932–33." *Bauwelt*, vol. 24, Apr. 1933.

———. "The Greater Bombay Scheme." *Marg*, Bombay, Dec. 1947.

———. "The Victory Hall in Bangalore." *Marg*, Bombay. Oct. 1950.

———. "Housing and Town Planning Problems of Burma." *Journal of the American Institute of Planners*, vol. 18, no. 1, Winter 1952.

———. "New Towns in India." *Town Planning Review*, vol. 23, no. 2, July 1952.

———. "Town Planning in India." *Eastern World*, London, Aug. 1953.

———. "Urban Planning in Tropical Climates." In German. In *Klima und Stadtebau*, E. Kuehn, ed. Munich, 1959.

KOENIGSBERGER, OTTO H., with CHARLES ABRAMS. *Housing Programme for Pakistan*. In two parts. New York: United Nations, 1957–58.

Koenigsberger, Otto H, with Carl Mahony and Martin Evans. *Climate and House Design*. Vol. 1. New York: U.N. Dept. of Economic and Social Affairs, 1971.

Koenigsberger, Otto H., with S. Groak, eds. *A Review of Land Policies*. Oxford, 1980. Originally published as *Habitat International*, vol. 4, nos. 4/5/6, 1979.

Konvitz, Josef W. *Cities and the Sea: Port City Planning in Early Modern Europe*. Baltimore: The Johns Hopkins Univ. Press, 1978.

Krautheimer, Richard. *The Rome of Alexander VIII 1655–1667*. Princeton, NJ: Princeton Univ. Press, 1985.

Kumar, Nita. *The Artisans of Banaras*. Princeton, NJ: Princeton Univ. Press, 1988.

Kumar, Ravinder. *Essays in the Social History of Modern India*. New Delhi: Oxford Univ. Press, 1983.

Lal, Kanwar. *Temples and Sculptures of Bhubaneswar*. Delhi: Arts and Letters, 1970.

Lampugnani, Vittorio Magnago. *Architecture and City Planning in the Twentieth Century*. New York: Van Nostrand Reinhold Co., 1980.

Lee, Robert, ed. *The Church and the Exploding Metropolis*. Richmond: John Knox Press, 1965.

Linn, Johannes F. *Cities in the Developing World: Policies for Their Equitable and Efficent Growth*. New York: Oxford Univ. Press, 1983.

Loomis, Samuel Lane. *Modern Cities and Their Religious Problems*. 1887. Rpt. New York: Arno Press, 1970.

Mahtab, Harekrushna. *The History of Orissa*. 2 vols. Enlarged 2nd ed. Cuttack: Students' Store, 1981.

———. *While Serving My Nation: Recollections of a Congressman*. Cuttack: Sri Pitambe Misra, 1986.

Mansinha, Mayadhar. *History of Oriya Literature*. New Delhi: Sahitya Akademi, 1962.

———. *The Saga of the Land of Jagannatha*. Cuttack: J. Mohapatra and Co., n.d.

Marshall, Werner. *Contemporary Architecture in Germany*. Trans. James Palmes. New York: Frederick A. Praeger, 1962.

Meck, Stuart, and Edith M. Netter, eds. *A Planner's Guide to Land Use Law*. Washington, DC: Planners Press, American Planning Assoc., 1983.

Mehta, V. C. *Civic Survey of Cuttack*. Orissa: Town Planning Organization, Govt. of Orissa, Sept. 1956.

Metcalf, Thomas R. *An Imperial Vision: Indian Architecture and Britain's Raj*. Berkeley: Univ. of California Press, 1989.

Miller, David M., and Dorthy Wertz. *Hindu Monastic Life: The Monks and Monasteries of Bhubaneswar*. Montreal: McGill-Queen's Univ. Press, 1976.

Ministry of Education and Culture, Govt. of India. *Our Cultural Fabric: Indian Architecture Through the Ages*. Faridabad: Govt. of India Press, 1982.

Mishra, Amareswar. *Urban Government and Administration in India*. Meerut, India: Anu Books, 1986.

MISHRA, G. N. *Urban Politics in India.* Meerut, India: Anu Books, 1984.

MISHRA, PRASANNA KUMAR. *The Political History of Orissa: 1900–1936.* New Delhi: Oriental Publishers and Distributors, 1979.

———. *Political Unrest in Orissa in the 19th Century.* Calcutta: Punthi Pustak, 1983.

———. *Evolution of Orissa and Her Culture.* Calcutta: Chaitali Press, 1984.

MISKIMIN, HARRY A., DAVID HERLIHY, and A. L. UDOVITCH, eds. *The Medieval City.* New Haven: Yale Univ. Press, 1977.

MISRA, B. B. *Administrative History of India.* New Delhi: Oxford Univ. Press, 1970.

———. *The Unification and Division of India.* New Delhi: Oxford Univ. Press, 1990.

MITRA, DEBALA. *Bhubaneswar.* 4th ed. New Delhi: Director General, Archaeologi cal Survey of India, 1978.

MITRA, RAJENDRALAL. *The Antiquities of Orissa.* Calcutta: Mukhopadhya, 1963.

MOHANTY, NIVEDITA. *Oriya Nationalism: Quest for a United Orissa 1866–1936.* New Delhi: Manohar Publications, 1982.

MOHAPATRA, R. P. *Archaelogy in Orissa: Sites and Monuments.* Delhi: B. R. Pub. Corp., 1986.

MONTAGU, EDWIN. *An Indian Diary.* ed. Venetia Montagu. London: William Heinemann Ltd., 1930.

MUKHERJEE, PRABHAT. *The History of Medieval Vaishnavism in Orissa.* Calcutta: R. Chatterjee, 1940.

———. *History of Orissa in the 19th Century.* Vol. 6 Utkal University History of Orissa Series. Cuttack: Utkal Univ. Pub., 1964.

———. *The Buddhist Remains of Orissa.* Bhubaneswar: Orissa Govt. Pub., [1964].

———. *History of the Chaitanya Faith in Orissa.* New Delhi: Manohar Pub., 1979.

MUMFORD, LEWIS. *The City in History.* Harmondsworth, Middlesex: Penguin Books, 1966.

MYRDAL, JAN. *India Waits.* Trans. Alan Bernstein. Chicago: Lake View Press, 1986.

NANDA, SUKADEV. *Coalitional Politics in Orissa.* 1st ed. New Delhi: Sterling, 1979.

NEALE, WALTER C. *Developing Rural India: Policies, Politics, and Progress.* Riverside, MD: The Riverdale Co., 1988.

NEUTRA, RICHARD. "City Planning and Architecture in India Today." *Marg,* Bombay, vol. 8, no. 3, June 1955.

NILSSON, STEN A. *European Architecture in India, 1750–1850.* Trans. Agnes George and Eleonore Zettersten. London: Faber & Faber, 1968.

———. *The New Capitals of India, Pakistan and Bangladesh.* Trans. Elisabeth Andereasson. Lund, Sweden: Studentlitteratur, 1973.

OLDNBURG, VEENA TALWAR. *The Making of Colonial Lucknow.* Princeton, NJ: Princeton Univ. Press, 1984.

Orissa History Congress. *Orissa History Congress: Proceedings of the Annual Session.* Joytivihar, 1978.

PADHI, A. P., ed. *Indian State Politics: A Case Study of Orissa*. Delhi: B. R. Pub. Corp., 1985.

PAGANO, MICHAEL A. *Cities and Fiscal Choices: A New Model of Urban Public Investment*. Durham: Duke Univ. Press, 1985.

PANIGRAHI, KRISHNA CHANDRA. *Archaeological Remains at Bhubaneswar*. Bombay: Orient Longmans, 1961.

———. *History of Orissa: Hindu Period*. Cuttack: Kitab Mahal, 1981.

PASQUARIELLO, RONALD D., DONALD W. SHRIVER, Jr., and ALAM GEYER, *Redeeming the City: Theology, Politics and Urban Policy*. New York: Pilgrim Press, 1982.

PATNAIK, B. K. *The Politics of Floor Crossing in Orissa*. Cuttack: Santosh Pub., 1985.

PATRA, KISHORI MOHAN. *Orissa Under the East India Company*. New Delhi: Munshiram Manoharlal, 1971.

———. *Orissa State Legislature and Freedom Struggle, 1912–47*. New Delhi: Indian Council of Historical Research, 1979.

PEREIRA, JOSE. *Elements of Indian Architecture*. New Delhi: Motilal Banarsidass, 1987.

POTTER, ROBERT E. *Urbanization and Planning in the Third World: Spatial Perceptions and Public Participation*. New York: St. Martin's Press, 1985.

PRADHAN, SADASIBA. *Agrarian and Political Movements: States of Orissa, 1931–1949*. New Delhi: Inter-India Publications, 1986.

PRAKASH, VED. *New Towns in India*. Durham: Duke Univ. Press, 1969.

PRESTON, JAMES. *Cult of the Goddess: Social and Religious Change in a Hindu Temple*. New Delhi: Vikas, 1980.

PURI, BAIJ NATH. *Cities of Ancient India*. Meerut: Meenakshi Prakashan, 1966.

RAMACHANDARAN, R. *Urbanization and Urban Systems in India*. New Delhi: Oxford Univ. Press, 1989.

RAO, P. R. RAMACHANDRA. *Bhuvanesvara: Kalinga Temple Architecture*. Hyderabad: Akshara, 1980.

RATH. S. N. *Development of a Welfare State in Orissa*. New Delhi: S. Chand and Co., 1977.

RAY, AMITA. *Villages, Towns and Secular Buildings in Ancient India, c. 150 B.C.–350 A.D.* Calcutta: Firma K. L. Mukhopadhya, 1964.

ROBERTS, BRYAN R. *Cities of Peasants: The Political Economy of Urbanization in the Third World*. Beverly Hills: Sage Pub., 1979.

RODWIN, LLOYD, and ROBERT M. HOLLISTER, eds. *Cities of the Mind: Images and Themes of the City in the Social Sciences*. New York: Plenum Press, 1984.

SAHU, N. K., ed. *A History of Orissa*. Rpt. 2 vols. By W. W. Hunter, Andrew Sterling, and John Beans. Calcutta: Susil Gupta, India, Ltd., 1956.

SAMAL, J. K. *Orissa Under the British Crown, 1858–1905*. New Delhi: S. Chand, 1977.

SANDERSON, GORDON. *Types of Modern Indian Buildings*. Allahabad: Govt. Press, United Provinces, 1913.

SENAPATI, N. "Rumblings on New Towns of Orissa," *Journal of the Institute of Town Planners, India*, nos. 49–50, Dec. 1966–Mar. 1967, pp. 52–54.

SEYMOUR, SUSAN, ed. *The Transformation of a Sacred Town: Bhubaneswar, India*. Boulder, CO: Westview Press, 1980.

SIMPSON, BARRY J. *Quantitative Methods for Planning and Urban Studies*. Aldershot, Hampshire, England; Brookfield, Vermont, USA.: Gower, 1985.

SINGER, MILTON. *When a Great Tradition Modernizes*. New York: Praeger Pub., 1972.

SINGH, R. L. and RANA P. B. SINGH. *Place of Small Towns in India*. Varanasi: The National Geographical Society of India, Banaras Hindu Univ., 1979.

SINHA, S. N. *Bhubaneswar: An Urban Study*. Part 6-B. Census of India 1971, Series-16, Orissa. Cuttack: Archana Press, 1978.

———. *Geography of Orissa*. 2nd ed. New Delhi: National Book Trust, 1981.

SISSON, RICHARD, and STANLEY WOLPERT, eds. *Congress and Indian Nationalism: The Pre-Independence Phase*. Berkeley: Univ. of Calif. Press, 1988.

SMITH, BRADWELL, and HOLLY BAKER REYNOLDS, eds. *The City as a Sacred Center*. Leiden: E. J. Brill, 1987.

SMITH, WALTER THOMAS. *The Muktesvara Temple at Bhubaneswar: A Contextual Study of its Artchitecture and Sculptural Program*. N.p.: n.p., 1984. Originally Ph.D. diss., Univ. of Iowa, 1984.

Social Science Research Institute, International Christian Univ. *Asia Urbanizing*. Tokyo: Simul Press Inc., 1976.

STERLING, ANDREW. *A History of Orissa*. See N. K. Sahu, ed.

STRETTON, HUGH. *Urban Planning in Rich and Poor Countries*. New York: Oxford Univ. Press, 1978.

SUTCLIFFE, ANTHONY. *Towards the Planned City: Germany, Britain, the United States and France, 1780–1914*. New York: St. Martin's Press, 1981.

SWAAN, WIM. *Lost Cities of Asia: Ceylon, Pagan, [and] Angkor*. New York: Putnam, 1966.

SYMONS, ARTHUR, *Cities and Sea Coasts and Islands*. New York: Brentano's, 1919.

TAUB, RICHARD. *Bureaucrats Under Stress: Administrators and Administration in an Indian State*. Berkeley: Univ. of Calif. Press. 1969.

TAYLOR, LISA, ed. *Cities: The Forces that Shape Them*. New York: Rizzoli, 1982.

THAPAR, ROMILA. *Asoka and the Decline of the Mauryas*. Oxford: Oxford Univ. Press, 1961.

TILLOTSON, G. H. R. *The Tradition of Indian Architecture: Continuity, Controversy, and Change Since 1850*. New Haven: Yale Univ. Press, 1989.

Two Bachelors of Arts. *The Oriya Movement: Being a Demand for a United Orissa*. Ganjam: Pub. by H. H. Panda, Secretary, Oriya Samaj Ganjam, 1919.

UNTERMANN, RICHARD K., with LYNN LEWICKI, asst. *Accommodating the Pedestrian: Adapting Towns and Neighborhoods for Walking and Bicycling*. New York: Van Nostrand Reinhold, 1984.

Vaz, Julius L. "Architecture of Bhubaneswar." *Journal of the Indian Institute of Architects*, vol. 20, no. 2, Apr.–June 1954.

Whyte, Iain Boyd. *Bruno Taut and the Architecture of Activism*. Cambridge: Cambridge Univ. Press, 1982.

Wolpert, Stanley A. *A New History of India*. New York: Oxford Univ. Press, 1989.

———. *India*. Berkeley and Los Angeles: Univ. of Calif. Press, 1991.

INDEX

Ravi Kalia is an associate professor of history, The City College of The City University of New York (CUNY). He received his B.A. (Honors) and M.A. degrees from Delhi University, India, and his Ph.D. and M.B.A. degrees from the University of California, Los Angeles. He is the author of *Chandigarh: In Search of an Identity*; his articles have appeared in *Habitat International* and *India Quarterly*, as well as in the *Oregonian, Los Angeles Herald Examiner, Morning Star, Hindustan Times* (New Delhi), and *Statesman* (New Delhi); and currently he is working on a study of Gandhinagar, the capital of Gujrat state, and an intellectual and cultural history of modern India.